Ovid, Aratus and A

The astronomical material in Ovid's *Fasti* h
ing the recent revival of scholarly interest i
which is the subject of this book. The auth
using the techniques of mathematical astronomy. Rather she aims to combine the methodology of recent 'programmatic' or genre-based readings with a broad cultural perspective. Arguing that the stars serve to align the *Fasti* with hexameter didactic poetry, she first tests the assumption that the *Fasti* is influenced by the *Phaenomena* of Aratus. A second task is to assess the value of such writing in Augustan Rome: the *Fasti* and its Aratean model may be removed from the literary-historical sphere and placed in the political setting of the later Augustan Principate, in which the stars had been appropriated to express a powerful connection between the Julian family and the cosmos.

EMMA GEE is Lecturer in Classics at the University of Exeter.

CAMBRIDGE CLASSICAL STUDIES

General Editors

OVID, ARATUS AND AUGUSTUS

OVID, ARATUS AND AUGUSTUS

Astronomy in Ovid's *Fasti*

EMMA GEE
University of Exeter

CAMBRIDGE
UNIVERSITY PRESS

CAMBRIDGE UNIVERSITY PRESS
Cambridge, New York, Melbourne, Madrid, Cape Town, Singapore, São Paulo, Delhi

Cambridge University Press
The Edinburgh Building, Cambridge CB2 8RU, UK

Published in the United States of America by Cambridge University Press, New York

www.cambridge.org
Information on this title: www.cambridge.org/9780521651875

First published 2000
This digitally printed version 2008

A catalogue record for this publication is available from the British Library

Library of Congress Cataloguing in Publication data

Gee, Emma, 1970–
Ovid, Aratus and Augustus: astronomy in Ovid's Fasti / Emma Gee.
p. cm. (Cambridge classical studies)
Includes bibliographical references and indexes.
ISBN 0 521 65187 5 (hardback)
1. Ovid, 43 B.C.–17 or 18 A.D. Fasti. 2. Rome – History – Augustus, 30 B.C.–14 A.D. – Historiography. 3. Ovid, 43 B.C.–17 or 18 A.D. – Knowledge – Astronomy. 4. Didactic poetry, Latin – History and criticism. 5. Politics and literature – Rome – History. 6. Astronomy, Ancient, in literature. 7. Aratus, Solensis. Phaenomena. 8. Aratus, Solensis – Influence. I. Title. II. Series.
PA6519.F9G44 2000
520′.937–dc21 99-30735 CIP

ISBN 978-0-521-65187-5 hardback
ISBN 978-0-521-10177-6 paperback

To my parents

CONTENTS

ILLUSTRATIONS

ACKNOWLEDGEMENTS

My colleagues in Exeter are responsible for this book being in its present form. I would particularly like to thank John Wilkins, Peter Wiseman, Anne Wiseman, Norman Postlethwaite, Chris Gill, Dave Braund, and Richard Seaford for their patience and support. However, its origin lies in Cambridge. My heartfelt thanks go to Michael Reeve for his meticulous but gentle filtering of ideas and correction of malapropisms, and for his continuing help; to John Henderson, who should take the credit for starting things off; to senior members of the Faculty of Classics who read and commented on parts of my work: David Sedley, Mary Beard, Christopher Kelly, and in particular Richard Hunter in his guise as Aratus scholar. Denis Feeney and Philip Hardie also provided invaluable advice.

My book would not exist but for my fellow graduates, who helped at the thesis stage by their proofreading, suggestions, and good-natured ridicule. They are too many to name individually, and in any case I would be in danger of accidentally leaving someone out, so I shall express my gratitude to the Cambridge Classics graduate community as a collective entity.

The Faculty of Classics and the executors of the Jebb Fund provided generous financial support, as did the Cambridge Commonwealth Trust and the University of Sydney. Corpus Christi College Cambridge gave support in every way; its members graciously put up with my singing over the years. My thanks go also to the British School at Rome and to its Director, Andrew Wallace-Hadrill, for the opportunity to study in Rome during Michaelmas term 1996. I am greatly indebted to my teachers at Sydney University, especially to Frances Muecke and Kevin Lee. Finally, thanks go to Mrs Joan Godwin, and, most of all, to my parents.

INTRODUCTION

The *Fasti* of Ovid is a syncrasis of the Roman religious calendar, Julian panegyric, and astronomical material, the risings and settings of stars in relation to the Roman year. When I first approached the *Fasti* I was puzzled by its astronomy. Why is there astronomy in Ovid's *Fasti* at all? Do the stars come into the *Fasti* because they are a natural part of the calendar? Does astronomy tell us something about the nature of Ovid's literary project? Is it representative of broader cultural and political factors? These questions give us several lines of approach to the text of the *Fasti* through astronomy: as a scientific or 'practical' text; as a manifestation of dialogue between Greece and Rome; and as an artefact reflective of cultural and political conditions outside itself. These lines of approach are by no means discrete; all will be essayed in this book.

The astronomical stratum of the *Fasti* has been left behind by the scholarly revival of Ovid's calendar poem. There are only two articles in existence which deal exclusively and comprehensively with astronomy in the *Fasti*, Ideler (1825) and Santini (1975). Ideler's approach was technical. His task was the 'correction' of Ovid's astronomical references, explaining which movement of a star, morning or evening, rising or setting, Ovid had intended to represent each time, had he not been impeded by his astronomical ignorance.[1] Santini's concern, on the other hand, was with poetic genre. His aim was to

[1] Ideler's approach was based on the assumption that Ovid's aim is exactitude. Because of this he took no account of the fact that the astronomical references occur in the context of an elegiac poem, and may therefore follow the dictates of theme and poetic fiction rather than accuracy. Frazer in his commentary of 1929 was reliant on Ideler for his astronomical information (see vol. I, xx), as Fantham still is in her commentary of 1998.

explore the *Fasti's* astronomy in the light of didactic poetry. To this end he collected and categorised many of Ovid's star references, subjecting them to detailed stylistic and lexical scrutiny in the light of comparative didactic material. Santini's approach is problematic in its segregation and exclusivity. He deals only with the individual astronomical nuggets (a divisive approach to the text), so that we cannot see whether the stylistic features enumerated are exclusive to these passages, or whether they hold good throughout the poem.[2]

Carole Newlands is the only scholar of three who have recently written monographs on the *Fasti*[3] who devotes a significant amount of space to the stars. She perceives a twofold function in the stars: articulation of the generic principles of the *Fasti*, and opposition to the 'normative values' of the Roman state.[4] Through the stars, Ovid introduces Greek mythic narrative into the Roman calendar in such a way as to fulfil the poem's 'elegiac agenda' of celebrating peace rather than war. Ovid's carelessness about dates is in reality a device calculated to give him the freedom to position his Greek star myths so they challenge the points of view encoded in the Roman material. Newlands' reading of the stars in the *Fasti* is subordinate to her theory as a whole, which sees subversion everywhere in the poem.

The enduring lack of attention to the *minutiae* of Ovid's astronomy among scholars is understandable, given the recalcitrance of Ovid's astronomical material, and the difficulty

[2] The problem of segregation has been rectified to an extent by more recent 'programmatic' or literary readings of individual astronomical passages, readings which look for connections with the surrounding material or with the programme of the poem as a whole. Hinds (1987a) 4–24, Newlands (1991), and Brookes (1994), for example, fall into this category. Hinds treats the myth of Pegasus (*Fasti* 3.449–58) and its programmatic function in the *Fasti* and the *Metamorphoses*. Newlands presents a programmatic reading of the rising of the Raven, Snake and Bowl (*Fasti* 2.243–66), and Brookes explores the myth of Chiron, who is also the constellation Centaurus (*Fasti* 5.379–414). These readings tend towards the other extreme from Santini: rather than segregating the astronomical parts from the rest of the poem, they seek thematic connection with surrounding material at the expense of the autonomous function, and particular literary history, of the astronomical material.

[3] Herbert-Brown (1994), Newlands (1995), Barchiesi (1997).

[4] Newlands (1995) 44. For a different interpretation of the function of the stars in relation to the Roman material, see Martin (1985).

of teasing out either an accurate picture of the state of the sky in the early years AD, or a definitive purpose, meaning and thematic function, from the stars in the *Fasti*. Sometimes Ovid records several different dates of rising or setting for the same constellation, dates which may have represented the work of different astronomers taking their calculations from different latitudes. At other times his astronomical references are wholly incorrect. Sometimes the stars seem to be connected thematically with the surrounding material, as when a dog is sacrificed to the Dog Star (at a date some five months too early for its rising) in the festival of the Robigalia at the end of *Fasti* 4;[5] sometimes it is discrete, as is often the case with the short astronomical soundbites which occur throughout the poem.

The *Fasti* was composed in the early years of the first century AD but abandoned when half complete as a result of the poet's exile in AD 8.[6] Ovid began to revise the *Fasti* while still in exile, apparently during the years surrounding Augustus' death in AD 14. At some stage before Ovid's own death in AD 17[7] the poem was re-dedicated to Augustus' younger heir, Germanicus, who was both a member of the imperial family and himself the author of an astronomical poem, the *Phaenomena*, a verse translation into Latin of Aratus' work of the same name.[8]

The *Phaenomena* of Aratus, itself a 'translation' into Hesiodic verse of a prose treatise on the stars and weather signs by Eudoxus, was commissioned *c.* 276 BC by Antigonus Gonatas, king of Macedon, and shows Stoic influence.[9] Ovid himself translated Aratus into Latin hexameters,[10] and the influence of Aratus' *Phaenomena* is discernible in the *Fasti*:

5 See Fantham (1998) *ad Fasti* 4.901–42.
6 See Syme (1978) 21–36, Fantham (1985), Alton, Wormell and Courtney (1988) v–vii, Newlands (1995) 235–6, Barchiesi (1997) 259–72, and Fantham (1998) 1–4.
7 See Thibault (1964) 22.
8 See Gain (1976), Herbert-Brown (1994) 176–8.
9 For the existing biographical material on Aratus, see Pfeiffer (1968) 120–2; Maass (1892) 328–9; Mair and Mair (1921) 359–63, Hutchinson (1988) 214–36, Green (1990) 183–6, Kidd (1997) 3–5.
10 On Ovid's own translation of Aratus, see below pp. 66, 68–70.

both works are in a sense calendars, both in a sense didactic poems;[11] in addition Ovid recalls Aratus at various points.[12]

My purpose in this book is twofold: firstly to unpick the scholarly assumption, which has been stated and re-stated but never explored, that the astronomy in the *Fasti* is indebted to Aratus,[13] and secondly to build a theory on Ovid's relationship with this particular model: in a nutshell, that the debt to the *Phaenomena* which is evident in the *Fasti* adds another register of meaning to Ovid's poem. This level of meaning may be seen as generated by the interaction between the *Fasti*, the *Phaenomena*, and Ovid's other long work, the *Metamorphoses*. The unified cosmos of Aratus' Stoic poem is fragmented across Ovid's Roman calendar, and at the same time tied in with the shifting universe of the *Metamorphoses*. To my mind Ovid's fragmentation of a poetic text which, as we shall see, carried political importance in Rome, and assimilation of it to a more anarchic world, runs counter to the Julian and Augustan impulse towards unity, particularly as manifest in the calendar reform of 46 BC.

My study falls in to two parts, the first of which (chapters 1–3) explores the generic and literary historical orientation of the *Fasti* and the *Phaenomena*, the second of which (chapters 4–6) modulates the literary, scientific, and philosophical tonality of the first part into a political key. My aim is not to ascertain the correctness of Ovid's astronomical references using the technical methods of mathematical astronomy. I believe that, while some knowledge of geocentric astronomy is

[11] See chapter 1 below for the calendrical aspect of the *Phaenomena*, chapter 2 for the didactic aspect of the *Fasti*.

[12] See appendix 1.

[13] For example, McKeown (1987–9) *ad Amores* 1.15–16: 'The astronomy in the *Fasti* is indebted to Aratus, as was presumably Ovid's own *Phaenomena*.' Things have not changed significantly in the 1990s: Newlands (1995) 29, says only, 'A precedent for treating the stars as a suitable subject for poetry was set by Aratus' *Phaenomena*, a didactic poem devoted to describing the geography of the sky through its star-signs.' She does not explore the relationship. Santini (1975) mentions the Hellenistic astronomical didactic poet Aratus as the *fons et origo* of the didactic style of the Latin poets with whom he compares Ovid: Cicero (*Aratea*), Virgil (*Georgics*), Manilius (*Astronomica*), and Germanicus. For Santini, Aratus' role was prototypical rather than direct. For this reason he does not deal fully with the relationship between Aratus and Ovid.

necessary to my topic, the astronomy of the *Fasti* is fundamental to an understanding of the poem not so much in its technical intricacies, as in its importance when seen against the symbolic value of astronomy in Augustan culture. My reading of the *Fasti* through its stars will aim to combine the technique of recent genre-based or 'programmatic' readings with the more general cultural-historical approach of work now being done on ancient astronomy and astrology by scholars such as Tamsyn Barton.[14]

Chapter 1 explores the question of calendrical precedents for the astronomy which we find in the *Fasti*. Despite the similarity in appearance of the poem, as it has been edited in the modern period, with the epigraphical calendar, the inscribed calendar does not provide astronomical material. For that, one must go to the prose agricultural writers of the Augustan period and later. The irony is that, for practical (agricultural) purposes, the Julian calendar rendered astronomical observation obsolete: one no longer needs to look at the stars if the written calendar is in line with them. We are left, therefore, with the question of why Roman authors cling to the fiction of celestial time-reckoning. This is a question which can be answered in both generic and political terms.

The purpose of chapter 2 will be to show that the *Fasti* is in some sense a didactic poem, and that one of its strongest underlying impulses is to be found in Aratus' *Phaenomena*. Chapter 3 aims at determining the nature of the *Phaenomena* in order to ascertain the symbolic value which may be assigned to it and which must be taken into account when determining how Ovid reacts to Aratus in the *Fasti*. I will argue here that Stoic theory provides a frame within which to talk about the unity, cohesion and order of Ovid's astronomical model. The prevailing themes of Aratus' poem will be discussed in the light of Stoicism, with the intention of showing how the repetition of these themes contributes to the poem's unity, which is in harmony with the Stoic world-view. Ultimately, however, it is the work's artistic unity, for which

[14] Barton (1994a), (1994b), (1995).

Stoicism provides an interpretative strategy, which enables it to be placed in potential opposition to the *Fasti*.

This opposition is demonstrated in chapter 4, which takes as its starting-point Ovid's Vestalia, *Fasti* 6.249–460. The round temple of Vesta is placed by Ovid in parallel with the Sphere of Archimedes. As well as being a model of the world, the Sphere of Archimedes will be seen to represent in some sense Aratus' poem, which a number of sources say was a description of just such a model globe rather than the result of direct observation of the universe. The Sphere has the potential to act in isolation as a symbol of poetic and cosmic order. However, it is placed by Ovid in a context which suggests the appropriation of the stars for political ends in the Augustan period. The Sphere is a Roman appropriation of Greek astronomy, and as such is parallel to Ovid's use of Aratus in the *Fasti*; but it undergoes a metamorphosis in symbolic value by the context in which it is placed, in which political forces subsume the scientific.

Chapter 5 aims to explore the functioning of astronomy against the background of the Augustan political world in which Ovid's poem was composed. Here I shall go outside the purely Aratean frame, and examine the stars in the *Fasti* in the light of the political use of the stars in Rome. The stars are one area of the integration of Greek culture into Rome. If they appear in the Roman calendar, it is partly at least because the calendar is itself an expression of cultural fusion. In their literary culture, however, the Romans seemed to like to express such cultural fusion by an opposition between Greece and Rome. The period in which this opposition was most clearly articulated is arguably the Augustan period, as we may see from the famous lines of Anchises' Speech in *Aeneid* 6, where *sidera* are one index of comparison between Greeks (the *alii*) and Romans:[15]

> [alii] caelique meatus
> describent radio et surgentia sidera dicent:
> tu regere imperio populos, Romane, memento ... (*Aeneid* 6.849–51)

[15] On Greek and Roman, traditional and 'scientific' elements in Anchises' Speech, see Habinek (1989).

In Virgil the stars are one arm of an opposition between Greece and Rome; but at the same time they seem already in the late Republican period to have been important in the articulation of the concepts of power in Rome. In his *Republic* Cicero uses an astronomical disquisition to introduce his treatise on Roman government;[16] in the second book of his *De Natura Deorum* the divinity of the stars and the theory of euhemerist apotheosis (when kings and heroes become stars on account of their *virtutes* and *beneficia* on earth) are placed in close juxtaposition by Cicero's Stoic speaker.[17] Both of these works were written in the decade before Ovid's birth.

In the Principate of Augustus, public divination had become obsolete, and private astrology had become public.[18] This may be seen in the emperor's building of his giant sundial, the Horologium, with its astronomical references in bronze lettering;[19] in his exploitation of his birth sign Capricorn and the publication of his horoscope; and in the appearance during this period of ruler-catasterism as one way of expressing imperial succession.[20] The meaning of catasterism (astral apotheosis) in the Augustan period might be defined as

[16] Cicero, *Rep.* 1.15–34.

[17] Cicero, *DND* 2.60–2.

[18] Barton (1994a) 38: 'Astrology emerged as the Roman Republican system began to collapse, a coincidence which, in my view, was no accident. Astrology belonged with the sole ruler, as the state diviners belonged with the Republic.'

[19] This was a giant sundial on the Campus Martius, which served as both clock and calendar, marking the hours, the length of the days, changes of season, and the sun's yearly path through the zodiac. Augustus' sundial was in some way (the degree of generality or specificity varies from scholar to scholar) part of a complex of monuments which included the Ara Pacis and probably the Mausoleum as well. Bibliography is now extensive: see (in chronological order) Buchner (1982); Wallace-Hadrill (1985); Horsfall (1985); Wallace-Hadrill (1987); Snodgrass (1987), 27–34; Buchner (1988); Schütz (1990); Barton (1994b), 45–7, (1995); Newlands (1995) 23–6; Wallace-Hadrill (1997) 16–17; Boyle (1997) 8; Feeney (1998) 127. It has recently become fashionable in *Fasti* scholarship to compare or contrast the Horologium with the *Fasti* (see Newlands (1995) 23 and Boyle (1997) 8). Such comparisons give an impression of certainty as to the functioning of the Horologium, certainty which, to my mind, cannot be maintained in the face of two obstacles to accurate mathematical calculation: we do not know the exact height of the obelisk in Piazza Montecitorio, which has been reconstructed, and we do not know its precise position on the Augustan paving, since what is left is a Domitianic rebuilding, and in any case only a small portion has been excavated. Feeney (1998) 127 n. 50 is right to sound a note of caution.

[20] See below, pp. 167–8.

hegemony, actual or prospective, over celestial as well as terrestrial space.

Finally, however, it will be seen in chapter 6 that, while imperial catasterism may be placed in superficial opposition to mythological catasterism of the kind that is found in the *Metamorphoses* as well as in the *Fasti*, in reality the oppositions between mythic and imperial catasterism, between philosophy and mythology, and between politics and myth, may not be as straightforward as they seem. The conclusion will be that these opposites in fact impinge on one another, and that the catasterised Julius and the apotheosised Augustus are closer to mythical star figures like Callisto[21] than rulers eulogised in imperial panegyric might comfortably be.

Because of its affiliations with a Hellenistic literature of ruler-catasterism, the *Fasti* is consonant with Augustan universalising panegyric. The effect of ruler-catasterism on the astronomical material in the *Fasti* is to bind the work tightly into Augustan soteriological discourse; but at the same time the *Fasti* pulls away from the unifying tendencies of this discourse, by its affinity with the *Metamorphoses*, in which catasterisms are amoral and part of a fluid world-view. By its fragmentation of the Aratean model and assimilation of it to the *Metamorphoses*, the *Fasti* resists Augustan universalising panegyric.

[21] The myth of the Bear, Callisto, is explored in chapter 6 below.

CHAPTER I

CALENDRICAL ASTRONOMY?

The reason for the existence of the stars in the *Fasti* may at first seem obvious: the stars are part of the calendar, especially after the Julian calendrical reform, which synchronised the celestial with the civil year.[1] What did the Julian reform entail? In 46 BC Caesar, with the help of the Alexandrian mathematician Sosigenes, had brought the Roman republican calendar, which consisted of alternately 355 and 377 or 378 days a year (based on lunar months and intercalation), into synchronisation with the solar year of 365 and a quarter days.[2] This system overcame the problem inherent in the archaic calendar, traditionally attributed to Numa,[3] which was a result of measuring the solar year on the basis of twelve lunar months: twelve lunations are shorter than the time-period that constitutes a solar year, and thirteen are longer. Thus the calendrical year would tend to creep ahead of, or fall behind, the solar year. In the Republic this was addressed by intercalation, but intercalation was prone to error, and could be used arbitrarily by the Pontifices, who had charge of its administration.[4]

The Republican system of sacred and secular days, its festivals changed as little as possible,[5] was placed by Caesar inside the solar year of 365 and a quarter days. Augustus

[1] On Caesar and calendrical reform, see (most recently) Domenicucci (1996) 85–8. For the epigraphical calendar and its importance for Ovid's *Fasti*, see Herbert-Brown (1994) 15–26.

[2] Sosigenes: Pliny, *NH* 18.211; Caesar's reforms: Plutarch, *Caes.* 59. The fullest description of the Caesarian reforms is in Macrobius, *Saturnalia* 1.14, written several hundred years after Caesar's activities.

[3] See *Fasti* 3.151–4.

[4] See Domenicucci (1996) 85.

[5] Herbert-Brown (1994) 21–2: 'For the dictator to move the festivals about in the process of his reform would have risked creating confusion in collective Roman identity, and affronting both patriotic sentiment and *ius divinum*.'

further corrected the calendar when he rectified the pontiffs' error in applying Caesar's leap year.[6] New festivals were added, primarily by Augustus, which commemorated deeds of the Julian family.[7] In 45 BC Quintilis was named Iulius, in 27 Sextilis became Augustus. These elements, combined, form the Julian year, six months of which Ovid set to verse.

Scholars have not questioned the affinity of the *Fasti* with the surviving epigraphical calendars of the Julian period; nor has the assumption that astronomy is part of the calendar been tested. It will be found that, while Ovid's *Fasti* does of course bear affinities to the *Fasti anni Iuliani* collected by Theodor Mommsen in volume I of the second edition of the *Corpus inscriptionum latinarum* (1863), the similarity in title and appearance does not fully accord with similarity in fact. What is more, a superficial structural similarity between the *Fasti* and the epigraphical calendar has been enhanced by editorial technique since 1851.[8]

Moreover, of the twenty or so inscribed Julian calendars collected by Mommsen, only two contain any astronomical references, and these references are extremely brief.[9] Was astronomy an essential element of the calendar? According to Carole Newlands, 'Surviving remains of Roman calendars suggest that information on the risings and settings of the stars was not an essential part of the state calendar, and, if provided at all, was rather scattered.'[10]

It is certain that astronomy is linked with the agricultural and nautical calendar, given the importance of the position of

[6] After Caesar's assassination in 44 BC the pontiffs misunderstood his directions for intercalation and inserted a leap year every three years instead of every four. In 9 BC Augustus, as Pontifex Maximus, decreed that intercalation be omitted for the next 16 years. This was put in motion in 8 BC, so that the first year of right functioning of the calendar was AD 8.

[7] On these new *feriae*, see Herbert-Brown (1994) 22–3.

[8] The division of the text of the *Fasti* with date-markings of a kind found in epigraphical calendars dates from Merkel's Teubner edition of 1851 (my thanks to Michael Reeve for this observation).

[9] These are the *Fasti Venusini* (Mommsen (1863) 300–1) and the *Fasti Antiates* (Mommsen (1863) 327–9). The *Fasti Antiates* as preserved carry only one very general astronomical reference, which concerns the sun's passage from one zodiacal constellation to another: A XV SOL INSAGITT (17 November, Mommsen (1863) 329).

[10] Newlands (1995) 28–9.

the stars for the commencement of seasonal agricultural tasks and for the dates of the sailing season, as well as for navigation.[11] Virgil in the first book of the *Georgics* provides primary evidence for this in the Augustan period (although it may be argued that astronomy as an agricultural and navigational tool has taken on the value of a poetic trope by this stage). For Virgil, one of the key moments in the development of man is when he names the stars (*Georgics*) 1.137–8:

> navita tum stellis numeros et nomina fecit
> Pleiadas, Hyadas, clarumque Lycaonis Arcton.

The reason why astronomy was originally vital to the agricultural calendar in Rome is obvious: the arbitrary intercalation which had been part of Republican time reckoning, and lack of synchronicity between the calendrical and solar years, had rendered the Republican calendar useless as a guide to seasonal agricultural tasks. Two surviving agricultural calendars illustrate this, the *Menologium Rusticum Vallense* and the *Menologium Rusticum Colotianum*.[12] Both are illustrated with astrological signs at the head of the column for each month,[13] and both give the place of the sun in the zodiac at any given time, as well as giving the number of days in each month and hours in the day and night, and festivals and agricultural activities throughout the year. These calendars bear little similarity to the *Fasti* apart from their astronomical notes (they do not of course give star myths).

Astronomy also appears in the Roman agricultural writers, Cato, Varro, Columella, and Pliny the Elder (*Naturalis Historia* Book 18). These writers collectively provide us with evidence for the effect of Caesar's reforms. Cato makes no

[11] See Santini (1975) 1. We shall see below that astronomical dates in Roman agricultural calendars were likely (at least in the Augustan period and later) to derive from Greek sources.

[12] Mommsen (1863) 358–60, Degrassi (1963) 284–98. For comments, see Santini (1975) 1, Newlands (1995) 28–9. I have not found any evidence that these calendars can be closely dated. They both apparently come from the same archetype, and, although according to Degrassi ((1963) 284) they are related to the pre-Caesarian agricultural calendar, in their present form they must be Augustan or later, since the month of August is named as such.

[13] Degrassi (1963) tab. LXXXI–LXXXII and LXXXIV–LXXXVI.

reference to any calendar, but assumes that his readers are following purely seasonal dates. Consider for example *De Agricultura* 41.1, of times for grafting: *pirorum ac malorum insitio per ver et per solstitium dies L, et per vindemiam.* Sometimes Cato refers to the movements or phases of the sun or moon, as in 37.3: *Nisi intermestri lunaque dimidiata tum ne tangas materiem. Quam effodies aut praecides abs terra, diebus VII proximis, quibus luna plena fuerit, optime eximetur.* Occasionally he will refer to the divisions of the lunar month, as at 143.2: *Kalendis, Idibus, Nonis, festus dies cum erit, coronam in focum indat, per eosdemque dies lari familiari pro copia supplicet.* The context here, however, is a religious one, about the duties of the housekeeper, which comprise various rituals. It seems that in Cato the seasonal year is important for agricultural tasks, the lunar months for religious observance: as one would expect in a writer who pre-dates the Julian reform, when for the first time the Roman calendar became useful for agriculture, since its dates tallied with the seasons.

Varro, on the other hand, explicitly juxtaposes the sidereal and solar year with the Julian calendar, as at *De Re Rustica* 1.28.1–2:

> dies primus est veris in Aquario, aestatis in Tauro, autumni in Leone, hiemis in Scorpione. cum unius cuiusque horum IIII signorum dies tertius et vicesimus IIII temporum sit primus et efficiat ut ver dies habeat XCI, aestas XCIV, autumnus XCI, hiems XXCIX, quae redacta ad dies civiles nostras, qui nunc sunt, primi verni temporis ex a. d. VII id. Febr., aestivi ex a. d. VII id. Mai., autumnalis ex a. d. III id. Sextil., hiberni ex a. d. IV id. Nov.

Varro's phrase *quae redacta ad dies civiles nostras, qui nunc sunt*, must refer to the Julian calendar, which had come into effect a few years before this was written.[14]

Columella borrows from Greek parapegmata,[15] as is shown

[14] On Varro and the Julian calendar see Domenicucci (1996) 96 n. 223.

[15] 'Parapegma' may be defined as an inscription on stone for public use, listing risings and settings on key dates for the year, together with notes on the weather to be expected. Holes were drilled in the stone against the lines of the text so that a peg could be moved from day to day to keep the calendar up to date. The name could also be given to written calendars. See Kidd (1997) 13–14, who provides bibliography.

both by his calculations and his citations, such as the following: *verum in hac ruris disciplina sequor nunc Eudoxi et Metonis antiquorumque fastus astrologorum, qui sunt aptati publicis sacrificiis: quia et notior est ista vetus agricolis concepta opinio; nec tamen Hipparchi subtilitas pinguioribus, ut aiunt, rusticorum literis necessaria est.*[16] Ideler believed that Columella worked through a Roman intermediary, perhaps the same source as used by Ovid in the *Fasti*,[17] since Columella and Ovid are frequently in agreement over star dates, even when these dates are erroneous.[18] Columella is useful in that he provides, in Book 11 of his *De Re Rustica*, an agricultural calendar in which astronomical dates for rural activities and the Julian calendar are reconciled. Throughout *DRR* 11, Columella gives Julian dates for the risings and settings of stars, combining natural and calendrical time in the same way as Ovid does in the *Fasti*.[19]

Book 18 of the Elder Pliny's *Naturalis Historia* is devoted to the principles of astronomy, and to the Julian year. In it Pliny deals with Caesar's reforms, the methods of astronomical observation, the solstices, times of sowing, and dates of risings and settings of stars throughout the four seasons. Pliny states throughout *NH* 18 that he is following Caesar for astronomical information correct for the latitude of Rome.[20]

It is possible to reconstruct the Caesarian calendar to some degree from Pliny. Some dates in the Julian calendar are erroneous when judged by the standard of exact astronomical

[16] *DRR* 9.14.12. For Meton and Eudoxus as parapegmatists, see Vitruvius 9.6.3, with Soubiran (1969) *ad loc.*, Kidd (1997) 14.

[17] Ideler (1825) 167.

[18] See Le Boeuffle (1964) 329–30.

[19] See, for example, *DRR* 11.2.4. The juxtaposition of Columella and Ovid occurs in one at least of the *Fasti* manuscripts (*Vaticanus Latinus* 3264, fifteenth century). In this manuscript, a calendar entitled *Columellae Annus*, which runs parallel with a six-month calendar possibly derived from the poem itself, is placed at the beginning of the *Fasti*. It seems that the fifteenth-century copyist also thought the two authors comparable. On this and other *Fasti* manuscripts in the Vatican Library, see Buonocore (1994).

[20] For example, *NH* 18.255 (and frequently elsewhere), the expression *Caesari*, 'according to Caesar'.

dates. While some errors may be the result of Pliny's own misunderstandings, mistakes may also be a result of calculations taken further south than Italy, or of consultation of Egyptian sources.[21] Caesar appears to have followed Greek and Egyptian calendars, and there were still many mistakes in the Caesarian calendar, which may have been due to the interpolation of calculations made from latitudes other than that of Rome, an observation which flies in the face of Pliny's own assertion at *NH* 18.214: *nos sequemur observationem Caesaris maxime: haec erit Italiae ratio.*[22]

The agricultural works we have looked at span a crucial period in the history of chronology. Cato lived from 234 to 149 BC, Varro 116–27 BC; the lifetime of Columella (4 BC–AD 65) overlapped with the composition of the *Fasti*, and Pliny was somewhat later (AD 23/4–79). Cato predates the Julian calendar; he works primarily on seasonal dates. Varro, Columella and Pliny the Elder were writing after its advent. They include the stars, but align them with the Julian year. It was only after the calendrical reforms of Caesar and Sosigenes in 46 BC that writers were able to combine festivals and dates of the Roman civil year with risings and settings of stars. The irony is that, after the advent of the Julian calendar, the stars were no longer needed for the practical keeping of time.

Pliny gives sowing dates by the movements of the stars, with an important qualification: *quidam omissa caelesti subtilitate temporibus definiunt* (18.205), 'Some people ignore the nice points of meteorology and fix limits by the calendar.'[23] The important fact is that, in the day-to-day keeping of time for commercial and even agricultural purposes, it was easier, after the synchronisation of civil and solar years, to use calendrical dates than to observe the stars.[24] The Julian calendar superseded astronomical time, replacing it with a system that could exist independently of the movements of the heavenly

[21] Domenicucci (1996) 96.
[22] See Ideler (1825) 166–9.
[23] Trans. Rackham (1950).
[24] Aujac (1979) 53–4, Domenicucci (1996) 15.

bodies, and made observation of the stars unnecessary. It is also apparent from Pliny that, far from unifying time, Caesar's reforms resulted in a greater plurality of systems than previously existed: *tres autem fuere sectae, Chaldea, Aegyptia, Graeca; his addidit quartam apud nos Caesar dictator annos ad solis cursum redigens singulos Sosigene perito scientiae eius adhibito.*[25]

What do we mean, then, when we talk about the Julian calendar in relation to the *Fasti*? Which calendar do we refer to when speaking of 'the' calendar? If we mean the epigraphical one, we must remember that it is not a single entity of monolithic authoritativeness.[26] All the Julian *Fasti* transcribed by Mommsen are fragmentary to some degree, rendering questionable attempts to discuss 'the' Julian year, as though it were a single entity rather than existing (apart from Ovid's *Fasti*) only as a series of fragmentary epigraphical representations. The date-markings which appear in modern editions of Ovid's *Fasti* are themselves not reflective of any one inscribed calendar, but an idealised *cento* of many. In addition the calendar, rather than being a 'source' for Ovid's *Fasti*, is parallel with it, a creative fusion. At any rate it is misleading to compare the *Fasti*, an extended elegiac poem, to the epigraphical calendar. Attempts to make the poem look like the epigraphical calendar are essentially false.

The Caesarian calendar was itself a pastiche of the work of different parapegmatists and astronomers; it should be considered not as a document canonical in the keeping of Roman time, but as a textualisation of the history of chronology up to that point. It is an expression of the cultural fusion between

[25] Pliny, *NH* 18.210–11.

[26] See Wallace-Hadrill (1987), Beard (1987), Scheid (1992). Contrast Feeney (1998) 104, 'These painted or carved calendars were themselves by no means religious or cult documents in any straightforward sense. They were memorials without authority. They alluded to, commented upon, and commemorated the mechanisms by which state cult was regulated, but they were not themselves those mechanisms', with Boyle (1997) 7, 'For the Roman calendar, decreed and inscribed, far from being a national, apolitical body of antiquarian lore, was a malleable system of political and ideological control, which Augustus especially used – almost to perfection.'

Greece and Rome. This is revealed in the sources cited by Varro and Columella, which include both Roman agricultural writers and Greek parapegmatists. For the technical chronologer, it is also revealed by the calculations the calendar contained, taken from different latitudes.

When we are dealing with 'the' Julian calendar we are actually discussing representations of many different kinds, often fragmentary, of a phenomenon which was by its very nature composite and manifold. The calendar is a true parallel for Ovid's *Fasti* in the sense of its multiplicity alone. We have seen two different manifestations of the calendar contemporary with the Julian period: the inscribed calendar, which did not include a significant amount of astronomy, and the agricultural calendar, which did, reconciled with the dates of the civil year. The irony is that, while Ovid's *Fasti* is more similar to the latter than the former, Ovid maintains the fiction of calendrical astronomy which the Julian year had actually rendered obsolete.

However, it is perhaps true to say that, whatever the multiplicity of the Julian calendar, there is almost certainly a body of astronomical theory which underlay it, even if this theory did not manifest itself in inscribed form. Ovid himself tells us that Caesar as calendrical reformer understood the stars, and, moreover, that this was because of his future divinity:

> sed tamen errabant etiam nunc tempora, donec
>   Caesaris in multis haec quoque cura fuit.
> non haec ille deus tantaeque propaginis auctor
>   credidit officiis esse minora suis,
> promissumque sibi voluit praenoscere caelum
>   nec deus ignotas hospes inire domos.
> ille moras solis, quibus in sua signa rediret,
>   traditur exactis disposuisse notis;
> is decies senos ter centum et quinque diebus
>   iunxit et a pleno tempora quinta die. (*Fasti* 3.155–64)

Caesar, not wanting to be a mere sojourner in the celestial palaces, but preparing himself for full privileges, worked out the exact dates of the summer and winter solstices (this I take to be the meaning of *moras solis, quibus in sua signa rediret*, the *signa* being Cancer and Capricorn, the sun's tropics) and the exact length of the solar year, three hundred and sixty five days and one fifth (as Ovid would have it). This is Caesar as parapegmatist.

Lucan in the *Pharsalia* has Caesar refer to his calendar as surpassing the *Fasti* of Plato's pupil, the astronomer Eudoxus (fourth century BC):

> stellarum caelique plagis superisque vacavi,
> nec meus Eudoxi vincetur fastibus annus. (*Pharsalia* 10.186–7)

Eudoxus is also mentioned among the parapegmatists by Vitruvius in *De Architectura* 9.6.3 (which we shall look at in a moment). He wrote the work which was versified by Aratus, the *Phaenomena*.[27] The scholia *ad* Lucan 10.187 posit a *Liber Fastorum* of Caesar; according to Domenicucci this was the *De Astris*, a treatise explaining the theoretical basis of the new calendar, possibly written in collaboration with Sosigenes.[28] This finds support in Macrobius, *Saturnalia* 1.16.39: *nam Iulius Caesar ut siderum motus, de quibus non indoctos libros reliquit, ab Aegyptiis disciplinis hausit, ita hoc quoque ex eadem institutione mutuatus est, ut ad solis cursum finiendi anni tempus extenderet.*[29]

What is the astronomical work of Caesar referred to here? The references may just be to the astronomical background to Caesar's reconciling of the civil and celestial years; but equally the evidence may point to a specific astronomical work. This work may have taken the form of a parapegma annotated with astronomical observations relating to the stellar phases and the zodiacal position of the sun. According to Domenicucci, it was possibly in two parts, namely a general astronomical section, incorporating astrothesis (star-mapping), and

[27] Or perhaps Aratus followed more closely the updated version of it, the *Enoptron* (Mirror of the Sky): see Kidd (1997) 15. Kidd 14–18 discusses the influence of Eudoxus on Aratus. For my own discussion, see below, pp. 109–14.
[28] Domenicucci (1996) 85–99.
[29] For the other ancient references, see Domenicucci (*ibid.*).

the movement of the celestial sphere and the heavenly bodies, followed by a precise *ordinatio anni*: a theoretical section, and a specific exposition of the astronomical calendar.

Domenicucci does not comment on an interesting fact: the striking similarity of his proposed reconstruction of the *De Astris* with the *Phaenomena* of Aratus. Looking at the most recent exposé of the structure of the *Phaenomena*, that of Douglas Kidd in his 1997 edition, this is easy to see.[30] Discounting the proem for the moment, lines 19–758 are theoretical (astrothesis, 19–461, and the principles of astronomical chronology, 462–757), whereas the second half of the poem, also known as the 'Diosemeiai', the 'Signs of Zeus', is practical, telling us what signs bring what sort of weather at what times of year, and which agricultural and nautical tasks accompany them (lines 758–1141).[31] Such similarity is logical, given a moment's thought: Caesar as parapegmatist is accomplishing a task similar to Aratus' when he transforms into verse the work of the parapegmatist Eudoxus.

Firmicus Maternus (*Math.* 8.5.2–3) links Aratus and Caesar in this way: *hae [stellae] in vicinis signorum regionibus collocatae, cum XII signis oriuntur et cum ipsis occidunt rursus, immutatum semper cursus sui ordinem reservantes. sed his stellis nomina veterum fabularum apposuit antiquitas. executus est etiam horum numerum siderum Graece Aratus poeta disertissimus, Latine vero Caesar et decus eloquentiae Tullius.* Firmicus here is talking about 'paratellonta', the non-zodiacal constellations that rise and set at the same time as the constellations of the zodiac: a celestial relative chronology. Much of Aratus is taken up with exposition of the same thing (*Phaenomena* 559–732). Synchronic risings and settings were thus an important part of celestial chronology, and their exegesis marks out both Caesar and Aratus as parapegmatists. Cicero (Tullius) is included in the list because he wrote a translation of Aratus, probably in the late eighties BC.

[30] Kidd (1997) 5–8.

[31] In chapter 3, I shall adopt an older division of the text of the *Phaenomena*, according to which the break between the sections comes at 732–3. This makes no difference to the basic two-part division articulated here. See below, p. 78.

This is something of a revelation: Aratus is an astronomical poet, but he is also the writer of an astronomical calendar like Caesar's. At *De Architectura* 9.6.3, Vitruvius lists Aratus among the famous Greek astronomical parapegmatists who provide him with the theoretical basis for his explanation of sundials in *De Architectura* 9. I have already referred to this passage; here it is in full:

de naturalibus autem rebus Thales Milesius, Anaxagoras Clazomenius, Pythagoras Samius, Xenophanes Colophonius, Democritus Abderites rationes, quibus e rebus natura rerum gubernaretur quemadmodum cumque effectus habeat, excogitatas reliquerunt. quorum inventa secuti siderum et occasus tempestatumque significatus Eudoxus, Eudemus, Callippus, Meto, Philippus, Hipparchus, Aratus ceterique ex astrologia parapegmatorum disciplinis invenerunt et eas posteris explicatas reliquerunt. quorum scientiae sunt hominibus suscipiendae, quod tanta cura fuerunt, ut etiam videantur divina mente tempestatium significatus post futuros ante pronuntiare.

In natural philosophy, Thales of Miletus, Anaxagoras of Clazomene, Pythagoras of Samos, Xenophanes of Colophon, Democritus of Abdera left elaborate theories on the causes by which nature was governed, and the manner in which each produced their effects. Eudoxus, Eudemus, Callippus, Meto, Philippus, Hipparchus, Aratus, and others followed up their discoveries, and, with the help of astronomical tables, discovered the indications of the constellations, of their setting, and of the seasons, and handed down the explanations to after times. Their knowledge is to be highly regarded by mankind, because they so applied themselves, that they seem by divine inspiration to declare beforehand the indications of the seasons.[32]

Precise measurement of the year had not been achieved until Meton and Euctemon in *c.* 430 BC devised a method of reckoning the days by months according to the passage of the sun through the zodiacal constellations.[33] They may have invented the parapegma itself. Aratus has previously been seen as something of an anomaly in this company. Jean Soubiran comments that Aratus introduces into this list of authentic parapegmatists an extremely disparate note; if the latter part of the 'Phainomena' and the 'Diosemeiai' resemble a parapegma in some ways (astronomy mixed with meteorology),

[32] Text and trans. Granger (1934).
[33] On Meton and Euctemon, see Kidd (1997) 13–14. On Hipparchus and others, see Kidd 18–23.

the form of Aratus' work, that of poetry, does not authorise Vitruvius to take him so seriously, and is in fact revealing of Vitruvius' ignorance as to the true state of science.[34]

However, if one looks at Aratus in the context of astronomical parapegmata, as translator of Eudoxus, he does not seem so anomalous. The idea of Aratus as an agricultural parapegmatist is supported by Virgil's use of him in the agricultural calendar of *Georgics* 1.[35] Aratus' task was similar to that of Julius Caesar: the ordering of the year according to the astronomical calendar. At the same time, Aratus' work begins to look very similar in its basic conception to Ovid's *Fasti*.

To conclude, then: in this chapter we have questioned, firstly whether the *Fasti* is like a Roman calendar, and secondly whether the Roman calendar as it was in Ovid's time has room for astronomy. We have seen that, while its affinities to the calendar are undeniable, one must guard against any over-schematic analogy between Ovid's *Fasti* and the Roman calendar, especially since the latter is itself a complex organism.

Equally, while astronomy might underlie the Roman calendar, not least in Julius Caesar's astronomical work, which may have formed part of a body of calendrical theory, the Julian calendar had the effect of doing away with the need to observe the stars, and this is perhaps why they do not appear in its inscribed manifestation. This in turn functions to remove astronomy from the sphere of practicality and place it in the realm of fiction.

This chapter has also carried us beyond the answers to our two initial questions. In it we have seen Aratus the astronomical poet and Caesar the writer of a calendar collapsed into one another, so that now we can equally well speak of Caesar the writer on astronomy and Aratus the calendar poet. One consequence of this is that the *Phaenomena* of Aratus looks very like the *Fasti* of Ovid. We shall return to this in chapter 3. Let us meanwhile continue the debate on the wider generic field.

[34] Soubiran (1969) *ad loc.* [35] Thomas (1988) 6–7.

CHAPTER 2

ASTRONOMY AND GENRE

The *Fasti* is a literary artefact; consideration of its genre and poetic models is as essential as exploration of its calendrical characteristics. Quintilian says at *Institutio Oratoria* 1.4.4 that poetry cannot be understood by one unversed in astronomy: *nec, si rationem siderum ignoret, poetas intelligat, qui (ut alia omittam) totiens ortu occasuque signorum in declarandis temporibus utantur.*[1] Astronomy in poetry is useful for indicating the passing of time, among other things. Astronomy is part of poetry in many genres and may not be confined to elegiac, epic or didactic writing. In this sense astronomy is a good way to study the generic fluidity of Ovid's *Fasti* itself. Nonetheless it is useful to isolate models in different genres, to see if they offer astronomical precedents for the *Fasti*. This will be our project in this chapter.

Ovidian scholars have tended to construe the *Fasti* in the light of a dichotomy between elegy and martial epic.[2] This opposition has broken down somewhat in recent decades under the subtle influence of scholars such as Stephen Hinds, who has argued that the 'genre-based poetics' of the *Fasti* do not so much allow categorisation as result in 'a sharpening of

[1] See Domenicucci (1996) 13–14.

[2] The lineaments of the debate are as follows. Heinze (1919) sought to establish a clear distinction between the epic narrative manner of the *Metamorphoses* and the elegiac style of the *Fasti*, arguing that the stylistic differences between the two poems are concomitant with their difference in metre. Otis (1970) 23 could still say, '[Heinze's] fundamental distinction remains as clear and self-evident as when he first propounded it in 1919.' According to the caustic reassessment of Little (1970), 'The differences exist not because the *Metamorphoses* is epic and the *Fasti* elegiac, but because the *Fasti* is a poem directed to a specific purpose, the exposition and celebration of Roman cult' (75). The work of Hinds (1987a) and (1992) and others follows from this reassessment, which allows for discussion of the mixing of, and tension between, genres. Nonetheless, the epic/elegy opposition maintains its hold on *Fasti* scholarship more strongly than one might expect; Boyle (1997) is a recent example.

generic sensibilities'. There appears, in Hinds' view, to be continual negotiation between elegiac form and the strain placed on that form by the subject matter of the poem, much of which is epic or epicising in nature.[3] Hinds' permutation of the binary opposition between elegy and epic involves the stars: 'Ovid self-consciously sets against the *arma* of martial epic two other formal opposites besides the ones normally associated with epic–elegiac oppositions in Augustan poetry: he opposes *arma* to *sacra* and *arma* to *sidera*.'[4] *Sacra* must incorporate Callimachean aetiology, *sidera* the astronomical didactic poetry of Aratus. This double opposition – between epic and aetiological elegy, and between epic and the stars – is present in the *Fasti* from its proem:

> Tempora cum causis Latium digesta per annum
> lapsaque sub terras ortaque signa canam. (*Fasti* 1.1–2)

The opening couplet of the *Fasti* could be read as a manifesto of generic fusion:[5] Ovid projects a religious-aetiological agenda (*tempora*, 'dates', 'fitting times', 'festivals'); but with *lapsaque sub terras ortaque signa* he also announces a programme which incorporates astronomy.

Astronomy is usually taken to mean not elegiac but didactic poetry. The double programme in Ovid's opening lines was recognised as long ago as 1955, by L. P. Wilkinson: 'The literary grandparents of the *Fasti* are, on the aetiological side, the *Aetia* of Callimachus, admired of all Roman elegists, and on the astronomical side the no less admired *Phaenomena* of Aratus.'[6] Both of these Hellenistic writers represent a development of the *epos* of Hesiod rather than that of Homer, Callimachus taking the *Theogony* as his model, Aratus the *Works and Days*:[7] both poets follow *non*-martial epic, but, while Callimachus writes elegy, Aratus writes didactic. In one sense, Ovid's project – the combination of aetiological elegy and didactic epic – resulted in a synthesis of these divergent

[3] Hinds (1987a) 115–34. [4] Hinds (1992) 113. [5] See Santini (1975) 6–7.
[6] Wilkinson (1955) 242. [7] On Aratus and Hesiod, see Hunter (1995).

branches of post-Hesiodic writing. There has been an asymmetry, however, in the scholarly treatment of these models, privileging Callimachus, which I intend to rectify in this book, by my treatment of Aratus.

The keynote of a recent subtle study of Roman literature and religion is multiplicity of available materials, and polysemy in the way poets represented them.[8] This way of studying the *Fasti* can be seen to have value in understanding the astronomy in Ovid's poem, since the concept of an opposition between erotic elegy and martial epic is not strictly applicable to the astronomical parts of the *Fasti*, as I hope to show. I do not believe it is valid to try to isolate a generic model for astronomy in the *Fasti* in a general or preconceived sense; what one may do, however, is to study individual models for astronomy, which may happen to occur in different genres. Let us begin with an elegiac model.

Elegy: Propertius 4.1[9]

Speaking of Propertius 4.1, Geraldine Herbert-Brown says, 'It must be remembered that, following the Callimachean precedent, Roman poets had made it a conventional motif to reject the epic genre in favour of the elegiac.'[10] This is broadly true, even if, following Alan Cameron, one does not believe that the epic/elegy opposition started with Callimachus, but with the Roman reception of him.[11]

Most critics agree as to the political importance of Ovid's decision to write in elegiacs.[12] Two quotations will serve as a

[8] Feeney (1998), especially 123–33.

[9] In this section all quotations from the text of Propertius are from Goold (1990) unless it is otherwise stated.

[10] Herbert-Brown (1994) 11. On Propertius and the Augustan programme, see *ibid.*, 10–14.

[11] Cameron (1995) chapter 18.

[12] On the *Fasti* and elegy generally, see (a few examples among many) McKeown (1984), Miller (1991), Barchiesi (1991), Hinds (1992), Holzberg (1997). The criticism in this section is not of these authors but with those who try to map Ovid's 'elegiac agenda' onto the stars.

sample: 'The choice of the elegiac genre for the *Fasti* has an ideological component. The Augustan elegiac love poets constantly defined their writing in terms of opposition to epic. As a corollary they made elegy the genre of opposing the state, contrasting the private pursuit of love with the public pursuit of civic duties.'[13] 'Rather than disguise the generic problem Ovid parades it, affirming ... the work's elegiac status, even as he simultaneously exhibits its *maius* subject matter. It would have been easy to write the work in hexameters. Ovid's choice of elegiacs is a self-consciously provocative one, and one whose provocativeness is underscored, whose creative transgression of Roman elegiac boundaries is deliberate and deliberated.'[14] This last is especially perplexing: what is the *Fasti* transgressing, an Augustan régime which expected epic, or a set of conventions belonging to elegy, the genre which *opposed* itself to the régime? Can it transgress both at the one time?

It is when applied to the stars that the opposition between epic and erotic elegy becomes particularly problematic, as in the following: 'The star myths also play a key role in articulating the generic ideals of the *Fasti*, for they commonly deal with the familiar themes of erotic elegy – love, rape and untimely death – and characteristically reveal violence of any kind as tragic. The star myths therefore contribute substantially to the dynamic tension in the poem between Ovid's former erotic preoccupation and his new national themes.'[15] This seems to mean that the stars pull against the Augustan subject matter of the *Fasti*, in that they employ the themes of elegy. We shall see later that star myths are not always subversive, and that the presence of the stars can be panegyrical. Nor is their family tree that of erotic elegy. It is ironic, given the assumption that elegy acts against the régime, that the elegiac model for the *Fasti* which is most commonly discussed in such contexts is Propertius' fourth book of elegies, a set of poems which takes the first hesitant steps towards *Augustan* aetiological elegy.

[13] Newlands (1995) 14. [14] Boyle (1997) 19. [15] *Ibid.*, 31–2.

The only remaining option is to consider Propertius himself as subversive to the régime, even in his fourth book. It is true that Propertius vacillates between erotic and aetiological elegy in the fourth book, and that the decision to write Roman elegy at the beginning of 4.1 was to be constantly re-negotiated; but, at the same time, it must be remembered that Propertius is Ovid's immediate model for his Roman aetiological project, a project which must harmonise at some level with the Augustan recuperation of the past.

There can be no doubt that Propertian aetiology is a precedent for the kind of elegy Ovid writes in the *Fasti*. The programme of Propertius' fourth book of elegies, *sacra diesque/deosque canam et cognomina prisca locorum* (4.1.69), has been compared by Barchiesi and, following him, Newlands, with Ovid's opening couplet in the *Fasti*, *Tempora cum causis Latium digesta per annum | lapsaque sub terras ortaque signa canam*. In echoing Propertius' programme, Ovid is said to align himself with the aetiological-antiquarian tradition of Propertius' fourth book of *Elegies*.[16]

In general terms, Propertius in 4.1 provides us not only with a sketch map of Rome and of his own fourth book, but with a plan for the *Fasti*. Lines 1–70 of Propertius 4.1 are composed of tableaux of Roman history and religion, beginning with the Augustan present and the Temple of Actian Apollo on the Palatine (*Navali ... sacra Palatia Phoebo*, line 3).[17] The religious cults mentioned by Propertius in lines 17–26, apart

[16] It must be pointed out that the similarity is not so striking if one adopts the emendation of *diesque* to *deosque* at Propertius 4.1.69, as Goold (1990) has done; one is not then presented with the match of Propertius' *dies* and Ovid's *dies* (*Fasti* 1.8). Reading *deosque*, Propertius, *Elegies* 4 seems not so much a model for the calendrical part of Ovid's undertaking as for the topographical and theological (although this of course incorporates *dies* in the sense of festivals, *pace* Herbert-Brown (1994) 10, 'Propertius does not live up to his claim. Not one of his subsequent elegies really concerns *dies* ...'). This *caveat* applies particularly to Newlands, who rests part of her argument on *dies*, said to have been used by Ovid at the beginning of the *Fasti* in imitation of Propertius 4.1.69 (Newlands (1995) 204). Barchiesi is more subtle, noting that the keywords of Propertius' programme, *canam, sacra, priscis* and *dies*, are separated across the first 8 lines of the *Fasti*, as is appropriate in allusion to a recent Roman model (Barchiesi (1997) 51).

[17] For the Temple of Apollo on the Palatine, see Propertius 4.6.

from all having been 'revivified by Augustus',[18] are treated by Ovid in the *Fasti*: the Parilia (*Fasti* 4.721–806), Vesta (*Fasti* 6.311–12), the Lupercalia (*Fasti* 2.267–452). The sacrifices mentioned in Propertius 4.1.22–4 might be related to Ovid's Agonalia (*Fasti* 1.317–456).

It is not only in general programme that the two poets coincide. There are individual echoes of Propertius 4, especially 4.1, throughout the *Fasti*. For example, the opening of Propertius 4.1, *hoc quodcumque vides, hospes, qua maxima Romast,* | *ante Phrygem Aenean collis et herba fuit*, is echoed by the old woman who speaks at *Fasti* 6.401: *hoc, ubi nunc fora sunt, udae tenuere paludes*. Likewise, Propertius 4.1.67, *Roma, fave, tibi surgit opus*, may be seen in *Fasti* 4.830, *hoc mihi surgat opus*, and 5.111, *ab Iove surgat opus*. Janus echoes Propertius' opening early Rome tableau at *Fasti* 1.243–4:[19]

> hic, ubi nunc Roma est, incaedua silva virebat,
> tantaque res paucis pascua bubus erat.

Likewise, Propertius' adjective *Tarpeius* (4.1.7) may come to mind at *Fasti* 1.79 (*Tarpeias itur in arces*). Propertius 4.1.30, *magnaque pars Tatio rerum erat inter oves*, might be compared with *Fasti* 1.204, *pascebatque suas ipse senator oves* (an ironic transfer of *priscae virtutes* from foe to friend?), or with the story of Tatius told by Janus at *Fasti* 1.259–76.[20]

The contrast between early Rome and the present day with which Propertius 4.1 began is the substance of Janus' speech at *Fasti* 1.191–254; the same contrast is exploited in Carmentis' rant in the Carmentalia (*Fasti* 1.463–542). At *Fasti* 1.465–6, when Ovid asks

> unde petam causas horum moremque sacrorum?
> deriget in medio quis mea vela freto?

[18] Butler and Barber (1933) *ad loc.*

[19] On Propertius and early Rome, see Fantham (1997).

[20] See Stahl (1985) 285 for Propertius' divergence from the usual version of the Tarpeia story. On further connections between 4.1 and 4.4, see Stahl (1985) 298–305. For Stahl, the dissonance between the frame of 4.4 and Tarpeia's monologue is intrinsically related to the dissonance between 4.1A and B: 'In the Tarpeia elegy, it seems to me, Propertius reveals that he has accepted Horos' warning' (304).

it is not impossible (though the nautical trope is common) that we may think of Propertius' *nunc tua vel mediis puppis luctetur in undis* (4.1.147); if so, the answer to Ovid's question, *deriget in medio quis mea vela freto?*, might be 'Propertius'. Who should direct Ovid's literary boat other than his Roman predecessor in this kind of elegy, whose craft had already sailed a shaky course through the same Roman aetiological waters? Indeed, Ovid's exiled Evander finds his ancestor in Propertius 4.1.4 (*Evandri profugae procubuere boves*); and the place where Carmentis' boat pulls into port in Ovid (*Tuscis obvius ibat aquis*, *Fasti* 1.500) is Propertius' Tiber (*et Tiberis nostris advena murus erat*, 4.1.8).

The *hospita tellus* which receives Evander and Carmentis at *Fasti* 1.511 itself takes on the role of the poet as host which was seen in Propertius 4.1.1 (*hoc quodcumque vides, hospes* ...).[21] The walls of Rome at *Fasti* 1.515 (*fallor, an hi fient ingentia moenia colles?*) are as important to Ovid's Carmentis as they were to Propertius at 4.1.55–8:

> optima nutricum nostris, lupa Martia, rebus,
> qualia creverunt moenia lacte tuo!
> moenia namque pio coner disponere versu:
> ei mihi, quod nostrost parvus in ore sonus!

Propertius 4.1.2, *collis et herba fuit*, reminds us of *Fasti* 1.539–40:

> puppibus egressus Latia stetit exul in herba:
> felix, exilium cui locus ille fuit!

At 4.1.67–8, Propertius prays for success in his undertaking:

> Roma, fave, tibi surgit opus; date candida, cives,
> omina; et inceptis dextera cantet avis!

At *Fasti* 1.513, Carmentis prays for good omens: *este bonis avibus visi natoque mihique*.

Propertius goes on to enunciate his programme – *sacra deosque canam et cognomina prisca locorum*, 4.1.69 – and

[21] And also Evander's own role as host in *Aeneid* 8, where he explains the cults in Propertius 4.1.17–26 (see below).

immediately afterwards has an astrologer chip in with an admonition: *quo ruis imprudens? fuge discere/dicere*[22] *fata, Properti!* (71).

At this point we discover that, as well as providing the model for Ovid's Roman aetiology, Propertius provides some sort of precedent for the astronomy in the *Fasti*. There is a precedent specifically for astronomy in Callimachean aetiological elegy. Book 4 of Callimachus' *Aetia* is where we find the *Lock of Berenice*, astronomical panegyric of the Ptolemaic dynasty, and a model for Ovid on both astronomical and panegyrical counts, as we shall see in chapter 6. Propertius, the self-appointed *Callimachus Romanus* (*Elegies* 4.1.64), also incorporates the stars in the aetiological programme of *Elegies* 4.1.

We have seen that, in *Elegies* 4.1, Propertius embarks on a new ambitious programme of building the city of Rome in verse, parallel to Augustus' project of re-building the city in marble. Both Propertius and Augustus anchor their foundations in Rome's past. But Propertius cannot sustain his attempt. Directly after the programme enunciated in 4.1.69–70, in a comic parody of the *recusatio* form, Propertius is interrupted by a seedy Egyptian Apollo, the astrologer Horos,[23] who with all manner of astrological gobbledegook exhorts him to write, not aetiological elegy, as Apollo had exhorted Callimachus in the first book of the *Aetia*, but erotic elegy pure and simple.[24] Horos thus uses the stars to *stop* Propertius writing Roman aetiological elegy.

The speech of Horos, which forms the substance of Propertius' *recusatio*, is astrological, containing a list of the planets, the heavenly bodies most essential to astrology:

[22] Goold (1990) adopts *discere*, although there is also manuscript authority for *dicere*. If we were to adopt the latter reading, Propertius would be engaging in a Carmentis-like prophecy when stopped by Horos.

[23] Propertius' choice of name may be significant, given the Egyptian origins of astrology. Horos is an Egyptian version of Apollo, who uses his native art to persuade the poet. For the identification of Apollo with the Egyptian god Horus, see Witt (1971) 51–2; for identification through Helios, see Turcan (1989) 124. On Horos as Apollo in Propertius 4.1, see Stahl (1985) 267–9.

[24] On the relationship of the two parts of Propertius' poem to one another, and the structure of Book 4 in general, see Stahl (1985) 265–305.

quo ruis imprudens? fuge discere fata, Properti!
  non sunt a dextro condita fila colo.
accersis lacrimas: aversus cantat Apollo:
  poscis ab invita verba pigenda lyra.
certa feram certis auctoribus, aut ego vates
  nescius aerata signa movere pila,
felicisque Iovis stellas Martisque rapacis
  et grave Saturni sidus in omne caput.
(Propertius 4.1.71–6, 83, 84)

Astrological imagery forms the substance of Horus' extended admonition to the poet:

quid moneant Pisces animosaque signa Leonis,
  lotus et Hesperia quid Capricornus aqua,
hoc neque harenosum Libyci Iovis explicat antrum,
  aut sibi commissos fibra locuta deos,
aut si quis motas cornicis senserit alas,
  umbrave quae magicis mortua prodit aquis:
aspicienda viast caeli verusque per astra
  trames, et ab zonis quinque petenda fides.
(Propertius 4.1.85–6, 103–8)

These lines take the form of an astronomical syllabus of the kind found in Aratus and his followers. Ovid also uses this kind of syllabus in the *Fasti*, as at *Fasti* 3.105–10:

quis tunc aut Hyadas aut Pliadas Atlanteas
  senserat, aut geminos esse sub axe polos,
esse duas Arctos, quarum Cynosura petatur
  Sidoniis, Helicen Graia carina notet,
signaque quae longo frater percenseat anno,
  ire per haec uno mense sororis equos?

Both poets indulge in what is essentially astronomical didactic parody.[25] Therefore, one might assume, Propertius 4.1 is

[25] Such lists are first found in *Theogony* 108–13 and the early cosmological poets Parmenides and Empedocles. Virgil's cosmological song of the bard Iopas incorporates one at *Aen.* 1.742–56. The convention is common in the astronomical poets, for example, Germanicus, *Phaenomena* 11–14. Brown (1990) 318 maintains that, 'This sort of programmatic summary, articulated primarily or partially by means of indirect questions, was a customary feature of Roman didactic poetry.... The conventional use of such synopses in didactic poetry accounts for their presence in certain non-didactic works where the poet wishes to imitate or evoke the didactic manner.' I believe this is Propertius' purpose here: didactic parody.

an astronomical model for Ovid, as well as an aetiological one.

A direct echo in astronomical material would seem to support this. Horos ends his exhortation with an astrological admonition:

> nunc tua vel mediis puppis luctetur in undis,
> vel licet armatis hostis inermis eas,
> vel tremefacta cavum tellus diducat hiatum:
> octipedis Cancri terga sinistra time! (Propertius 4.1.147–50)

There is an element of astronomical truth in this: Manilius tells us Cancer rises back first (*aspice ... | testudine Cancrum | surgere*, Manilius 2.198–200), hence perhaps Propertius' *terga* denotes its rising.[26] The first constellation in Ovid's *Fasti* is Cancer. Paradoxically, it cannot be seen, because on that date it will disappear 'head first' (*praeceps*, the opposite way from its rising in Propertius):

> octipedis frustra quaerentur bracchia Cancri:
> praeceps occiduas ille subibit aquas. (*Fasti* 1.313–14)

Ovid's allusion to Propertius is beyond doubt, since the adjective *octipes* occurs only in these two passages.[27]

But astronomical comparison between Ovid and Propertius gives rise to a problem. On the astronomical level, the relationship between the two writers of Roman aetiological elegy must be one of opposition, since Propertius places the stars in conflict with his aetiological project, while Ovid incorporates them in his. This oppositional relationship is perhaps symbolised by Ovid's *oppositio in imitando* at *Fasti* 1.313–14. Propertius' use of astrology as a means of opposition to his Augustan programme may seem to explain views such as that of Newlands (quoted above), who sees Ovid's stars too as being in opposition to Augustan Rome.

Newlands extends this interpretation to Cancer, interpreting Ovid's allusion to Propertius as follows: 'By referring emphatically to the baleful Crab's sudden disappearance from

[26] On the difficulties of *terga*, see Stahl (1985) 375–6 n. 13.
[27] The first to flag the Propertian intertext here was Barchiesi (1991) 1–3.

the sky, Ovid suggests, perhaps, that whereas Propertius does indeed avoid the stars in his Roman aetiological poetry, he himself is free from astrological malign influences: indeed, he avoids the subject of astrology and integrates the stars within his poem through an account not of their influence on human lives but of their mythical origins.'[28] The underlying assumption here seems to be that Cancer stopped Propertius from writing about *the stars*, but that once he makes it disappear, Ovid can in fact write about the stars, albeit on the mythical rather than astrological level.

Newlands shortly afterwards appears to have shifted her ground on the nature of the opposition between Propertius and Ovid. She notes that the threatening Crab disappears as Ovid embarks on his project, but re-appears at the end of the poem, where Ovid should be referring to its setting, 'a malign sign that seems in keeping with a poem left unfinished'.[29] Now we have moved from the Crab as a warning in Propertius not to write the stars into his Roman elegy, and its absence as permission for Ovid to do so, to the Crab as symbolising Ovid's inability to continue writing Roman aetiological elegy at all, not just the astronomical parts of the *Fasti*.

Newlands' second opposition is closer to what Propertius himself is saying in 4.1, since implicit in it is the idea that astrology is used by Horus to dissuade the poet from writing serious elegy, and persuade him to write love elegy instead. As Stahl puts it, 'Horos' warning to Propertius is ... basically a *vaticinium ex eventu*, which cautiously tells the reader why the Roman Callimachus did not finish his *Aetia*.'[30] When the crab rises in Book 6 of the *Fasti* (as opposed to its setting at the beginning of the work), Ovid too is dissuaded from his Roman aetiological project, but instead of writing erotic elegy, he is silenced altogether.

There are several problems in Newlands' reading which

[28] Newlands (1995) 36. Note Newlands' use of the word 'integrates'; this articulates her approach to astronomy, which is to read the astronomical sections with an eye for connections with surrounding material.

[29] *Ibid.*

[30] Stahl (1985) 277.

must be clarified, since they affect our interpretation not only of these two passages in Propertius and Ovid but of the two works themselves, the model (*Elegies* 4) and its re-interpretation (the *Fasti*), and the place of the stars in them. One might firstly object that Cancer is not the last sign in the *Fasti*, but Orion; the *Fasti* as we have it continues for 100 lines or so after Cancer rises at 6.727. Secondly, Newlands does not say why the sign is 'malign'. Consultation with Manilius is unhelpful, since it turns out, as in most astrology, that the sign can be both positive and negative; a good emblem, perhaps, of the way I would like to see the *Fasti* and its stars, and a *caveat* against overly prescriptive astronomical reading.[31]

Again, astrology does not dissuade Propertius from writing aetiological elegy, since the very next elegy in Book 4 is an aetiological one, although in the same book he also gives us erotic elegies, such as (most notably) 4.7, the appearance of Cynthia's ghost. So what exactly is the astrologer objecting to in Propertius, and does this affect how we see him as an astronomical model for the *Fasti*?

Context is important here. Horus objects to Propertius' project just after he begins to tell the future (4.1.67–8). Likewise, *non ... a dextro ... colo* (72) responds to Propertius' wish in 68, *inceptis dextera cantet avis*. The notable fact is that Propertius places astrology in opposition to other kinds of divination (the watching of birds is a particular target, perhaps because Romulus did it before founding Rome). The truth of astrology over divination is the issue here. None of the divinatory practices Horos mentions in 103–18 can compete with the *verus per astra* | *trames* (107–8).

[31] Cancer is the sign of the summer solstice and brings the harvest (Manilius 1.568ff.). Cancer as a sign is lacking in eyes (2.259–60); therefore his natives can be born blind if in addition that part of the sign which is covered by the 'cloud' (cluster) Praesaepe rises at their birth (4.530ff.). Mercury rules the Crab, and that is perhaps why its natives are skilled in trade (2.440, 4.162–75). The Crab is hostile to some of the signs favoured in Augustan astrology, including Capricorn, Libra and Virgo (2.547–53). At the same time, it gives rise to war, perhaps because ancient warfare took place in summer (*tunc et bella fero tractantur Marte cruenta*, 3.632), or because the sign itself is hot(-blooded?). Cancer-generated war, however, is against the adversaries of Rome, Scythia, Germany and Egypt, and so is not necessarily a bad thing (3.632–6).

The new opposition we have found, between astrology and divination, is germane to the discussion, since it reflects a cultural phenomenon with which we will be concerned in later chapters, namely the supersession of traditional divination by astrology at precisely this point in the early Empire.[32] Propertius might use astrology to dissuade himself from writing Roman aetiology (which nonetheless he goes on to do, albeit with some hesitation); but at the same time he reflects a phenomenon current in the Augustan period, the new prominence of astrology over divination.

In this respect 4.1 is consonant with the cultural climate of the Principate. Augustus published his horoscope by edict in 11 BC (Dio 56.25.5); his Principate saw the first in a long series of imperial edicts banning private astrological consultation.[33] Roman emperors always had an ambiguous relationship with astrology. Like the press by the modern monarchy, astrology was both exploited and feared by the Julio-Claudians and their successors. Why should the poetry of both Propertius and Ovid not reflect such ambiguity?

Let us summarise the debate. A straightforward reading of the stars in Propertius and the stars in Ovid cannot, we see, be produced from looking at Propertus 4.1 and the *Fasti*. The relationship between the two is partly one of opposition, partly one of consonance. An answer to the question of whether the Callimachean/Roman aetiological idiom, as we see it in Propertius 4.1, holds a place for the stars, is equally not straightforward. Certainly Callimachus' Berenice sat happily in the rag-bag of *Aetia* 4, but the Roman tradition looks somewhat different. Propertius 4.1 does *not* provide a generic precedent for the stars in Roman elegy, except in so far as the poet shows his skill in writing astrology into his elegy, while subordinating it to the programmatic *recusatio*. At the same time, Propertius has shown us that the stars are enough of a part of the cultural climate for him to use them in a way which exploits the comic potential of the

[32] Barton (1994) 38. See above, p. 7.

[33] Domenicucci (1996) ch. 2.

contemporary substitution of Greek astrology for Roman divinatory practice.

Finally, although they write in the same genre, the generic tensions in Propertius are different from those in Ovid. The opposition in Propertius is one of elegy to elegy (aetiological to erotic), much more like the original Callimachean opposition as interpreted by Cameron.[34] At the same time, Propertius has incorporated a divination/astrology opposition which makes his poem contemporary for anyone reading it in the Augustan period, when divination was being superseded by astrology, and astrology was in turn a means of articulating the power of the Princeps. In Ovid, astronomy takes its place alongside divination, as we have seen it in Carmentis' speech (*Fasti* 1.513). These alternative world-views both belong in the *Fasti*, as part of its set of competing media. Nor can the stars in Ovid be seen as part of an elegiac opposition to epic, as I shall go on to show.

Epic: Virgil's Shield of Aeneas

It is implicit in the orthodoxy that has developed in *Fasti* scholarship since the eighties that Ovid is negotiating a double opposition in the *Fasti*: between peace and war, and between elegy and epic. Ovid is usually said to be in favour of the first element in each pair. We have already seen from Propertius 4.1 that the situation is more complex. That is not to say that an adversative relationship between elegy and epic in the *Fasti* must be ruled out altogether: such a relationship is clearly one component of Ovidian poetic language across his entire *oeuvre*. A parallel opposition between epic and didactic will be seen to emerge strongly from discussion of *Fasti* 1.295–310 later in this chapter.

Aeneid 8 is an *epic* model common to both the *Fasti* and Propertius, *Elegies* 4.[35] The Propertian/Ovidian opposition

[34] Above, n. 11.

[35] On Propertius 4.1 and *Aeneid* 8, see Butler and Barber (1933) *ad* 4.1.1–70, Stahl (1985) 256. Hardie (1986) 354 points out in addition that Propertius' Actium elegy (4.6) is closely dependent on the Virgilian Shield.

between early Rome and the present day takes its hexameter origin from *Aeneid* 8. The festivals which Propertius and Ovid talk about are present in *Aeneid* 8. In addition, the Shield of Aeneas can tell us something about the contemporary significance of the astronomy in the *Fasti*.

First, let us briefly consider *Aeneid* 8 in its entirety as a model for Ovid's *Fasti*. Ovid follows the least 'epic' (in the martial sense) and most Callimachean (in the aetiological sense) book of the *Aeneid*, and this is as one would expect, since the *Fasti* is a religious aetiological work about Rome. Ovid has magnified *Aeneid* 8 under the lens of the *Fasti*. Ovid's six existing books enlarge the aetiological, religious, historical and panegyrical content of *Aeneid* 8.

In *Aeneid* 8, Evander takes Aeneas on a tour of the future Rome, the prevailing theme of which, like Propertius 4.1.1–70 and the corresponding passages of the *Fasti* which we examined above, is the progression from small to great, Evandrian to Augustan.[36] This tour is to a large extent reduplicated in the scenes on the Shield of Aeneas which ends *Aeneid* 8. The Shield thus becomes a synopsis of *Aeneid* 8. Ovid's *Fasti*, because it is an enlargement of *Aeneid* 8, is also a magnified Shield of Aeneas, with all that entails, including (as we shall see) the stars. The elements of Virgil's narrative topography in the walk around Rome are distilled into scenes on the Shield of Aeneas; it is easy for Ovid then to transfer the same tableaux into a festival aetiology such as the *Fasti*.

The connection between the walk around Rome in the early part of *Aeneid* 8, and the *Fasti*, is most pronounced in the Carmentis episode of *Fasti* 1.461–586, which we have studied above in connection with Propertius. At *Aeneid* 8.99–100, Aeneas and Evander see Evander's dwelling:

> tecta vident, quae nunc Romana potentia caelo
> aequavit, tum res inopes Evandrus habebat.[37]

[36] On the topography of the walk, and parallels with the *Fasti*, see Gransden (1976) 29–36, and notes *ad Aen.* 8.341, 630.

[37] Compare line 100 with Propertius 4.1.4, and see also *Aen.* 8.359f., *tecta | pauperis Evandri.*

Ovid uses the same term, *tecta*, in his Carmentalia (*Fasti* 1.541–2):

> nec mora longa fuit: stabant nova tecta, nec alter
> montibus Ausoniis Arcade maior erat.

Tecta might be considered ambiguous here; while it certainly refers to the Evandrian buildings, the *tecta* of the new Rome surely come to mind, the more so since Carmentis has already looked forward to Augustan Rome at *Fasti* 1.515–17:

> fallor, an hi fient ingentia moenia colles,
> iuraque ab hac terra cetera terra petet?
> montibus his olim totus promittitur orbis.

The starting-point of Virgil's tour of Rome is the *Ara Maxima* (*Aen.* 8.271), which is commemorated at *Fasti* 1.581–2. The walk in *Aeneid* 8 reaches the Temple of Jupiter Capitolinus at *Aeneid* 8.347–8:

> hinc ad Tarpeiam sedem et Capitolia ducit
> aurea nunc, olim silvestribus horrida dumis.

The temple of Jupiter Capitolinus was traditionally built on the site of Tarpeia's tomb by Tarquinius (Plutarch, *Romulus* 18.1) and restored by Augustus.[38] It is alluded to by Ovid at *Fasti* 1.85–6, in the context of Roman world empire:

> Iuppiter arce sua totum cum spectet in orbem,
> nil nisi Romanum quod tueatur habet.

Between these two landmarks comes a topography of Roman cult. At *Aeneid* 8.285–305, the Salii, the leaping priests of Mars, give thanks for Hercules' defeat of Cacus. The *Caci | speluncam* of *Aen.* 8.303–4 is presumably the same cave as at *Fasti* 1.550, *traxerat aversos (boves) Cacus in antra ferox*. Ovid gives the Salii a long episode, at *Fasti* 3.259–392, which I shall deal with presently.

Virgil's religious topography also includes the Lupercal (*Aen.* 8.343, *gelida monstrat sub rupe Lupercal*), a site connected both with the Lupercalia of *Fasti* 2.381ff., and with the

[38] See *Res Gestae* 19.

upbringing of Romulus and Remus, a theme throughout Ovid's Roman aetiological poem.[39] Suetonius, *Augustus* 31.4 says that these were among the cults Augustus restored: *nonnulla etiam ex antiquis caerimoniis paulatim abolita restituit, ut ... sacrum Lupercale*. Virgil's walk thus includes the locations of the Augustan religious restoration, the subject of Ovid's *Fasti*.

The Salii, the Lupercal and the twins all reappear later on the Shield of Aeneas. The first scene on the Shield is that of Romulus and Remus (*Aen.* 8.626–34), and the cave in 630 is the Lupercal. The Salii and Luperci are juxtaposed at *Aeneid* 8.663–5:

> hic exsultantis Salios nudosque Lupercos
> lanigerosque apices et lapsa ancilia caelo
> extuderat ...

The *apices* and *ancilia* both belonged to the Salii; the *apices* are their priestly hats, the *ancilia* the shields carried by the Salii, the prototype of which fell from heaven during the reign of Numa as a gift from Jupiter.[40] The Shield of Aeneas can itself be taken (partly at least) as a synopsis of the cults restored by Augustus.

So far, this exploration of *Aeneid* 8 as a model for Ovid's *Fasti* has shown us an overlap in terms of Roman cult, but has left unanswered the question of the stars. Aeneas' Shield is cosmological, as Philip Hardie in particular has shown.[41] It is not overtly astronomical; its key literary model, however, Homer's Shield of Achilles (*Iliad* 18.483–608), does incorporate the stars, and does so in a prominent position at the beginning of the ekphrasis:

> ἐν μὲν γαῖαν ἔτευξ', ἐν δ' οὐρανόν, ἐν δὲ θάλασσαν,
> ἠέλιόν τ' ἀκάμαντα σελήνην τε πλήθουσαν,
> ἐν δὲ τὰ τείρεα πάντα, τά τ' οὐρανὸς ἐστεφάνωται,
> Πληιάδας θ' Ὑάδας τε τό τε σθένος Ὠρίωνος
> Ἄρκτον θ', ἣν καὶ Ἄμαξαν ἐπίκλησιν καλέουσιν,
> ἥ τ' αὐτοῦ στρέφεται καί τ' Ὠρίωνα δοκεύει,
> οἴη δ' ἄμμορός ἐστι λοετρῶν Ὠκεανοῖο. (*Iliad* 18.483–9)

[39] See also Propertius 4.1.26. [40] See below, pp. 41–7. [41] Hardie (1986) 359.

On it he [Hephaistos] made the earth, and sky, and sea, the weariless sun and the moon waxing full, and all the constellations that crown the heavens, Pleiades and Hyades, the mighty Orion and the Bear, which men also call by the name of Wain: she wheels round in the same place and watches for Orion, and is the only one not to bathe in Ocean.[42]

Astronomy is present at a substrate level in the Shield of Aeneas, through its model, the Shield of Achilles. As Hardie showed, Homer's Shield was developed by Hellenistic interpreters into an allegory for the scientific universe; furthermore, this world picture was open to monarchical exploitation as a symbol of world empire, in iconography as well as in literature.[43] Such exploitation began in the Hellenistic kingdoms (perhaps as far back as Alexander), particularly the Attalid kingdom of Pergamum, and carried over into the Roman period. It is in the cosmological-panegyrical tradition that Virgil's Shield belongs.

The grandly cosmological aspect of the Shield is connected with the issues of catasterism and world empire we shall explore in chapters 5 and 6. It is present in Virgil's Shield from the scene of its forging. At *Aeneid* 8.427, the Cyclopes are interrupted from their making of a *fulmen* (one of Jupiter's thunderbolts). *Fulmina* are the epic *arma* of Zeus from Homer onwards, *toto genitor quae plurima caelo | deicit in terras* (*Aen.* 8.427–8).[44] These same artisans, then, turn from their stocking of Jupiter's arsenal to the manufacture of Aeneas' Shield, something else which will fall from the heavens. They form the Shield from concentric circles of metal, *septenosque orbibus orbis | impediunt, Aeneid* 8.448–9. This is how shields in Homer were fashioned too, for example Agamemnon's Shield at *Iliad* 11.33: ἣν πέρι μὲν κύκλοι δέκα χάλκεοι ἦσαν.[45] But

[42] Trans. Hammond (1987).
[43] Hardie (1985a) 11: 'The image of the cosmos becomes an emblem of the power, actual or anticipated, of the king.'
[44] See *Fasti* 3.439–40: *fulmina post ausos caelum adfectare Gigantas | sumpta Iovi: primo tempore inermis erat*. On *fulmina* and epic, see Hardie (1986) 183–7.
[45] See also Idomeneus' Shield at 13.406–7.

orbis in Virgil can also mean the starry heaven.[46] The latter is its meaning elsewhere, as at *Aeneid* 8.136–7:

> Electram maximus Atlas
> edidit, aetherios umero qui sustinet orbis.

For the Augustan reader the massive circular structure of the Shield could have been suggestive of the *orbis terrarum*: 'The sphere is an ambiguous symbol, for it can refer either to the spherical earth or to the spherical universe; as a symbol of power it can thus stand either for control of the *oikoumene* or for a more ambitious claim to cosmic might.'[47] The globe as a symbol of power in Roman iconography fudges the boundary between the map-like *orbis terrarum*, the *oikoumene* or inhabited world over which the domination of Rome extended, and the *orbis* in its three-dimensional form, the *sphaira*, model of the natural-philosophical universe.[48] Domination of the *oikoumene* is translated into domination of the universe.

In the *Aeneid*, an analogy develops between Aeneas, Augustus and Atlas as shoulderers of world burdens.[49] At *Aeneid* 8.136, Atlas is described as *maximus Atlas* | ... *aetherios umero qui sustinet orbis*. In the closing lines of *Aeneid* 8, Aeneas raises the Shield onto his shoulders (*Aen.* 8.729–31):

> Talia per clipeum Volcani, dona parentis,
> miratur rerumque ignarus imagine gaudet
> attollens umero famaque et fata nepotum.

Imagine in 730 might signal Virgil's recognition of an allegorical tradition which interpreted the Shield of Achilles, the precursor of that of Aeneas, as a κόσμου μίμημα (*imago*

46 Gransden (1976) *ad loc.*: there is a play on two specific meanings of *orbis* here, the circular plates of the shield, and the circling heavens.

47 Hardie (1986) 267.

48 See chapter 4 below. The globe as a symbol of the *orbis terrarum* is first found on coins of the seventies BC, and became common under Caesar (see Hardie (1986) 368 and Weinstock (1971) 42–5). Augustus appears with a globe in Hardie (1986) pl. 5. According to Hardie, the globe on top of the Horologium (*ibid.* pl. 6) signified the Princeps' direction of time as part of world empire. See also Brendel (1977), L'Orange (1953).

49 See Gransden (1976) *ad Aen.* 8.136–7, Hardie (1986) 374.

mundi).[50] Ovid later heralds his own recognition of such a tradition by describing the Shield of Achilles at *Metamorphoses* 13.110 as a *clipeus vasti caelatus imagine mundi*.[51]

At *Aeneid* 6.792–7, Augustus, who sustains the limits of Roman power (which are the same as the outer limits of the universe), is a kind of Atlas figure, since his power extends outside the physical universe, to where Atlas shoulders the world:

> Augustus Caesar, divi genus, aurea condet
> saecula qui rursus Latio regnata per arva
> Saturno quondam, super et Garamantas et Indos
> proferet imperium; iacet extra sidera tellus,
> extra anni solisque vias, ubi caelifer Atlas
> axem umero torquet stellis ardentibus aptum.

The world Atlas sustains is star-studded, as was Homer's Shield of Achilles. When Aeneas, Atlas or Augustus shoulder their burdens, they shoulder the stars as well.

Stars are associated with divinity,[52] not least in the case of Julius Caesar at *Aeneid* 1.286–8:

> nascetur pulchra Troianus origine Caesar,
> imperium Oceano, famam qui terminet astris,
> Iulius....

Not only will Caesar's *imperium* fill the limits circumscribed by the River of Ocean (which runs around the edge of Homer's world), but his reputation will fill the universe. *Famam qui terminet astris* also plays with the idea of Caesar's catasterism, his turning into a star after his death in 44 BC.[53]

At *Iliad* 18.485 the constellations on the Shield of Achilles are described as τείρεα: monsters or portents. The word can also mean meteor or comet (since comets tended to have portentous status in antiquity); and indeed it is a comet that ap-

[50] The Greek phrase is used of the Shield of Achilles by the scholia on Aratus, *Phaenomena* 26: see below, p. 112.

[51] Much later, Eustathius (the allegoriser probably following Crates of Mallos) describes the Shield of Agamemnon in *Iliad* 11 as a μίμημα τοῦ κόσμου. See Hardie (1985a) 16. Ovid's expression may hark back to the Cratetean allegory.

[52] See Hardie (1985a) 11.

[53] See below, chapter 6.

pears on Virgil's Shield, the *Sidus Iulium*, which was taken to signify the ascent of the dictator's soul, and the sanctification of Octavian as his successor.[54] The star appears on Augustus' helmet: *patriumque aperitur vertice sidus* (*Aen.* 8.681). A literary prototype for the starry helmet is the simile of Diomede's helmet at *Iliad* 5.5, which is like an ἀστὴρ ὀπωρινός ('a midsummer star'). The star referred to may well be Sirius, a fierce, hot star which rises in August and announces the 'Dog Days'. In similar vein, Aeneas, with his burning crest, is compared to a comet, or the Dog Star itself:

> ardet apex capiti cristisque a vertice flamma
> funditur et vastos umbo vomit aureus ignes:
> non secus ac liquida si quando nocte cometae
> sanguinei lugubre rubent, aut Sirius ardor
> ille sitim morbosque ferens mortalibus aegris
> nascitur et laevo contristat lumine caelum. (*Aeneid* 10.270–5)

Aeneas' head burns (*ardet apex capiti*), just as at *Aeneid* 8.681, the flame of the *patrium sidus* rested on the head of Augustus. In *Aeneid* 10, Aeneas recalls Augustus fighting at Actium, as we saw him on the Shield in Book 8. Actium is where Augustus vindicates his claim as a world ruler; it is here that the astral imagery of Homer's Shield emerges from its substrate level to become explicit in Virgil's, adapted to the Roman context.

So far we have seen the astronomical associations of Virgil's Shield of Aeneas, and this has taken us some way from Ovid; but there is a point of intersection between the Virgilian Shield and the *Fasti*. In *Fasti* 3, Ovid introduces his own heavenly shield into his calendar poem: the *ancile*, the sacred shield which fell from heaven in the reign of king Numa. Copies of this shield were carried by the Salii in their ritual dance. The *ancilia* from *Aeneid* 8.664 are given a long episode at *Fasti* 3.259–392 in which they might be seen to act as Ovid's equivalent of Aeneas' Shield. In Ovid, the peaceable ruler seeks an apotropaic ritual for Zeus' epic *arma*, his

[54] Pliny, *NH* 2.94.

fulmina. In the end he obtains *caelestia arma*[55] of his own which, like Aeneas' Shield, fall as a gift from heaven. Unlike Aeneas' Shield, the *ancile* is a religious, not a military shield, since it is destined to be used in Roman cult. It reflects Ovid's religious project in the *Fasti* in the same way that Virgil's Shield represents his epic project.

Let us look in more detail at *Fasti* 3.259–392. In this passage Ovid summons the nymph Egeria, the wife of King Numa, to help him solve a religious riddle: why do the leaping priests, the Salii, carry Mars' heavenly arms and sing 'Mamurius' (*Fasti* 3.259–60)? Egeria is the goddess of the Arician Grove, where Hippolytus had been deposited after being ripped apart by his horses: hence no horse is allowed in (*Fasti* 3.261–6). In this grove priests reign while they are strong enough to avoid being killed by potential successors (271–2).

Numa comes at a point in Roman history when bellicose ways were exchanged for religious ritual (277–84). It so happened that he was present during a portentous shower of thunderbolts (*Fasti* 3.285–8). Egeria advises the king to seek advice about expiating the thunderbolts from two old Roman deities, Picus and Faunus. The two gods are duly caught and forced to summon Jupiter so that he might tell Numa how to expiate the thunderbolt (289–328).

There follows a remarkable dialogue between Numa and the god (339–46). Jupiter asks for a head (*caput*), to which Numa replies that an onion (*cepa*) will be substituted. The god insists that a man's head is meant, and Numa says 'You shall have the hair of a man.' Jupiter asks for a life, and Numa agrees: 'A fish's life.' Jupiter laughs and replies that he will let Numa buy him off in this way, and that in addition, on the next day, he will provide the king with a pledge of empire.

Numa and the citizens line up and wait; in due course they

[55] It is Livy who dubs them thus, speaking of the religious reforms of Numa: *Salios item duodecim Marti Gradivo legit [Numa], tunicaeque pictae insigne dedit et super tunicam aeneum pectori tegumen; caelestiaque arma, quae ancilia appellantur, ferre ac per urbem ire canentes carmina cum tripudiis sollemnique saltatu iussit* (Livy 1.20.4).

are rewarded: thunder and lightning (line 369 – *ter tonuit sine nube deus, tria fulgura misit*) herald the fall of a shield, the *ancile*, from heaven. Having followed correct sacrificial procedure (lines 375–6), they pick up the shield. Numa orders the craftsman Mamurius to make eleven exact duplicates, to defeat any prospective thief in his attempt to take the original (381–6). As a reward, Mamurius asks that his name be sung by the Salii every year (389–92).

There are many mysteries in this passage, some of which I have explored elsewhere.[56] Relevant here is the analogy with the Shield of Aeneas. In both cases the shields are *munera* from heaven (*Aen.* 8.613 and *Fasti* 3.365, 375). At *Fasti* 3.346, 354, and 379, the shields are *imperii pignora.* Likewise Virgil's Shield of Aeneas was both a guarantee of victory over Turnus and a guarantee of the world empire it represents.[57] At *Fasti* 3.367–8 the descent of the *ancile* is described in the sort of cosmic language we have been dealing with in the case of Virgil's Shield of Aeneas:

> totum iam sol emoverat orbem,
> et gravis aetherio venit ab axe fragor.

Note especially *orbis* (the starry heavens) and *axis*, with their Atlantean overtones.

The descent of the *ancile* in Ovid may even remind us of the prospective catasterism of Augustus and thus be connected with the astronomical-monarchical side of the Shield of Aeneas. Compare *Fasti* 3.371, *a media caelum regione dehiscere coepit*, with Virgil, *Georgics* 1.33–5, of the catasterism of Augustus: *qua locus Erigonen inter Chelasque sequentis | panditur (ipse tibi iam bracchia contrahit ardens | Scorpius et caeli iusta plus parte reliquit)* . . . The road between earth and heaven is two-way; things can come down (like the Shields) and also go up (like Julius Caesar and Augustus). It is also possible that the *ancile* in Ovid is like Caesar's catasterism in that both are the result of something bad (a shower of thunderbolts, a

[56] *Antichthon* 32 (1998): 64–90.   [57] Hardie (1986) 367.

comet) turned into something good (a pledge of empire, astral apotheosis).

The form of the Ovidian *ancile* as an *imago mundi* is made explicit when the poet gives its etymology. Numa is the namer of the Shield: Ovid places its etymology in the mouth of the king (*Fasti* 3.377–8):[58]

> idque ancile vocat, quod ab omni parte recisum est,
> quaque notes oculis **angulus omnis abest**.

The shape of the shields here appears to be round, rather than figure-of-eight shaped as the shields of the Salii are described elsewhere (Plutarch, *Numa* 13.5):

Αὐτὰς δὲ τὰς πέλτας ἀγκύλια καλοῦσι διὰ τὸ σχῆμα· κύκλος γὰρ οὐκ ἔστιν οὐδὲ ἀποδίδωσιν, ὡς πέλτη, τὴν περιφέρειαν, ἀλλ᾽ ἐκτομὴν ἔχει γραμμῆς ἑλικοειδοῦς, ἧς αἱ κεραῖαι καμπὰς ἔχουσαι καὶ συνεπιστρέφουσαι τῇ πυκνότητι πρὸς ἀλλήλας ἀγκύλον τὸ σχῆμα ποιοῦσιν· ἢ διὰ τὸν ἀγκῶνα περὶ ὃν περιφέρονται.

The bucklers themselves are called 'ancilia' from their shape; for this is not round, nor yet completely oval, like that of the regular shield, but has a curving indentation, the arms of which are bent back and united with each other at top and bottom; this makes the shape 'anculon', the Greek for *curved*.[59]

One imagines that Plutarch's shields are figure-of-eight shaped. We can surmise that Ovid, on the other hand, intends the *ancile* to be round because the phrase with which he describes its shape is identical to his later description of the *globe* of the earth suspended in the middle of the universe at *Fasti* 6.271–2, a description we shall return to in chapter 4:[60]

> ipsa volubilitas libratum sustinet orbem,
> quique premat partes **angulus omnis abest**.

Why does Ovid make the *ancilia* round? The obvious answer, given the echo at *Fasti* 6.271, would be that he wants them to

[58] In Varro, *ancile* is from *am(bo)cisum*, cut away on both sides: Varro, *Ling*. 7.43: '*ancilia*' *dicta ab ambecisu, quod ea arma ab utraque parte ... incisa*. See Maltby (1991), '*ancile*'.
[59] Trans. Perrin (1967).
[60] See below, pp. 101–4.

be a model of the universe.[61] Like the Shield of Aeneas, the *ancile* is an *imago mundi* which is also a guarantee of Roman rulership over the world it represents: a *pignus imperii*.

Working along these lines, we might try to fit the *ancilia* into Augustan panegyric. Their Numan origin fits nicely with the *Pax Augusta*.[62] At *Fasti* 3.281 Numa is law-giver after the martial rule of Romulus: *exuitur feritas, armisque potentius aequum est*. However, the shields are not obtained without a degree of violence, which emerges at the capture of Picus and Faunus: *nec sine vi tradent*, *Fasti* 3.289. They are themselves *arma*, as we remember, albeit symbolic (religious) weapons. They are thus a good image for the later Principate, a peaceful régime based on former conquest: the expiation of the thunderbolt which results in the *pignora imperii* does involve violence, just as the establishment of the *Pax Augusta* did. All this is part of a delicate balance of war and peace in the Augustan Principate: 'Peace is the inevitable consequence of the achievement of world empire ... and in Augustan ideology the themes of universal rule and the *pax Augusta* ... go hand in hand.'[63]

The *ancilia* in Ovid can be *pignora imperii* without also being martial shields: they represent the transformation of Virgil's martial Shield of Aeneas into a part of religious ritual. Furthermore, while the story of the *ancilia* can be read symbolically as the sublimation of military *arma* (the Shield of Aeneas or the weapons of Octavian's civil wars) in religious

[61] Illustrations of the figure-of-eight type are found on coins dated *c.* 17 BC (see Frazer (1929) *ad Fasti* 3.377); the shields could apparently also be depicted as round bucklers rendered slightly oblong by chopping off the top and bottom end: Ovid's shape is not, therefore, without parallel (for an illustration of this type, see Harrison (1912) 194–6).

[62] Galinsky (1996) 36 connects a Numa coin issue with Augustus' original plan to hold Secular Games in 23 BC. According to Galinsky, the Numa bronzes look forward to a theme of Augustan coinage: a de-emphasis of military subjects in favour of themes of peaceful consolidation. At the same time, Galinsky introduces a qualification: 'This does not mean ... the projection of a blissful "Golden Age" or a renunciation of world conquest because *pax* and *victoria* remained closely linked. It was simply that the former now received as much expression as the latter, often with the help of emblems of a religion that had originated with Numa.'

[63] Hardie (1986) 358.

ritual (the *ancilia* of Numa, the religious restoration of Augustus), it can also be read generically as a parable defining the *Fasti* as a religious-elegiac work of epic proportions. In the same way that Virgil's Shield of Aeneas might be said to distil the themes of Virgil's epic poem, Ovid's *ancilia* are a parallel for the *Fasti*: these are not martial shields, but cultic shields: the form of militarism (or of epic) without its function. Appropriately, the feather-like shield which wafts down from the sky at *Fasti* 3.373 is *levis* (not *durus*, as would befit a martial or, in poetic terms, epic shield).[64] Numa in *Fasti* 3 can be read as parallel to Ovid, who does not write hexameter epic but uses its materials (such as cosmology) in cultic aetiology.

One theme of the passage we have studied will be seen to be of importance later: that of Jupiter and his thunderbolts.[65] It is worth reading on in the Ovidian text, to see how this theme is developed after the Numa passage. The following entry is a record of the dedication of two temples to Veiovis, the young Jupiter. Here we are back with the Propertian theme of the growth of Rome; note at *Fasti* 3.432, *o quam de tenui Romanus origine crevit*. Veiovis is himself a representative of the theme of origins, as we see from his etymology, at 437–44:

> Iuppiter est iuvenis: iuvenales aspice voltus;
>   aspice deinde manum: fulmina nulla tenet.
> fulmina post ausos caelum adfectare Gigantas
>   sumpta Iovi: primo tempore inermis erat;
> ignibus Ossa novis et Pelion altius Ossa
>   arsit et in solida fixus Olympus humo.
> stat quoque Capra simul: nymphae pavisse feruntur
>   Cretides, infanti lac dedit illa Iovi.

Appropriately enough for the preceding Numa episode, Jupiter here carries no *fulmina*. He became an epic god only after the gigantomachy. Ovid's poem, being about origins, is an alternative to epic, and epic is a genre of poetry which could be represented by gigantomachy.[66] The youth of Jupiter is a

[64] For the *levis/durus* opposition in poetic programme, see Hinds (1987a) 4–24, Newlands (1991).
[65] Below, pp. 146–53.
[66] As we shall see in the following section.

theme in Ovid's poem, returning at *Fasti* 5.111–28.[67] Jupiter without his *fulmina* (which, remember, the Cyclopes were hammering out in *Aeneid* 8 just before they turned to the making of Aeneas' Shield) can act as a symbol parallel to the *ancilia*, denoting the politics of peace and the poetry of origins.

To draw together the threads of this section: here we have studied *Aeneid* 8 as an epic model for the stars in Ovid's *Fasti*. At first, the aetiological connection seems clear, the astronomical link tenuous, the more so since the only point at which astronomy is explicit in the Shield of Aeneas is the appearance of the *Patrium Sidus* on Augustus' helmet at Actium. However, this is a moment of fundamental importance, and opened up for us an entire stratum of astronomical imagery in the *Aeneid*, a type of imagery which, connected as it is with universal empire, will become important when we discuss Ovid's stars in the light of their cultural context, in chapters 5 and 6 below. It is possible to argue that some of the epic importance of the stars in the *Aeneid* must carry over into the *Fasti*, the more so since Ovid may be reacting to the Shield of Aeneas in *Fasti* 3.259–392.

The didactic tradition

Our study of Numa and the *ancilia* has shown us a modified version of the epic/elegy dichotomy: Ovid rejects martial epic but uses its materials in religious aetiology. It is not erotic elegy which is opposed to epic, but aetiological writing. Didactic poetry is also part of the generic repertoire of the *Fasti*, and it too may be placed in opposition to martial epic. In fact, didactic is arguably the dominant genre in the *Fasti*, and undoubtedly provides a place for the stars.

Ovid's first astronomical entries (*Fasti* 1.311–16) are preceded by their own quasi-proem (henceforward to be referred

[67] This passage is discussed in chapter 5 below. Ovid's *feruntur* at *Fasti* 3.443 signals, as often in *Fasti*, the poet's choice between alternatives in the literary tradition, and indeed, as we shall see, the youth of Jupiter, which is a theme in panegyric from Callimachus onwards, came in different versions.

to as the Eulogy of Astronomers), which presents the poet as following didactic precedents:

Quid vetat et stellas, ut quaeque oriturque caditque,
 dicere? promissi pars sit et ista mei.
felices animae, quibus haec cognoscere primis
 inque domos superas scandere cura fuit!
credibile est illos pariter vitiisque locisque
 altius humanis exseruisse caput.
non Venus et vinum sublimia pectora fregit
 officiumque fori militiaeve labor;
nec levis ambitio perfusaque gloria fuco
 magnarumque fames sollicitavit opum.
admovere oculis distantia sidera mentis
 aetheraque ingenio supposuere suo.
sic petitur caelum, non ut ferat Ossan Olympus
 summaque Peliacus sidera tangat apex.
nos quoque sub ducibus caelum metabimur illis,
 ponemusque suos ad vaga signa dies. (*Fasti* 1.295–310)

As Newlands points out, 'When Ovid says at the conclusion of his panegyric on astronomy, *nos quoque sub ducibus caelum metabimur illis* (309), his true *duces* are not only nameless astronomers but first and foremost his predecessors in Roman didactic poetry.'[68] Through the Eulogy, one may argue that the emphasis which hitherto in scholarship has been placed upon the aetiological elegiac models for the *Fasti*, Callimachus and Propertius, should be applied to its hexameter didactic ancestry. Some of the predecessors of Ovid's Eulogy, namely Virgil's *recusatio* at *Georgics* 2.458–540, and Lucretius' praise of Epicurus, particularly in *De Rerum Natura* 1, have already been studied,[69] so I shall merely mention Virgil, as he enters my own argument, introduce some new ideas about Lucretius, and then proceed to study some didactic parallels which have not yet been explored.

The result of my discussion will be a reading of the passage as a network of didactic allusions; from this will emerge an agenda based on the importance of the Aratean model.

[68] Newlands (1995) 36.
[69] Newlands (1995) 34. Another model is the proem to the second book of Lucretius' *DRN* (Schilling (1992–3) *ad loc.*).

Aratus enters the programme of the Eulogy of Astronomers in several different ways, giving us a cumulative and complex picture of how the Aratean material in the *Fasti* will function. At the same time the Eulogy brings us into a tradition of Stoic exegesis, which has not been considered by earlier scholars writing on the *Fasti*, but which is an essential component in its machinery.

First, Virgil's *Georgics*:

> o fortunatos nimium, sua si bona norint,
> agricolas! quibus ipsa procul discordibus armis
> fundit humo facilem victum iustissima tellus;
> si non ingentem foribus domus alta superbis
> mane salutantum totis vomit aedibus undam,
> nec varios inhiant pulchra testudine postis
> inlusasque auro vestis Ephyreiaque aera,
> alba neque Assyrio fucatur lana veneno,
> nec casia liquidi corrumpitur usus olivi ... (*Georgics* 2.458–66)

The closest point of comparison between the Virgilian *recusatio* and Ovid's Eulogy is the convention of beatitude (*makarismos*). The initial line of Ovid's eulogy of astronomers, *felices animae, quibus haec cognoscere primis*, recalls both *Georgics* 2.458 and *Georgics* 2.490, *felix qui potuit rerum cognoscere causas*. The immediate comparison in Virgil between the two kinds of people who are apostrophised is that the first group are farmers, the second philosophers, or rather a philosopher (*qui potuit rerum cognoscere causas*). More will be said on the latter presently. For now, we should note that the two apostrophes set up the opposition on which Virgil's *recusatio* hinges: farmers and scientists are both blessed (*fortunatos, felix*), but Virgil is only capable of praising the former appropriately, since he is a writer of agricultural rather than scientific poetry. Ovid's use of the beatitude in the *Fasti* is an answer to this, in that it praises scientists, and Ovid is at least in part a writer of scientific (astronomical) poetry. This much is common currency of *Fasti* scholarship.[70]

Likewise, Ovid echoes the prevailing *topoi* of Virgil's

[70] See, for example, Newlands (1995) 37.

recusatio: compare *Fasti* 1.299–306, the theme of luxury, and military and political activity, with *Georgics* 2.459–66. The common model for both Virgil and Ovid in this respect is Lucretius' eulogy of the simple enlightened life at *DRN* 2.1–60, where the objects of criticism are also luxury, military activity, and political ambition. Ovid is closer to Lucretius, whose philosophers shun these things, than to Virgil, whose farmers do without. Ovid has reverted to the Lucretian opposition between philosophy and public life, whereas Virgil's contrast in these lines is one of urban and rural existence, his overall opposition being between agricultural and scientific poetry. At the same time, Ovid responds to Virgil in that he reapplies the imagery of luxury and ambition from Virgil's *agricolae* to his own *felices animae*, astronomers. Echo of Virgil's beatitude thus performs the function of doubly orientating Ovid in the tradition of didactic poetry, the more so since the *felix* of *Georgics* 2.490 may be Lucretius.[71]

Often the Lucretian material on which Virgil draws is specifically astronomical. This is particularly obvious in *Georgics* 2.475–82:

> me vero primum dulces ante omnia Musae,
> quarum sacra fero ingenti percussus amore,
> accipiant caelique vias et sidera monstrent,
> defectus solis varios lunaeque labores;
> unde tremor terris, qua vi maria alta tumescant
> obicibus ruptis rursusque in se ipsa residant,
> quid tantum Oceano properent se tingere soles
> hiberni, vel quae tardis mora noctibus obstet.

Georgics 2.478 – *defectus solis varios lunaeque labores* – recalls the programmatic beginning of Lucretius' astronomical exposition, *DRN* 5.751, *solis item quoque defectus lunaeque latebras*, and *DRN* 5.774–5:[72]

> solis uti varios cursus lunaeque meatus
> noscere possemus quae vis et causa cieret ...

[71] Hardie (1986) 40.

Similarly, one may compare the list of *topoi* at *Georgics* 2.479–82 with the subject matter of the fifth and sixth books of the *DRN*, which deal with astronomy and meteorology. *Georgics* 2.479–82 may also remind us of Lucretius' jingle at *DRN* 6.83–5:

> est ratio caeli ⟨species⟩ que tenenda,
> sunt tempestates et fulmina clara canenda,
> quid faciant et qua de causa cumque ferantur ...

These passages of Lucretius and Virgil are both examples of the kind of syllabus common in didactic poetry, used to set out the parameters of the poet's enquiry in a series of indirect questions.[73] Think of *Georgics* 1.1–5:

> quid faciat laetas segetes, quo sidere terram
> vertere, Maecenas, ulmisque adiungere vitis
> conveniat, quae cura boum, qui cultus habendo
> sit pecori, apibus quanta experientia parcis,
> hinc canere incipiam.

In *Georgics* 2.479–82, as at the beginning of the poem, Virgil is writing in the conventions of didactic; in *Georgics* 2.479–82, the former passage, the immediate didactic model is scientific or astronomical.

What is more, Virgil apparently chooses in his *recusatio* to echo passages from *DRN* in which Lucretius is at his most Aratean. Several of the Lucretian examples quoted above are from *DRN* 5 and 6. In these books Lucretius is treating the same subjects as his Hellenistic didactic predecessor Aratus, and in the same order: astronomy followed by meteorology.[74]

In fact, the *recusatio* of *Georgics* 2 gives us a double dose of Aratus: indirectly, by allusion to Lucretius 5 and 6, where Lucretius is writing in the Aratean tradition, and also by di-

[72] Both these passages may be compared with the cosmological Song of Iopas in *Aeneid* 1, where Virgil assumes the didactic voice under the cover of his epic narrative. For example, *Aen.* 1.742, *hic canit errantem lunam solisque labores*, recalls *Geo.* 2.478 and its Lucretian model. On the song of Iopas and the Homeric Shield of Achilles, see Hardie (1986) 63 n. 72, and Brown (1990) 325–6 and n. 17.

[73] See above, n. 25.

[74] It is not important for this purpose that Lucretius is philosophically opposed to the Stoic Aratus; he belongs by his subject matter in *DRN* 5 and 6 to the Aratean tradition of astronomical didactic.

rect allusion, since in it Virgil imitates Aratus' tableau of Justice (*Dike*) quitting the earth appalled by the evil of man:[75]

> extrema per illos
> Iustitia excedens terris vestigia fecit.
> (*Georgics* 2.473–4)

> καὶ τότε μισήσασα Δίκη κείνων γένος ἀνδρῶν
> ἔπταθ' ὑπουρανίη, ταύτην δ' ἄρα νάσσατο χώρην,
> ἧχί περ ἐννυχίη ἔτι φαίνεται ἀνθρώποισι
> Παρθένος ἐγγὺς ἐοῦσα πολυσκέπτοιο Βοώτεω.
> (Aratus, *Phaenomena* 133–6)

Then Justice, conceiving a hatred for the generation of these men, flew up to the sky and took up her abode in that place, where she is still visible to men by night as the Maiden near conspicuous Bootes.

Virgil's astronomical Muses are close to the Muses invoked by the astral poet Aratus in his proem:

> me vero primum **dulces** ante omnia **Musae**,
> quarum sacra fero ingenti percussus amore,
> accipiant caelique vias et **sidera monstrent** . . .
> (*Georgics* 2.475–7)

> χαίροιτε δὲ **Μοῦσαι,**
> **μειλίχιαι** μάλα πᾶσαι· ἐμοί γε μὲν **ἀστέρας εἰπεῖν**
> ᾗ θέμις εὐχομένῳ τεκμήρατε πᾶσαν ἀοιδήν.
> (*Phaenomena* 16–18)

And hail, Muses, all most gracious! In answer to my prayer to tell of the stars in so far as I may, guide all my singing.

It seems that Virgil is not being entirely honest in the wistful beatitude of *Georgics* 2.490; not only is he capable of being a scientific poet if he chooses, but he has done it in this very passage, with the beautifully worked pastiche of astronomical didactic in lines 475–82.[76]

A similar case could be made for the Speech of Anchises in *Aeneid* 6, with its antithesis between liberal arts and war at lines 847–53. Virgil's Anchises exhorts future Romans to

[75] Aratus is responding in turn to the Hesiodic departure of Aidos and Nemesis, *WD* 199.

[76] And of course in the Aratean Book 1 of the *Georgics*, which takes up the *quo sidere* motif of *Geo.* 1.1.

pursue the military path in the language of astronomical didactic: *caelique meatus* (*Aen.* 6.849), *surgentia sidera* (850). Here too Virgil could be seen as writing the astronomical didactic poetry he had claimed himself incapable of composing in the *recusatio* of *Georgics* 2, but doing this behind the veil of Roman militarist panegyric.[77] Virgil may not wholly agree with the words of Apollo to Iulus at *Aeneid* 9.641–2:

> macte nova virtute, puer, sic itur ad astra,
> dis genite et geniture deos.

Here the way to the stars is by military achievement alone. Ovid's *sic petitur caelum*, *Fasti* 1.307, answers this: the way to the stars is not by military achievement but by scientific learning; his poetic programme is, congruently, a didactic one. However, this need not be in direct antithesis to the various Virgilian passages we have studied here, nor, as we shall see, need it be antithetical to the prevailing spirit of the Augustan Principate.[78]

Ovid is able to make use of Virgil's language and themes to pitch his camp in the region of didactic poetry, recalling Virgil and Lucretius and at the same time echoing their model Aratus. Ovid imitates Virgil's *recusatio* in a passage of the *Fasti* which is apparently a proposal to do what Virgil had left undone in the *Georgics*: to write astronomical poetry. Ovid's alternative path was already inherent, however, in the Virgilian *recusatio*. Virgil's network of astronomical allusion in the *recusatio* of *Georgics* 2 is a clever ploy; at *Georgics* 2.483–6 he excuses himself from writing the astronomical poetry he has in fact already written in the *cento* of astronomical didactic in lines 475–82. Ovid's choice of the astronomical path is not necessarily antithetical to the Virgilian model; in fact it can be seen to respond to something already present in Virgil's *recusatio*, and indeed elsewhere in Virgil's *oeuvre*: Virgil seems to share the ambiguous reaction to astronomical learning which

[77] On scientific and traditional elements in the Speech of Anchises, see Habinek (1989).
[78] *Pace* Newlands (1995) 39–40.

we have noted above in Propertius. Ovid seems to comment on Virgil rather than write in opposition to him.

Another way in which Ovid expresses his generic alignment with didactic in the Eulogy is by exploiting the theme of gigantomachy:

> sic petitur caelum, non ut ferat Ossan Olympus
> summaque Peliacus sidera tangat apex. (*Fasti* 1.307–8)

This is an image from Homeric epic:[79]

> Ὄσσαν ἐπ' Οὐλύμπῳ μέμασαν θέμεν, αὐτὰρ ἐπ' Ὄσσῃ
> Πήλιον εἰνοσίφυλλον, ἵν' οὐρανὸς ἀμβατὸς εἴη. (*Odyssey* 11.315–16)

It was their ambition to pile Mount Ossa on Olympus, and wooded Pelion on Ossa, to make a stairway up to heaven.[80]

In the Eulogy it enables the poet to make an adversative connection between two ways of reaching the sky, through military endeavour or through scientific learning: ***sic** petitur caelum*. The astronomers of *Fasti* 1 touch the stars not with a polemical mountain peak, but with their *ingenium* (*Fasti* 1.304). As when he converts the Shield of Aeneas into Numa's *ancilia* in *Fasti* 3, so here Ovid's technique is to appropriate a martial epic image and situate it in a context which diverges from its original genre.

The *topos* seems to have become a metaphor for high-style poetry in the Augustan *recusatio*.[81] Propertius had already given us an elegiac gigantomachy at *Elegies* 2.1.19–20:

> non ego Titanas canerem, non Ossan Olympo
> impositam, ut caeli Pelion esset iter ...

Here Propertius announces his intention to sing of love, in elegiac metre, rather than of war, in hexameters. Thus in Ovid's Eulogy, in the words of Barchiesi, 'Titanomachy and gigantomachy are rejected as emblematic of the "lofty" poetry associated with war and an Augustan commission, as in Propertius' celebrated model.'[82] Ovid is writing in the *recu-*

[79] As well as being a subject for Hesiodic aetiology, in the *Theogony*.
[80] Trans. Rieu (1946).
[81] See also Propertius 2.1.39–40, 3.9.47–8, Horace, *Odes* 2.12.6–12.
[82] Barchiesi (1997) 179.

satio tradition; however, Ovid's substitution is different from Propertius': *didactic* for epic.

Substitution of learning for gigantomachy as a way of aspiring to the stars is a topos in didactic poetry from Lucretius on.[83] Consider Lucretius' praise of Epicurus at *DRN* 1.62–79:

> humana ante oculos foede cum vita iaceret
> in terris oppressa gravi sub religione
> quae caput a caeli regionibus ostendebat
> horribili super aspectu mortalibus instans,
> primum Graius homo mortalis tollere contra
> est oculos ausus primusque obsistere contra,
> quem neque fama deum nec fulmina nec minitanti
> murmure compressit caelum, sed eo magis acrem
> irritat animi virtutem, effringere ut arta
> naturae primus portarum claustra cupiret.
> ergo vivida vis animi pervicit, et extra
> processit longe flammantia moenia mundi
> atque omne immensum peragravit mente animoque,
> unde refert nobis victor quid possit oriri,
> quid nequeat, finita potestas denique cuique
> quanam sit ratione atque alte terminus haerens.
> quare religio pedibus subiecta vicissim
> obteritur, nos exaequat victoria caelo.

Ovid in his Eulogy repeats the key words and concepts of Lucretius' praise of Epicurus. In *DRN* 1.62 we have *humana ante oculos*, in *Fasti* 1.300 *humanis*, in 305 *oculis* (also at *DRN* 1.66). In *DRN* 1.64 Lucretius wrote *caput a caeli regionibus*; in *Fasti* 1.300 Ovid writes *caput*, and in 309 *caelum* (also at *DRN* 1.69, 79). Ovid's *quibus ... primis* (*Fasti* 1.297) recalls both Epicurus (*DRN* 1.66, 67, 71) and Empedocles (*DRN* 1.716), establishing the didactic theme of the πρῶτος εὑρετής, the 'first discoverer'. The imagery of *DRN* 1.74, *omne immensum peragravit mente animoque*, is akin to *Fasti* 1.306, *aetheraque ingenio subposuere suo*, and perhaps *Fasti* 1.305, *oculis* ...

[83] Something which has not been noted before in connection with Ovid's Eulogy, although Newlands (1995) 34 touches on Lucretius' praise of Epicurus as one of its general models.

mentis,' the eyes of the mind': all these expressions pertain to the metaphorical journey of the intellect.[84]

Most importantly for the present discussion, Epicurus' role is expressed through gigantomachic imagery, at *DRN* 1.68–9. He did not fear the weapons of the Olympians, Jupiter's *fulmina*, but instead, unlike the giants, who were defeated by the thunderbolts, succeeded in storming heaven, in 'a lawful epic battle ending in victory'.[85] Lucretius' *fulmina* are the bolts of superstition, since it is phenomena such as lightning which cause men to be subject to *religio*.[86] Perhaps Numa's expiation of thunderbolts in *Fasti* 3 is related to this passage of Lucretius, since Numa, like Epicurus, does not fear Jupiter's thunderbolts, but brings them under human control, albeit using proper ritual rather than the power of philosophy.

In Lucretius the gigantomachy is not rejected but subsumed, becoming part of the poet's arsenal for expressing the achievements of the great founding sage; Roman triumphal and military imagery is added to it at *DRN* 1.75 (*victor*), 78 (*religio pedibus subiecta*), and 79 (*nos exaequat victoria caelo*). Again at *DRN* 5.114–21 gigantomachy becomes a symbol of scientific endeavour, with Reason as stormer of the heavens; here the poet puts forward the punishment of the giants as unjust retribution for legitimate aspirations, a reversal of its hubristic connotations.

After Lucretius, Virgil re-mythologised the gigantomachy, in the Battle of Actium on the Shield of Aeneas, and reverted to its original moral significance. In *Aeneid* 8, the Egyptian gods who battle the Roman pantheon are, like the giants,

[84] See also Horace, *Odes* 1.28.1–6, on the Pythagorean Archytas:

> te maris et terrae numeroque carentis harenae
> mensorem cohibent, Archyta,
> pulveris exigui prope litus parva Matinum
> munera, nec quicquam tibi prodest
> **aerias temptasse domos animoque rotundum**
> **percurrisse polum** morituro.

On Archytas, see Dicks (1970) 76.

[85] Hardie (1986) 209. Hardie (1986) 210ff. lists points in common between gigantomachy and the eulogy of Epicurus.

[86] See *DRN* 5.1188–93, *DRN* 6.379–422.

monstrous and non-anthropomorphic (*Aen.* 8.698).[87] Gigantomachic imagery is used for the clash of the fleets. The model for *Aeneid* 8.692, *montis concurrere montibus*, is *DRN* 4.136–9, where the giants are illusory forms which obscure the sun:

> nam saepe gigantum
> ora volare videntur et umbram ducere late,
> interdum magni montes avulsaque saxa
> montibus anteire et solem succedere praeter ...

Virgil re-applies Lucretian imagery to make a point morally opposed to the earlier poet: for Virgil the giants are once again enemies in the fight for order, an example of how not to aspire to heaven. The right way is still military endeavour, but accompanied by *virtus* after the pattern of Hercules or Aeneas (*sic itur ad astra*).[88]

Actium is where Augustus assumes his burden of world rulership, winning the fight for cosmic control. Elsewhere in Augustan poetry the same analogy between Augustus and the giant-conquering Jupiter was exploited.[89] Virgil's Actium ekphrasis belongs to a tradition with its origins in the Hellenistic kingdoms in which the victories of a city and its rulers are compared to victory of gods over giants.[90] We shall see more of this theme, as it appears elsewhere in the *Fasti*, in chapter 5 below.

What is Ovid's position in the Eulogy? It seems that he must have taken both Lucretius and Virgil into account. His position is close to Lucretius in that scientific as opposed to military endeavour has primacy, but close to Virgil in that he rejects gigantomachy outright rather than seeing it as a metaphor for legitimate scientific aspiration. He has to reject gigantomachy, even while keeping various other motifs from Lucretius' praise of Epicurus, since Epicurus, as a 'giant', was on the other side from Augustus as Jupiter. Ovid is closest to

[87] Hardie (1986) 98, and (1986) 97–110, 351 treats Virgil's Actium as a gigantomachy.
[88] See Hardie (1986) 209 n. 135 for bibliography on right and wrong ways of getting to heaven.
[89] See Innes (1979), Hardie (1986) 85–156. The gigantomachy of Horace, *Odes* 3.4.42–64, functions as an allegory for Augustan supremacy.
[90] Hardie (1986) 86 n. 5.

Lucretian didactic in that he applies military imagery to the flight of the mind: *sub ducibus illis* (*Fasti* 1.309) picks up the victory metaphors of *DRN* 1.75, 78 and 79. Ovid in the Eulogy is playing a substitution game which goes back to Lucretius: philosophical for military exploits, didactic for epic poetry.

I now move to the other material which I think is important in our understanding of Ovid's Eulogy, and of his astronomy in the *Fasti*. Lucretius' Epicurus is a sage divinised through his wisdom (*DRN* 5.8–9, *deus ille fuit, deus, inclute Memmi*), and, ironically, not so unlike philosophically opposed Stoic heroes, who might be apotheosised for their achievements. Monica Gale sees the Stoic poet Manilius' praise of Mercury as *protos heuretes* of astronomy at *Astronomica* 1.25–112 as direct polemic against the Lucretian idea of Epicurus as a god.[91] Consider *Astronomica* 1.25–34:

> quem primum interius licuit cognoscere terris
> munere caelestum. quis enim condentibus illis
> clepsisset furto mundum, quo cuncta reguntur?
> quis foret humano conatus pectore tantum,
> invitis ut dis cuperet deus ipse videri, 29
> sublimis aperire vias imumque sub orbem, 32
> et per inane suis parentia finibus astra? 33
> tu princeps auctorque sacri, Cyllenie, tanti; 30
> per te iam caelum interius, iam sidera nota 31
> nominaque et cursus signorum ...[92] 34

Manilius answers Lucretius: the human intellect cannot know the universe on its own: we must have the help of the divine. How could Epicurus have been a god, unless by the will of the gods? 'Who of but human understanding would have essayed so great a task as to wish against heaven's wish to appear a god himself; to reveal paths on high and paths beneath the bottom of the earth and stars obedient to appointed orbit through the void?', as Goold translates lines 28–31.

The terms in which the astrological poet responds to Lucretius are similar to those of Ovid's Eulogy, which may have

[91] Gale (1994a) 197 n. 140.
[92] All quotations of Manilius are from the text of Goold (1985).

been written just a few years before the *Astronomica*. Manilius' *primum* (25), and *princeps* (30) is like Ovid's *primis* (*Fasti* 1.297). The *sublimia pectora* of Ovid's astronomers may lie behind Manilius' *humano pectore*. Manilius' passage displays other similarities to Ovid's Eulogy as well: the *regalis animos*, the minds of the Chaldean kings who discovered astrology, are like Ovid's *felices animae*:

> et natura dedit vires seque ipsa reclusit
> regalis animos primum dignata movere
> proxima tangentis rerum fastigia caelo,
> qui domuere feras gentes oriente sub ipso,
> [quas secat Euphrates, in quas et Nilus abundat]
> qua mundus redit et nigras super evolat urbes. (*Astronomica* 1.40–5)

Stoic euhemerism conferred quasi-divine status on the kings (here Zoroaster and Belus, among others[93]) who first practised science. Again they are the first founders:

> hi tantum movere decus **primique** per artem
> sideribus videre vagis pendentia fata. (*Astronomica* 1.51–2)

Compare this to *Fasti* 1.310, *ponemusque suos ad vaga signa dies.*[94]

In Manilius, personified *Ratio* shares the role of Ovid's astronomers; compare *Astronomica* 1.96–7, *nec prius imposuit rebus finemque modumque | quam caelum ascendit ratio*, to *Fasti* 1.298. Manilius' *Ratio* is responsible for the imposition of limitations and order on the universe; likewise Ovid's astronomers are responsible for the delimiting of time, the astronomical calculations required for the reconciling of civil and solar years.

Manilius has the same substitution of scientific for military exploits, expressed through gigantomachy, as do Lucretius and Ovid. At *Astronomica* 1.104 *Ratio* robbed Jupiter of his

[93] Housman (1903–30) *ad Astronomica* 1.41.

[94] The adjective *vaga* must be employed differently in Ovid from Manilius, however, since according to Housman, *vaga sidera* in Manilius usually denotes the planets, which had (to the ancient understanding) no fixed courses. On the other hand, Ovid's *vaga signa* must be the fixed stars, by which the *dies* are calculated, as in Julius Caesar's *De Astris*, the role of which we have considered above. *Vaga* in Ovid may perhaps just mean 'moving'.

thunderbolt, *eripuitque Iovi fulmen viresque tonandi*. One might also think of Ovid's Numa here, and his substitution of religious for bellicose ways. In addition, Numa is specifically one who delimited time, in his capacity as calendar reformer. Early Romans in the time of Romulus did not have much grasp of the stars (*non illi caelo labentia signa tenebant, Fasti* 3.113), until Numa reformed the calendar. At *Fasti* 3.151–2, it is Numa who appears in the role of the Lucretian/Manilian First Founder:

> primus, oliviferis Romam deductus ab arvis,
> Pompilius menses sentit abesse duos.

There follows the passage we have considered in chapter 1, on Julius Caesar as calendar reformer (*sed tamen errabant etiam nunc tempora, donec | Caesaris in multis haec quoque cura fuit, Fasti* 3.155–6). As well as being the founding king or sage, Numa in Ovid acts as the prototype of Caesar. Caesar, as we saw above, reformed the calendar by virtue of his *cognatio caeli*, his kinship with the heavens. In this respect, he is the latest in a long line of sages. In Vitruvius 9.6.3, a passage we have already discussed,[95] the philosophers listed seem, like Ovid's astronomers, with their *sublimia pectora* (*Fasti* 1.301), and Manilius' sages (*regalis animos, Astronomica* 1.41), to be endowed with divine mind (*quorum scientiae sunt hominibus suscipiendae, quod tanta cura fuerunt ut etiam videantur* ***divina mente*** *tempestatium significatus post futuros ante pronuntiare*). Ovid's astronomers can be seen as euhemerist heroes, Stoic sages who managed to climb into the heavenly dwellings by their intellect (*Fasti* 1.298). Bearing the passage of Vitruvius in mind also, Ovid's astronomers are particularly those who fixed the limits of the calendar, the parapegmatists, including Julius Caesar.

In Manilius there may be allusion to the divinity of Caesar. *Quis foret humano conatus pectore tantum, | invitis ut dis cuperet deus ipse videri?* (*Ast.* 1.28–9) might be taken of Manilius' confirmation of the divine ratification of Caesar's apo-

[95] Quoted above, with translation, p. 19.

theosis, as well as a response to Lucretius. On this reading, Caesar is a true god, since his divinity was not accomplished *invitis dis*. Manilius' passage might be read as legitimating Caesar, and perhaps also the deified Augustus by this time, linking them with Stoic sages divinised through scientific knowledge.

Manilius provides a good commentary on Ovid's Eulogy, which is now seen to incorporate Caesar as calendar reformer, as well as the founding fathers of astronomy. Numa, Caesar, and also Germanicus, who translated Aratus' astronomical calendar, all take their place among the *felices animae* through their knowledge of the delimitation of time. This reading of Ovid's Eulogy can be supported using another Stoic text, the second book of Cicero's *De Natura Deorum*.

In the Eulogy, Ovid is said to develop an antithesis between philosophy and war (or didactic and epic poetry) by the use of military language to describe the act of following the astronomers' achievements:

> nos quoque sub ducibus caelum metabimur illis,
> ponemusque suos ad vaga signa dies. (*Fasti* 1.309–10)

Carole Newlands notes that *metabimur* belongs to the diction of military surveying, and says: 'In his application of military language here to the study of the stars, Ovid quietly reminds us that although his subject is no longer the war of love, he is nonetheless an elegiac poet, interested in challenging social norms and promoting alternatives to warfare.'[96] There may indeed be a superficial antithesis between war and science; however, scholars have overlooked a model evoked by the verb *metari* which I believe is fundamental to understanding the Eulogy: Cicero, *DND* 2.153–5.[97]

The metaphorical usage of *metari* ('to measure out a camp') in the Ovidian passage, of 'marking out' the paths of the heavenly bodies, is the only occurrence of the transferred meaning of this verb; but the same meaning, attached to a

[96] Newlands (1995) 39.
[97] For the significance of the Stoic book of the *De Natura Deorum* elsewhere in the *Fasti*, see below, pp. 99–104, 108–9, 117–18.

compound form of the verb, *dimetari*, had already been applied (uniquely it seems) to star-gazing by Cicero, *DND* 2.155:[98]

iam vero circumitus solis et lunae reliquorumque siderum, quamquam etiam ad mundi cohaerentiam pertinent, tamen et spectaculum hominibus praebent; nulla est enim insatiabilior species, nulla pulchrior et ad rationem sollertiamque praestantior; eorum enim cursus **dimetati** maturitates temporum et varietates mutationesque cognovimus. quae si hominibus solis nota sunt, hominum facta esse causa iudicandum est.

Again, the revolutions of sun, moon and other heavenly bodies admittedly form part of the organic structure of the universe, but they also offer a spectacle to the human race. This is supremely the sight of which we never tire; it is more beautiful and reflects greater reason and intelligence than all others, for by **measuring** their courses, we become aware of the due arrival of the seasons, and of variations and changes in them. Since only humans have this awareness, we must infer that this is a dispensation made for their sake.[99]

Cicero had already used this verb once, applied metaphorically to the disposition of constellations at *DND* 2.110: *atque ita **dimetata signa sunt** ut in tantis descriptionibus divina sollertia appareat* ... Given the rarity of the metaphorical usage of *(di)metari*, which occurs only in these two instances in Cicero, and in Ovid, it is possible that Ovid had this passage of Cicero in mind when he wrote his Eulogy.

If one pursues *DND* 2.153–5 as a model for Ovid's Eulogy, additional similarities become apparent. At *DND* 2.153 Cicero's speaker Balbus moves from talking generally about the heavenly bodies as evidence for the divine, to a direct connection between the sky and human *ratio*, particularly the power of mankind to order time:

Quid vero? hominum ratio non in caelum usque penetravit? soli enim ex animantibus nos astrorum ortus, obitus, cursusque cognovimus, ab hominum genere finitus est dies, mensis, annus, defectiones solis et lunae cognitae praedicataeque in omne posterum tempus, quae, quantae, quando futurae sint.

[98] The verb *dimetor* is rare even in the literal sense, occurring only at Livy 8.38.7, *locum castris dimetari iussit*.
[99] Trans. Walsh (1997).

Then again, has not our human reason advanced to the skies? Alone of living creatures we know the risings, settings, and courses of the stars. The human race have laid down the limits of the day, the month, the year; they have come to recognise eclipses of the sun and moon, and have foretold the extent and the date of each occurrence of them for all days to come.

The metaphor *hominum ratio non in caelum usque penetravit* is similar to Ovid's *vitiisque locisque | altius humanis exseruisse caput* (*Fasti* 1.299–300) and *aetheraque ingenio subposuere suo* (306); Cicero and Ovid are talking the same language here. The ordering of time described by Cicero's Stoic speaker, which is made possible by observation of the heavenly bodies, places us firmly within the territory of the *Fasti*. Arthur Stanley Pease, commenting on *DND*, believed that *dies mensis annus* (2.153) refers to Caesar's calendrical reform, which had taken place shortly before the composition of Cicero's work.[100]

If this is so, this passage of *DND* sheds light on the relation of Ovid's astronomical programme, his Eulogy of Astronomers, to the project of the *Fasti* as a whole. Ovid's poem is about the relationship between astronomy and Roman time, taking as an ostensible starting-point empirical astronomy and its *utilitas* in determining temporal cycles. Given this component of the underlay to the *Fasti*, Carole Newlands' opinion that 'The proem to the stars suggests that astronomical notices and their attendant myths will not function in thematic isolation, rather, the different sets of values they encode will provide a counterpoint to those enshrined in the civil calendar'[101] may seem questionable. While it is true that some of the individual star myths, such as the one which we shall study in chapter 6, Callisto, the Bear, may look strange against the Roman religious calendar, it cannot be said that the stars in themselves 'provide a counterpoint' to the calendar: they are involved in it at its deepest level. Nor does the Eulogy have to be anti-Augustan in its substitution of scientific for military exploits, since it is appropriate that, in a calendrical work, the *personae* of members of the royal house as parapegmatists

[100] Pease (1955–8) *ad DND* 2.153. [101] Newlands (1995) 50.

should be emphasised. Indeed, Caesar as calendar reformer, and Caesar as a star, may be implicit in it.

To conclude: Ovid's Eulogy of Astronomers is where the generic strands we have seen in this chapter intersect. In it, one might detect a hint of Propertius' opposition of the stars to early Rome, if indeed the stars are at loggerheads with the kind of military achievement which was a hallmark of portraits of early Rome in Augustan poetry. This opposition surfaces, if anywhere, at *Fasti* 1.302 (*officiumque fori militiaeve labor*). However, the stars are also important in that they define the astronomers (who include Caesar and Germanicus) as heroes, if not fully in the epic mode, then in the Lucretian or indeed Stoic euhemerist mould.[102]

It is arguable whether such modes of heroism are unepic, since we have seen how astronomical learning forms a strand in Virgil, not only in the *recusatio* of *Georgics* 2, but also in the Speech of Anchises in *Aeneid* 6, and in the Shield of *Aeneid* 8. The epic importance of astronomy, which is a substratum of Virgilian epic, despite the surface conflict between arms and the stars, enters into the *Fasti* on the level of imperial panegyric and world rulership: to be among the stars, rulers (like Caesar) have to understand the stars. Study of Manilius in this connection provides a good opening for themes we shall discuss later, namely catasterism and astral apotheosis, with its Platonic-Stoic foundation. Finally, consideration of Cicero's *DND* as a predecessor of the *Fasti*, and Manilius' *Astronomica* as a successor of it, reveals an underlying stratum of Stoicism in the *Fasti*. This, as well as the calendrical and astronomical material, sets the scene for Aratus.

There is no reason why Ovid's education should not have acquainted him with Stoic texts. One of the most obvious roads into philosophical study for a Roman of Ovid's day must have been the philosophical writings of Cicero (even if their impact has been significantly underestimated by modern

[102] These do not necessarily cancel each other out; Ovid has drawn on both literary traditions.

scholars, especially Ovidians), and among these the *DND* contained Stoic ideas in its second book. Evidence that Ovid read the Stoic book of the *DND* comes from the Eulogy itself, in his echo of the verb *metari*, used twice by Cicero in connection with the delimitation of the astronomical year. Aratus' Stoic system may have been one feature of his astronomical poem which made it attractive to the Romans, and in particular to Ovid in the *Fasti*, where reference to the *Phaenomena* may serve to confer upon Ovid too, as one familiar with astronomical literature, the status of the *felices animae*.

CHAPTER 3

VERSE AND UNIVERSE IN ARATUS' *PHAENOMENA*

Introduction: Aratus and Ovid

So far, we have encountered Aratus on several levels. In chapter 1 he was seen as a parapegmatist, and as such, a forerunner of Caesar the calendar reformer and writer of a work of astronomical theory. In chapter 2, we saw how he came into Ovid's poetic programme. He is encapsulated in the *lapsaque sub terras ortaque signa* of *Fasti* 1.2; he is present indirectly in the didactic models of the poem, especially at its underlying Stoic level, since for the Stoics and kindred schools of philosophy, the importance of the stars lay in their *utilitas* for determining the cycles of time, and the provident nature of the gods in revealing them to man.

In acknowledging his debt to the didactic tradition in the Eulogy of Astronomers, Ovid also acknowledges affiliation with the kind of poetry written by his dedicatee Germanicus, translator of the *Phaenomena*. Carlo Santini was the first to treat the question of the relationship between the *Fasti* and the *Phaenomena* of Germanicus,[1] which later became the preoccupation of Elaine Fantham in her article of 1985, 'Ovid, Germanicus and the Composition of the *Fasti*', which dealt with the dates of the composition and revision of Ovid's incomplete poem.[2] Fantham believes that Ovid knew, or at least knew of, the *Phaenomena* of Germanicus, and that this work was important to him, especially since Germanicus himself may have relied to some extent on Ovid's own *Phaenomena*. If this is so, it is remotely possible that all of the as-

[1] Santini (1975) 2–4.
[2] Fantham (1985). See also Herbert-Brown (1994) 173–212.

tronomy of the *Fasti* was added at the revision stage, at the same time as the work was re-dedicated to Germanicus.[3]

Germanicus in the *Fasti* is invoked as a proemial god (*dexter ades, Fasti* 1.6).[4] The invocation recalls the beneficence of Zeus in Aratus' proem, who δεξιὰ σημαίνει (*Phaenomena* 6). Ovid invokes a shared interest with Germanicus in his role as poet at *Fasti* 1.25 (both are 'bards': ***vates*** *rege* ***vatis*** *habenas*), by implication aligning himself with a tradition of astronomical poetry of which Germanicus, as translator of Aratus, forms a part.

The future *princeps*, as well as being the god presiding over the poem, is its *principium* also, the ἀρχή of Aratus' ἀρχώμεσθα (*Ph.* line 1), the ruling principle of the poem. It is therefore right that Aratus' Muses should cede to him tutelage of the poem:

> si licet et fas est, vates rege vatis habenas,
> auspice te felix totus ut annus eat. (*Fasti* 1.25–6)

> χαίροιτε δὲ Μοῦσαι,
> μειλίχιαι μάλα πᾶσαι· ἐμοί γε μὲν ἀστέρας εἰπεῖν
> ᾗ θέμις εὐχομένῳ τεκμήρατε πᾶσαν ἀοιδήν. (*Phaenomena* 16–18)

And hail Muses, all most gracious! In answer to my prayer to tell of the stars in so far as I may, guide all my singing.

Si licet et fas est corresponds to ᾗ θέμις, *auspice te* roughly to τεκμήρατε, *totus annus* to πᾶσαν ἀοιδήν, since Ovid's *carmen* is also the Roman *annus* (*Fasti* 2.1). Germanicus is thus the equivalent of Virgil's astronomical muses of *Georgics* 2.475–82: the Muse of astronomical didactic poetry, who will preside over the *Fasti*. Aratus' initial invocation of Zeus has been displaced in the *Fasti* by the twin forces of Germanicus and Janus, who together stand in for the Zeus invoked at *Phaenomena* 1–18.

Another element of Ovid's flattery of his royal dedicatee

3 Fantham (1985) does not advance this theory, nor, to my knowledge, has any other scholar done so.

4 The same address is used in the invocation of Janus at *Fasti* 1.67. On the proemial role of Janus in the *Fasti*, see Hardie (1991).

might be the inclusion of subject matter congenial to him. At the same time, Ovid places his work in a tradition of didactic poetry which extends from Aratus to Manilius and beyond, and from Greece to Rome, the 'Aratean tradition'. This could be seen to include, apart from Germanicus, the translations of Aratus by Cicero and Varro Atacinus, Books 5 and 6 of Lucretius' *De Rerum Natura*, which deal with celestial and meteorological phenomena, Julius Caesar's *De Astris*, the first book of Virgil's *Georgics*, with its translation of Aratus' celestial calendar, and Manilius' *Astronomica*.[5] While Ovid is closer in the *Fasti* to his Hellenistic source, the *Phaenomena*, than to his Roman predecessors, nonetheless he is the successor of the Roman Arateans with regard to his astronomical subject matter; they form, so to speak, the horizontal axis of the astronomical literary history of the *Fasti*, the vertical axis of which is Ovid's direct ancestor, Aratus.

Germanicus is part of the internal evidence in the *Fasti* which helps to link the *Fasti* with the *Phaenomena* and its Latin translations. As well, we have the allusions to Aratus in the *Fasti* which I have collected in appendix 1 and will study in chapters 5 and 6. There are in addition two pieces of external evidence for Ovid's affiliation with Aratus. Ovid himself mentions Aratus in the *sphragis* to the first book of his *Amores*: *cum sole et luna semper Aratus erit* (*Amores* 1.15.16). The line may mean both 'Aratus will survive as long as the sun and moon', or 'Aratus will be with the sun and moon forever.' Ovid's reference, in epigrammatic style, both takes up the *topos* of poetic immortality, and plays on the *topos* of catasterism, a subject treated by Aratus himself.[6]

The second piece of external evidence is the record of a translation of Aratus by Ovid. No clue is provided to the date

[5] There is also a shorter poem by Quintus Tullius Cicero on stars and weather signs, on which see Courtney (1993) 179–81. On Varro of Atax, see Courtney (1993) 235–53. On the tradition generally, see Reeve (1983). Scholars have been bemused by the prevalence of Aratus in Rome; I hope the following chapters may go some way towards replacing bemusement with fascination at the marriage between Aratus and Rome.

[6] For McKeown's comments on this passage of the *Amores*, see above, p. 4 n. 13.

of composition of Ovid's *Phaenomena* similar to Cicero's attestation of the youthfulness of his *Aratea*.[7] But by analogy with Cicero's poem one would be tempted to see Ovid's translation of Aratus as belonging to the poet's youth.[8] This impression may be strengthened by Ovid's reference to Aratus in the *Amores*, showing interest by Ovid early in his literary career. However, Franz Bömer posits the near-contemporaneity of Ovid's *Fasti*, *Phaenomena*, and *Metamorphoses*.[9] Bömer implies in addition that Ovid's connection with Aratus might be expressed in terms of a generic affiliation to astronomical-aetiological literature rather than Roman national poetry (by which one might understand epic in the Ennian/Virgilian mode).

There are two extant fragments of Ovid's *Phaenomena*, which may be quoted in their entirety:

Pleiades ... quarum mentionem facit Ovidius in Phaenomenis dicens de Perseo:

> Pliades ante genus septem radiare feruntur,
> sex tamen apparent, sub opaca septima nube. (Probus *ad* Virgil, *Georgics* 1.138)

Ovidius ... eum librum quo Phaenomena breviter comprehendit his tribus versibus terminavit:

> tot numero talique deus simulacra figura
> imposuit caelo perque atras sparsa tenebras
> clara pruinosae iussit dare lumina nocti. (Lactantius, *Divinae Institutiones* 2.5.24)

7 *'Utar', inquit [Balbus], 'carminibus Arateis, quae a te admodum adulescentulo conversa ita me delectant quia Latina sunt ut multa ex iis memoria teneam'* (*DND* 2.104).

8 It is logical that translating Aratus' *Phaenomena* might have been a good way of cutting one's poetic teeth, since part of Roman education, which incorporated astronomy, could have been the memorisation of this poem as a way of learning the constellations and their positions (Clavel (1868) 104–5). It would also have been a good exercise in versification, containing many detailed descriptions and Greek names. Hinds (1987a) 13 believes that this was the case: 'It is natural to assume that it was an early work: the translation of the well-known Hellenistic poem is surely the sort of exercise that Ovid would have set himself while first trying out his powers, rather than in his maturity, when daring innovation in subject matter was his rule.' Hinds believes in addition that many of Ovid's allusions to Aratus in the *Fasti* may be through his own translation, which was also a source for Germanicus.

9 Bömer (1957–8) vol. I, 14.

These quotations correspond to Aratus, *Phaenomena* 257–8 and 451–3.[10] They do not alone tell us much about what Ovid's *Phaenomena* was like; they are important in that they attest Ovid's familiarity with Aratus. I hope that the study of Aratus in this chapter will be a preliminary step towards showing what it might have been about Aratus that made him attractive to the Romans.

The Stoic themes of Aratus' *Phaenomena*

I shall demonstrate here that the *Phaenomena* achieves by an overall uniformity of language, imagery and themes, a unified whole, for which one interpretative model (perhaps the ideal one) is early Stoic cosmology. It must be stated at the outset that scholarly opinion is divided as to the extent of Stoic influence on the *Phaenomena*.[11] Lack of evidence for the details of early Stoic doctrine is an obstacle. In addition, most of the scholarly argument hinges on the status of the proem, which no one denies to be heavily Stoic, in relation to the rest of the work, the Stoicism of which is debated. Douglas Kidd, for example, the most recent to join the debate, notes Stoic influence in the proem; at the same time he points out that Zeus appears in many different guises throughout the *Phaenomena*, including as the Hesiodic anthropomorphic god.[12]

On the other hand, Effe argued that Aratus was on a philosophical crusade to promote Stoic doctrine by showing how celestial phenomena reflect divine providence; thus whenever Zeus is named elsewhere in the poem, there may be a suggestion of the god of the proem.[13]

My purpose here will be to show just how tightly Stoic ideas are bound into the literary frame, to create a poem of a

[10] See Courtney (1993) 308–9.

[11] For a cross-section of opinion, see Martin (1956a) 3, James (1972) 28, Effe (1977) 40–56, Kenney (1979), Bulloch (1985) 600–2, Hopkinson (1988) 137, Hunter (1995) 4–5, Kidd (1997) 10–12.

[12] Kidd (1997) 10–11. For a way of reconciling anthropomorphism and abstraction through Stoic allegory, see chapter 4 below.

[13] Effe (1977), with the critique of Kenney (1979).

thoroughgoing unity which reflects that of the Stoic cosmos. I shall integrate the proem into the work, rather than treating it as in some way separate from it, showing how the themes adumbrated in the opening 'Hymn to Zeus' branch out across the poem. What happens to Aratus' unified entity when it becomes part of the Roman year will be the subject of chapters 4, 5 and 6.

Three Stoic ideas are useful in demonstrating the unity of the *Phaenomena*: the concept of the divinity of the heavenly bodies, the idea of 'universal sympathy' (contingent on a pantheistic theology), and the Stoic theory of language. Let us see how Aratus' poem reflects each of these.

For the Stoics, the regular and predictable movements of the heavenly bodies provided evidence of the existence of a providential creator; in addition, the heavenly bodies were considered by the Stoics to be divine in themselves:[14]

Ζήνων τὸν ἥλιόν φησι καὶ τὴν σελήνην καὶ τῶν ἄλλων ἄστρων ἕκαστον εἶναι νοερὸν καὶ φρόνιμον, πύρινον ⟨δὲ⟩ πυρὸς τεχνικοῦ. δύο γὰρ γένη πυρός, τὸ μὲν ἄτεχνον καὶ μεταβάλλον εἰς ἑαυτὸ τὴν τροφήν, τὸ δὲ τεχνικόν, αὐξητικόν τε καὶ τηρητικόν, οἷον ἐν τοῖς φυτοῖς ἐστι καὶ ζῴοις, ὃ δὴ φύσις ἐστὶ καὶ ψυχή. τοιούτου δὴ πυρὸς εἶναι τὴν τῶν ἄστρων οὐσίαν.

Zeno says that the sun and moon and each of the other stars are intelligent and prudent and have the fieriness of designing fire (πυρὸς τεχνικοῦ). For there are two kinds of fire: one is undesigning and converts fuel into itself; the other is designing, causing growth and preservation, as is the case in plants and animals where it is physique and soul respectively. Such is the fire which constitutes the substance of the stars.[15]

According to Zeno, the stars are sentient and prudent and therefore divine, to be identified with 'creative fire' (πῦρ τεχνικόν). This kind of fire is the active manifestation of Zeus, the world deity.[16] The world was said to have evolved from two generative forces (or one primal substance of two aspects), active θεός – Zeus, the πῦρ τεχνικόν – and the passive matter (οὐσία). From interaction of these in cosmogony, the four

[14] On the divinity of the heavenly bodies for the Stoics, see Cicero, *DND* 1.39, 2.39–42. At Plato, *Timaeus* 40b (and elsewhere) the stars are divine beings.

[15] Long and Sedley (1987) 46D.

[16] See Long and Sedley (1987) 46A.

elements came about.[17] The πῦρ τεχνικόν is still present in the upper echelons of the universe: this is what stars are made of.

If the fire of which the sun, moon and stars are made is τεχνικόν, and therefore to be identified with Zeus, then for Aratus to write about the stars *is* for him to speak of the Stoic Zeus, not only in the proem, but constantly throughout his work. He begins as he means to go on – from the sky (ἐκ Διὸς ἀρχώμεσθα, line 1), setting up an ambivalence between god and sky which continues throughout the *Phaenomena*.[18] An essential unity of Aratus' poem can already be seen in the fact that the Zeus of the proem is the same as the astronomical subject of the work.

Chrysippus, it seems, identified θεός, which was also divine reason or λόγος, with the cosmic πνεῦμα, the ordering force with which the universe is shot through.[19] God, Δία (the ἀρχή, λόγος, θεός, πῦρ τεχνικόν or πνεῦμα), pervades (διά + ἥκω[20]) the universe. Thus Aratus can say at *Phaenomena* 2–4:

μεσταὶ δὲ Διὸς πᾶσαι μὲν ἀγυιαί,
πᾶσαι δ' ἀνθρώπων ἀγοραί, μεστὴ δὲ θάλασσα
καὶ λιμένες· πάντη δὲ Διὸς κεχρήμεθα πάντες.

Filled with Zeus are all highways and meeting-places of people, filled are the sea and harbours: in all circumstances we are dependent on Zeus.

A force of cohesion, known as τόνος ('universal sympathy'), is imparted to the universe through all-pervasive λόγος.[21] Ovid's near-contemporary, the Stoic Manilius, was to express the concept thus (*Astronomica* 2.60–6):

[17] See Long and Sedley (1987) 46B and C.

[18] See, for example, *Ph.* 223–4, ὁ Ἵππος | **ἐν Διὸς** εἰλεῖται, and 253, [Πέρσεος] ἴχνια μηκύνει κεκονιμένος **ἐν Διὶ πατρί**. According to Kidd (1997) 11, this wordplay 'can suggest both the primitive god and the Stoic god, and in the phrase ἐν Διὶ πατρί (253) these two extremes are amusingly merged with the mythological god who is known as the father of Perseus'.

[19] See Long and Sedley (1987) 46A.

[20] In the Aratean scholia the Zeus of the proem is ⟨ὁ⟩ διὰ πάντων διήκων κατὰ τοὺς Στωϊκούς (Maass (1898) 335).

[21] See Long and Sedley (1987) 47G and J. On τόνος in Cleanthes, see James (1972) 32.

namque canam tacita naturae mente potentem
infusumque deum caelo terrisque fretoque
ingentem aequali moderantem foedere molem,
totumque alterno consensu vivere mundum
et rationis agi motu, cum spiritus unus
per cunctas habitet partes atque irriget orbem
omnia pervolitans corpusque animale figuret.

The all-pervasiveness of λόγος implies connectedness among all parts of the universe, including between heavenly and earthly phenomena. Hence also the unity of the two parts of Aratus' poem, the 'Phainomena' proper (lines 1–782), which deals with the stars, and the 'Diosemeiai', 'Weather Signs' (783–1154): by universal sympathy stars and weather signs are connected, the heavenly bodies being capable of exerting meteorological effect.[22]

Λόγος is also the rationality which gives rise to the structures of language. The later Stoic Epictetus uses the expression τὰ τοῦ λόγου στοιχεῖα, 'the elements of reason', and speaks of the way in which they are fastened to one another.[23] There lies behind his rhetoric a perceived connection between rightness of reason, and the parts of speech with their ordering syntax, which reflect human rationality. This reason is reflected in speech just as the divine λόγος is reflected in the syntax of the universe, which is revealed by the layout of its parts. Human reason and its product, language, are as much a part of the order of nature as are the structures of the cosmos. Thus Aratus' Stoic poem is related to the universe in a way which goes beyond the mere fact that it is its linguistic microcosm (as an armillary sphere would be its geometrical microcosm): it is a cosmos itself.[24]

Because it was a fundamental tenet of Stoic grammar that the relationship between names and that which they signify is

[22] See Pliny, *NH* 2.105.
[23] *Discourses* 4.8.12.
[24] See Hunter (1995) 5–10. This idea is not exclusive to Stoicism: see Friedländer (1941) on Lucretius' *DRN* as a verbal construct which models the universe it describes.

a natural one,[25] etymology (the practice of linguistic archaeology) reveals for the Stoics a substratum of cosmological truth. The study of linguistic relationships is thus a study of the structures of the cosmos as they were revealed to the wise men who originally named the elements of the universe. The poet has the power to reveal connections through the language that he wields. For example, in Aratus, the constellation of the Eagle (Ἀητός or Αἰητός) 'is blown' (from ἄημι):

σχεδόθεν δέ οἱ ἄλλος ἄηται
οὐ τόσσος μεγέθει, χαλεπός γε μὲν ἐξ ἁλὸς ἐλθὼν
νυκτὸς ἀπερχομένης· καί μιν καλέουσιν Ἀητόν. (*Phaenomena* 313–15)

Close to it another bird is wafted (ἄηται), inferior in size, but stormy when it rises from the sea at the departure of the night; and men call it the eagle, (Ἀητόν).

οὐ μὴν Αἰητοῦ ἀπαμείρεται, ἀλλά οἱ ἐγγὺς
Ζηνὸς ἀητεῖται μέγας ἄγγελος. (*Phaenomena* 522–3)

It (the equator) is certainly not bereft of the Eagle (Αἰητοῦ): it has the great messenger of Zeus flying (ἀητεῖται) nearby.

The etymology of the Eagle explains the storms which accompany it. Likewise, the star Sirius (Σείριος) 'burns' (σειριάει):

ἡ δέ οἱ ἄκρη
ἀστέρι βέβληται δεινῷ γένυς, ὅς ῥα μάλιστα
ὀξέα σειριάει· καί μιν καλέουσ' ἄνθρωποι
Σείριον. (*Phaenomena* 329–32)

... but the tip of its (the Dog's) jaw is inset with a formidable star, that blazes most intensely: and so men call it the Scorcher.

Sirius is a very bright star; it is also of course the star whose rising heralds the hottest days of summer (the 'Dog days'). Aratus shows us that the relationship between star signs and their attendant meteorological phenomena is in the name.

Given the premise that language reflects objective reality rather than existing as an arbitrary system, it is consistent to look for connections between linguistic phenomena, as manifest in a poem, and features of nature. This works in Aratus

[25] E.g. Origen, *Contra Celsum* 1.24; the same idea is found in the academic Varro, *Ling.* 6.3.

on the macrocosmic as well as the microcosmic level. In his article on Stoic grammar, Frede sees reason to believe that even in early times the field was divided into two parts, dealing firstly with individual words in isolation, and secondly with the assembly of words into sentences, or syntax.[26] An analogy may be found in the structure of Aratus' work, in which the connections between things become tighter as one moves through the poem, the morphology of the universe (the positions of the individual constellations, lines 1–558) giving way to its syntax in the 'Synanatolai' (559–732) and 'Diosemeiai' (733–1154), where the simultaneous risings and settings of constellations are noted, and weather signs must be watched in combination.

The divinity of the heavenly bodies, universal sympathy, and the relationship between language and nature, are all Stoic ideas which help us to express the unified structure of Aratus' *Phaenomena* on the general level. Let us now move to the debated area of the connection between the proem, which no one denies to be Stoic, and the rest of the work. Here I shall show in more detail how Aratus constructs his Stoic cosmos thematically, setting up in the proem (*Ph.* 1–18) the thematic elements of the rest of the poem.

One thematic group is composed of ideas of plenitude, inclusiveness and permanence. In *Phaenomena* 2–4, repetition and variation are used to give the impression of diverse things unified by the all-pervasiveness of Zeus. This effect is achieved by the chiastic arrangement of μεσταί/πᾶσαι/πᾶσαι/μεστή, and by the similarity of forms in ἀγυιαί/ἀγοραί. In addition, the dominant concept here is πᾶς, pantheism, god immanent in all.

In line 9 the time is right to cast 'every kind of seed', σπέρματα πάντα, so that, in line 13, 'everything may grow without fail', ἔμπεδα πάντα φύωνται. And at 16–18, all the Muses, gracious as they are, are exhorted to direct the entire poem (Μοῦσαι | μειλίχιαι μάλα πᾶσαι ... | πᾶσαν ἀοιδήν). The language of constancy and universality is continuous throughout the proem: ἁπάντη in line 22 picks up πάντη in line 4.

26 Frede (1978) 59.

Likewise, in lines 19–20, though the stars are many and follow diverse paths, their movements are constant. This is expressed by re-iteration of the idea of 'always' in threefold *variatio* (πάντ' ἤματα συνεχὲς αἰεί), the repetition serving to illustrate the concept of continuity to which it gives expression.

Mankind's hymning of Zeus (τῷ μιν **ἀεὶ** πρῶτόν τε καὶ ὕστατον ἱλάσκονται, line 14) is as permanent as is the fixed position of the earth's axis (ἄξων **αἰὲν** ἄρηρεν, line 22).[27] The constancy of the world's need for Zeus is emblematised in the steadfastness of the earth's axis, forever holding the world in equipoise. The axis of the earth is in a sense symbolic of the equilibrium between divine providence and human need.

Two other thematic kernels take root in the proem, to put out branches across the rest of the work. These are the themes of god and man, and of speech, signs, and seasons. In the first, the connection between god and man which exists in actuality, through divine Providence, is achieved verbally, by positioning words for mortals and immortals near one another. Διός and ἄνδρες in line 1 are picked up by a group of words denoting the human race, a notable feature in the proem to a work on celestial phenomena: the places of men are full of Zeus (Διὸς | ἀνθρώπων, 2–3); he is gentle to men (ἀνθρώποισιν, 5); like Hesiod's good Eris at the beginning of the *Works and Days* he arouses people (λαούς, line 6) to work; he marks out the stars which reveal the seasons to men (ἀνδράσιν, line 13), and he is a great blessing to humanity (μέγ' ἀνθρώποισιν ὄνειαρ, line 15).

The theme of speech begins with ἄρρητον in line 2; Zeus is 'not unspoken', nor is he silent in return (λέγει, lines 7–8), since the sky, the visible Zeus, has its own rhetoric of signs. The human/divine dialogue takes place through the mediation of Ἄρατος, expounder of the heavens, by whom Zeus is οὐδε-

[27] Also at Callimachus, *Hymn to Zeus* 1–2 there is a possible play on ἀείδειν and αἰέν: Ζηνὸς ἔοι τί κεν ἄλλο παρὰ σπονδῇσιν ἀείδειν | λώιον ἢ θεὸν αὐτόν, ἀεὶ μέγαν, αἰὲν ἄνακτα.

ποτ' Ἄρρητον.[28] At line 6 it is the turn of the god to speak (albeit in sign language), giving men favourable indications (δεξιὰ σημαίνει). In 8–9 he tells the right seasons for various agricultural activities (λέγει δ' ὅτε δεξιαὶ ὧραι). Aratus' use of δεξιός both to qualify the signs given by the god and for the seasons for agricultural tasks emphasises the continuity between celestial and terrestrial spheres of activity.[29]

Σημαίνει in line 6 is picked up in lines 10–13. Here the signs have become specifically star signs. They enable men to plant at due season for growth:[30]

> αὐτὸς γὰρ τά γε σήματ' ἐν οὐρανῷ ἐστήριξεν
> ἄστρα διακρίνας, ἐσκέψατο δ' εἰς ἐνιαυτὸν
> ἀστέρας οἵ κε μάλιστα τετυγμένα σημαίνοιεν
> ἀνδράσιν ὡράων, ὄφρ' ἔμπεδα πάντα φύωνται.

For it was Zeus himself who fixed the signs in the sky, making them into distinct constellations, and organised stars for the year to give the most clearly defined signs of the seasonal round to men, so that everything may grow without fail.

Aratus' verbal dexterity puts Zeus and the farmer into a position of reciprocity which transcends the categories of active and passive: the men in line 9 set the saplings upright in trenches (φυτὰ γυρῶσαι) and scatter the seed (σπέρματα βαλέσθαι); Zeus in 10–13 makes fast the σήματα in the heavens and distributes (διακρίνας) the stars which mark the seasons.[31] By association of σπέρματα and σήματα, the cycles of the heavens and of agriculture, of godly and of human activity, are intertwined, the lives of men being lived in harmony with the cosmic cycles. A relationship of reciprocity between macrocosm (Zeus, the world) and microcosm (man) has been achieved by the poet's use of juxtaposition and parallelism at

[28] Callimachus in *Epigram* 29 writes Aratus' name as Ἄρητος, perhaps alluding to the latter's own wordplay: χαίρετε λεπταὶ | ῥήσιες, Ἀρήτου σύντονος ἀγρυπνίη. On the pun see Kidd (1981) 355, Hopkinson (1988) 139, Bing (1990), *id.* (1993) 105–8.

[29] For *dexter* of Germanicus, see above, p. 67.

[30] Virgil paraphrases these lines of Aratus at *Geo.* 1.351–5.

[31] The idea of 'scattering' the stars is found explicitly at *Ph.* 393–4: οἵη τίς τ' ὀλίγη χύσις ὕδατος ἔνθα καὶ ἔνθα | σκιδναμένου. Ovid uses this motif in his own *Phaenomena* (quoted in full p. 69), with *perque atras* ***sparsa*** tenebras.

this point of the poem, its cosmogony, or the genesis of its language in the proem.

We are beginning to see how the themes of the proem extend across the *Phaenomena*. The 'Diosemeiai', the second main section of the poem, which passes from the layout of the constellations to their practical use as weather signs, is heralded by its own introductory passage, which matches the work's proem. This 'second proem' (733–77),[32] like lines 1–26, sets out the specifications of the universe, this time in a way which shows the poet to be mindful of the reading of weather signs in addition to star signs.

These lines use the language of the exordium, which there described the seasons of the solar year, to describe the phases of the moon. Line 732, πάντη γὰρ τά γε πολλὰ θεοὶ ἄνδρεσσι λέγουσιν ('for everywhere the gods give these many predictions to men'), marks the beginning of the transition. Λέγουσιν picks up the λέγει of the proem (line 7): the phases of the moon and weather signs, as well as the star signs, are a cosmic rather than verbal language. At 738–9 the multiplicity of the moon's phases is like that of the stars in the proem:

> αἰεὶ δ' ἄλλοθεν ἄλλα παρακλίνουσα μέτωπα
> εἴρει ὁποσταίη μηνὸς περιτέλλεται ἠώς.

As she continually changes her aspect with different phases, she tells which day of the month is taking its course.

As the moon tells (εἴρει, line 739) what day of the month it is, so the twelve signs of the zodiac are useful in telling the hours of the night, as well as the phases of the seasonal year (740–3):

> ἄκρα γε μὴν νυκτῶν κεῖναι δυοκαίδεκα μοῖραι
> ἄρκιαι ἐξειπεῖν. τὰ δέ που μέγαν εἰς ἐνιαυτόν,
> ὥρη μέν τ' ἀρόσαι νειούς, ὥρη δὲ φυτεῦσαι,
> ἐκ Διὸς ἤδη πάντα πεφασμένα πάντοθι κεῖται.

[32] My structuring of the two halves of the poem is slightly different from that of Kidd (1997) 425–44: he has the Weather Signs proper begin at 758, calling 758–77 the 'second proem'. Following what Kidd ((1997) 425) refers to as 'an old tradition', I include the preceding passage (733–57) under that rubric, since there too motifs can be detected which go back to the original proem.

For declaring the endings of nights those twelve signs of the zodiac are certainly reliable. But as for the times of the great year, the time to plough fallow land, the time to plant trees, these are already all available as revealed by Zeus.

Εἰς ἐνιαυτόν (741) echoes line 11 of the proem. Likewise, ὥρη ... ἀρόσαι | ὥρη ... φυτεῦσαι (742) brings to mind lines 7–9 of the proem. Ἐκ Διός (743) recalls line 1. Proximity of god and man is found at 756–7:

> οἵ τε Ποσειδάωνος ὁρώμενοι ἢ **Διὸς** αὐτοῦ
> ἀστέρες **ἀνθρώποισι** τετυγμένα σημαίνουσι.

... and the stars which, when sighted in Poseidon's realm or in that of Zeus himself, give clearly defined signs to men.

Line 757 reminds us of lines 12–13 of the proem, ἀστέρας οἵ κε μάλιστα τετυγμένα σημαίνοιεν | ἀνδράσιν ὡράων. The action of men in perceiving the stars at 756–7 is parallel to the action of the providential Zeus in setting them up. Σημαίνουσιν at 757 looks forward to the σήματα in 760 and 772, and at the same time causes us to recall that, in line 6 of the proem, Zeus σημαίνει. The idea is re-iterated at 768–72:

> πάντα γὰρ οὔπω
> ἐκ Διὸς ἄνθρωποι γινώσκομεν, ἀλλ' ἔτι πολλὰ
> κέκρυπται, τῶν αἴ κε θέλῃ καὶ ἐς αυτίκα δώσει
> Ζεύς· ὁ γὰρ οὖν γενεὴν ἀνδρῶν ἀναφανδὸν ὀφέλλει
> πάντοθεν εἰδόμενος, πάντη δ' ὅ γε σήματα φαίνων.

For we men do not yet have knowledge of everything from Zeus, but much still is hidden, whereof Zeus, if he wishes, will give us signs anon; he certainly does benefit the human race openly, showing himself on every side, and everywhere displaying his signs.

Note echoes of the proem here: Πάντα (768), πολλά (769), πάντοθεν | πάντη (772); the juxtaposition of Διός and ἄνθρωποι (769) and the proximity of Ζεύς to the γενεὴν ἀνδρῶν (771); the echo of line 1 in line 769 (ἐκ Διός). The theme is Zeus as ἤπιος ἀνθρώποισιν (*Ph.* line 5), from observation of whose signs one derives profit, ὀφέλλει, line 771.[33] Ἀναφανδόν is important: the reason Zeus can be said to aid men 'openly'

[33] Also ὄφελος, line 463.

is that he does it through σήματα, now both star and weather signs. This theme resounds throughout the *Phaenomena* from line 10 (αὐτὸς γὰρ τά γε σήματ' ἐν οὐρανῷ ἐστήριξεν) onwards.

By repetition and development of ideas from the opening of the poem, the 'second proem' links the latter half with its first section. As the ideas of the proem informed our reading of the 'Phainomena', so, now doubly enforced, will they dictate our view of the 'Diosemeiai'. Another way in which the *Phaenomena* is unified is by repetition of features of the opening and second proem at the end of the work, or ring composition on the large scale. Consider *Phaenomena* 1153–4:

τῶν ἄμυδις πάντων ἐσκεμμένος εἰς ἐνιαυτὸν
οὐδέποτε σχεδίως κεν ἐπ' αἰθέρι τεκμήραιο.

If you have watched for these signs all together for the year, you will never make an uninformed judgement on the evidence of the sky.

Note ἄμυδις πάντων: simultaneity and totality.

Ἐσκεμμένος εἰς ἐνιαυτόν recalls ἐσκέψατο δ' εἰς ἐνιαυτόν in line 11. In the proem the subject of ἐσκέψατο was Zeus, who 'saw to it' that the stars should give fixed indications of the seasons; at the close of the work the participle agrees with the addressee, who must simultaneously perceive the signs and order them for himself.

The same effect of unity is produced by τεκμήραιο (1154, the final word of the poem) and τεκμήρατε (line 18, the last word of the proem).[34] The Muses in the proem are asked to 'oversee' Aratus' work, but ultimately it is the addressee who

[34] The unity of the Aratean poetic inheres in techniques of lexical, as well as thematic, repetition. This verb is one component of Aratus' repetitive lexical arsenal, exploited for all its various meanings. At line 38, the Greeks 'look to' (τεκμαίρονται) Helice; there is no need, at 142, to'conjecture' (ἐπιτεκμήραιο) which stars make up the Great Bear; at 170, one can 'distinguish' (τεκμήραιτο) by certain signs the head of the Bull; the verb is used in 801–2 of 'forecasting' (τεκμαίρεο | τεκμήραιο) the weather; in 1063 the farmer 'predicts' (τεκμαίρεται) harvest time from the budding of white blossom; cows 'bear witness' (τεκμαίρονται) to storms at 1121, and, finally, in 1129, the addressee is himself taught to 'predict' storms, προτέροις ἐπὶ σήμασι τεκμήραιο. Σῆμα is another keyword. Maass (1893) lists in his appended concordance 45 occurrences of the noun in its various forms, and at least 10 of the verb σημαίνω. Likewise Aratus repeats the imperative σκέπτεο (75, 778, 799, 832, 880, 892, 994, etc.), which calls upon the addressee both to observe the sky and to read the poem.

must look back across the whole poem, in order to read all the signs together. Repetition of the verb τεκμαίρομαι at the beginning and end of the poem calls attention to the Aratean poetic, and serves to assimilate the writing of the poem with the Muses' aid to the act of perception by the addressee. Recognition of linguistic and thematic repetition causes the reader to identify with the process of poetic composition at the same time as he assimilates the information and advice which provides the material for this compositional process, just as recognition of the pattern in the stars caused the addressee to participate in the divine ordering process.

Aratus and Cleanthes

So far, looking at the *Phaenomena* through Stoic ideas has shown the essential unity of the work, a unity which is parallel to that of the Stoic cosmos. The Stoic connection can be strengthened by considering similarities between Aratus' *Phaenomena* and Cleanthes' *Hymn to Zeus*.[35] This work enables us to see how a Stoic who was Aratus' near-contemporary accommodated the language and forms of poetry to the world-view of his theology, and to place Aratus in the same tradition.

The same themes may be discerned in Cleanthes as in Aratus. Words of plenitude, inclusiveness and permanence occur throughout the *Hymn*: πολυώνυμε παγκρατὲς αἰεί (line 1), πάντα (line 2), πᾶσι (3), πᾶς ὅδε κόσμος (7), πάντ' ἔργα (11), πάνδωρε (32). At lines 12–13, Zeus is διὰ πάντων | ... μιγνύμενος and at line 14 βασιλεὺς διὰ παντός. Cleanthes rings changes on the theme of permanence: σὸν κράτος αἰὲν ἀείσω (line 6),[36] ἀειζώοντα, of Zeus' thunderbolt in line 10, ἕνα γίγνεσθαι πάντων λόγον αἰὲν ἐόντα (line 21). At line 37, the constancy of men in praising Zeus (ὑμνοῦντες τὰ σὰ ἔργα διηνεκές) leads up to the final ἀεὶ ... ὑμνεῖν in the closing line of the poem. Likewise, the interconnectedness of things

[35] See Kidd (1997) 10 for some skeletal references.
[36] See n. 27 above for αἰέν/ἀείδειν wordplay.

expressed in *Phaenomena* 2–4 is also seen in Cleanthes, *Hymn* 15–16:

> οὐδέ τι γίγνεται ἔργον ἐπὶ χθονὶ σοῦ δίχα, δαῖμον,
> οὔτε κατ' αἰθέριον θεῖον πόλον, οὔτ' ἐνὶ πόντῳ ...

No deed is done on earth, god, without your offices, nor in the divine etherial vault of heaven, nor at sea ...[37]

The adjectives which qualify πόλος ('heaven') render it the most significant of the three zones: it is θεῖος because Zeus for the Stoics is both immanent in, and to be identified with, the heavens. Since Zeus is also the πῦρ τεχνικόν, the sky is also αἰθέριος, 'burning' (αἴθω).

The second of the thematic groups examined above was that of god and man, reflective of providence and universal sympathy. This is also to be found in Cleanthes. The idea of mortals and immortals (ἀθανάτων ... Ζεῦ ... θνητοῖσι) seals off lines 1–3 as an introductory unit. This is a device which recurs towards the end of Cleanthes' *Hymn*, in the context of Zeus as πρόνοια (Providence):

> ἀλλὰ **Ζεῦ** πάνδωρε κελαινεφὲς ἀργικέραυνε
> **ἀνθρώπους** ῥύου ⟨μὲν⟩ ἀπειροσύνης ἀπὸ λυγρῆς (32–3)

Bountiful Zeus of the dark clouds and gleaming thunderbolt, protect mankind from its pitiful incompetence.

Zeus as Providence appears at Cleanthes line 25, where he leads men to the βίον ἐσθλόν, the 'good life', the abstract version of Aratus' concrete 'livelihood' (βιότοιο) of *Phaenomena* 7.

The third theme adumbrated above was that of speech and signs. In Cleanthes, the poet and mankind seem at first sight to be the most emphatic speakers, through their cultic acts: πολυώνυμε (1), προσαυδᾶν (3), καθυμνήσω ... ἀείσω (6), ὑμνοῦντες (37), ὑμνεῖν (39). Then Zeus, the λόγος, engages with men in a dialogue of honour at line 36: ὄφρ' ἂν τιμηθέντες ἀμειβώμεσθά σε τιμῇ. Aratus' providential Zeus speaks directly to men through his setting out of σήματα; Cleanthes'

[37] Text and translation of the *Hymn to Zeus* as in Long and Sedley (1987) 54I.

Zeus sets up the heavenly bodies through the agency of the universal reason (κοινὸς λόγος, *Hymn to Zeus* 12).

The heavenly bodies can lead to a closer parallel between Aratus' *Phaenomena* and Cleanthes' *Hymn to Zeus* than has previously been essayed. Consider the passage in which Cleanthes speaks of them:[38]

σοὶ δὴ πᾶς ὅδε κόσμος ἑλισσόμενος περὶ γαῖαν
πείθεται ᾗ κεν ἄγῃς, καὶ ἑκὼν ὑπὸ σεῖο κρατεῖται·
τοῖον ἔχεις ὑποεργὸν ἀνικήτοις ἐνὶ χερσὶν
ἀμφήκη πυρόεντ' αἰειζώοντα κεραυνόν·
τοῦ γὰρ ὑπὸ πληγῆς φύσεως πάντ' ἔργα βέβηκεν,
ᾧ σὺ κατευθύνεις κοινὸν λόγον, ὃς διὰ πάντων
φοιτᾷ μιγνύμενος μεγάλῳ μικροῖς τε φάεσσιν
†ὡς τόσσος γεγαὼς ὕπατος βασιλεὺς διὰ παντός.† (*Hymn to Zeus* 7–14)

All this cosmos, as it spins around the earth, obeys you, whichever way you lead, and willingly submits to your sway. Such is the double-edged fiery ever-living thunderbolt which you hold at the ready in your unvanquished hands. For under its strokes all the works of nature are accomplished. With it you direct the universal reason which runs through all things and intermingles with the lights of heaven both great and small ...

The reference in line 13 is to the heavenly bodies, both large (the sun) and small (the stars); the κοινὸς λόγος which mixes with them is the πῦρ τεχνικόν. This brings us back to the divinity of the heavenly bodies, and their identification with Zeus. Cleanthes' heavenly bodies occur in a context which Alan James, in his philological commentary on the passage, demonstrated to be that of Stoic cosmogony. Πυρόεντα (line 10) signifies the cosmic πῦρ of Stoicism, which, we remember, is also the substance of the stars.[39] Zeus' thunderbolt is 'starry' as well as 'fiery'.

The compound adjective ἀειζώοντα was probably coined by Cleanthes after Heraclitus' πῦρ ἀείζωον.[40] 'Philosophically ἀειζώοντα κεραυνόν represents the familiar Stoic concept of the material aspect of the divine, the "creative fire", πῦρ

[38] On the textual problems, see James (1972) 32.

[39] Coined by Cleanthes perhaps after the analogy of ἀστερόεις, 'starry', as of the Crown of Ariadne at Apollonius Rhodius, *Argon.* 3.1003, ἀστερόεις στάφανος.

[40] James (1972) 32. On Heraclitus and Cleanthes, see Long (1975–6).

τεχνικόν, derived from Heraclitus' "ever-living fire", which ... was actually pictured by Heraclitus as "the thunderbolt that steers all things", τὰ δὲ πάντα οἰακίζει κεραυνός. A strictly philosophical point has been conveyed naturally enough in the traditional language and imagery of poetry.'[41]

The heavenly bodies in Cleanthes are to be identified with πῦρ τεχνικόν, the active manifestation of Zeus. This supports the assertion made above in connection with Aratus, that every word spoken about the stars constitutes speaking about Zeus. The similarity between Aratus and Cleanthes reinforces both the Stoic subtext of the *Phaenomena* and the unity of Aratus' poem.

The artist in Aratus

Aratus' poem acts as a unified artistic entity by virtue of the kind of thematic repetition we have seen above. Such repetition is most prominent at crucial points in the poem: the beginning, the point of transition between the 'Phainomena' and the 'Diosemeiai,' and the end. It is through repetition that Aratus builds his poetic cosmos, a universe in which the structures of language act as the elements of nature.

Aratus, as a Stoic poet who works with the elements of language, 'builds' the cosmos.[42] It is my view that he can be seen as meditating on this act of cosmic construction in two passages which have hitherto been seen as 'digressions'. The first of these is *Phaenomena* 367–85, on the naming of stars. In this passage, Aratus directs us to recall his unified poetic, by re-iteration of the language and ideas already dominant in the *Phaenomena*. It is my view that the Namer of Stars, the τις ἀνδρῶν οὐκέτ' ἐόντων, acts as a trope for the poet himself. The Namer of Stars can be seen as a figure which Aratus uses to talk about his art, and the relation of that art with the cosmos – a natural one, since the structures of language are

[41] James (1972) 32.
[42] On the poet as demiurge, see Hardie (1985b), Lieberg (1982).

generated in accordance with what is in the natural world, and themselves construct it. Here is the passage in full:[43]

οἱ δ' ὀλίγῳ μέτρῳ ὀλίγῃ δ' ἐγκείμενοι αἴγλῃ
μεσσόθι πηδαλίου καὶ Κήτεος εἱλίσσονται,
γλαυκοῦ πεπτηῶτες ὑπὸ πλευρῇσι Λαγωοῦ,
νώνυμοι· οὐ γὰρ τοί γε τετυγμένου εἰδώλοιο
βεβλέαται μελέεσσιν ἐοικότες, οἷά τε πολλὰ
ἑξείης στιχόωντα παρέρχεται αὐτὰ κέλευθα
ἀνομένων ἐτέων· τά τις ἀνδρῶν οὐκέτ' ἐόντων
ἐφράσατ' ἠδ' ἐνόησεν ἅπαντ' ὀνομαστὶ καλέσσαι
ἤλιθα μορφώσας· οὐ γὰρ κ' ἐδυνήσατο πάντων
οἰόθι κεκριμένων ὄνομ' εἰπεῖν, οὐδὲ δαῆναι.
πολλοὶ γὰρ πάντῃ, πολέων δ' ἐπὶ ἶσα πέλονται
μέτρα τε καὶ χροιή, πάντες γε μὲν ἀμφιέλικτοι·
τῷ καὶ ὁμηγερέας οἱ ἐείσατο ποιήσασθαι
ἀστέρας, ὄφρ' ἐπιτὰξ ἄλλῳ παρακείμενος ἄλλος
εἴδεα σημαίνοιεν· ἄφαρ δ' ὀνομάστ' ἐγένοντο
ἄστρα, καὶ οὐκέτι νῦν ὑπὸ θαύματι τέλλεται ἀστήρ·
ἀλλ' οἱ μὲν καθαροῖς ἐναρηρότες εἰδώλοισι
φαίνονται, τὰ δ' ἔνερθε διωκομένοιο Λαγωοῦ
πάντα μάλ' ἠερόεντα καὶ οὐκ ὀνομαστὰ φέρονται.

Other stars covering a small area, and inset with slight brilliance, circle between Argo's steering-oar and the Monster, lying below the flanks of the grey Hare, without a name; they are not cast in resemblance to the body of any well-defined figure, like the many that pass in regular ranks along the same paths as the years complete themselves, the constellations that one of the men who are no more devised and contrived to call all by names, grouping (μορφώσας) them in compact shapes: he could not, of course, have named or identified all the stars taken individually, because there are so many all over the sky, and many alike in magnitude and colour, while all have a circling movement; therefore he decided to make the stars into groups, so that different stars arranged together in order could represent figures; and thereupon the named constellations were created, and no star-rising now takes us by surprise; so the other stars that shine appear fixed in clear-cut figures, but those beneath the hunted Hare are all very hazy and nameless in their courses.

The fundamental contrast here is between things named and unnamed: νώνυμοι (370), ὀνομαστὶ καλέσσαι (374), ὄνομ' εἰπεῖν (376), ὀνομαστά (381), οὐκ ὀνομαστά (385). At the risk of over-schematisation, it would be possible to fit this into the

[43] On the chiastic structure of the passage, with bibliography, see Kidd (1997) *ad loc.*

Aratean theme of speech and naming which we have studied above. Lines 370–3 show in addition that the tendency of certain stars to form figures 'like limbs' is just as important a criterion for their naming as is their brightness or obscurity; in other words, whether a place can be found for them in a comprehensive system, like words in their syntactical structure or syntactical units in poetic form.

The artistic analogy is what is important here. This is contained in the metaphorical use of μορφόω, 'to shape', of the defining act of the Namer. The idea is that the stars can be 'formed' into 'figures' (εἴδωλοιο, 370; εἰδώλοισιν, 383; εἴδεα, 381), as a sculptor would work with clay or stone. Εἴδωλον means 'phantom' in Homer;[44] εἶδος, its cognate, Homeric 'appearance' or 'form',[45] can already carry connotations of visual art in Hesiod. At *WD* 60–4 it is used of the form of Pandora which Hephaistos models:

> Ἥφαιστον δ' ἐκέλευσε περικλυτὸν ὅττι τάχιστα
> γαῖαν ὕδει φύρειν, ἐν δ' ἀνθρώπου θέμεν αὐδὴν
> καὶ σθένος, ἀθανάτῃς δὲ θεῇς εἰς ὦπα ἐίσκειν
> παρθενικῆς καλὸν **εἶδος** ἐπήρατον . . .

. . . and he told renowned Hephaistos at once to mix earth with water, to add in a human voice and strength, and to model upon the immortal goddess' aspect the fair and lovely form of a maiden.[46]

Hephaistos, we remember, was also the artisan of the Shield of Achilles, with its engraved constellations, in *Iliad* 18.[47] Given this context, the verb μορφόω (375), a term of sculpture, no longer appears quite so odd when used to describe the activity of naming the constellations verbally. Aratus is giving us here what almost amounts to an ekphrasis, the description of the naming of constellations as though it were the creation of a work of art, such as the Shield of Achilles.[48]

[44] As at *Il.* 5.449 and 451, *Od.* 4.796, 11.476. The word also came to be used of the constellations, as by Apollonius Rhodius at *Argon.* 3.1004, where the Crown of Ariadne 'whirls among the heavenly forms', οὐρανίοισιν ἑλίσσεται εἰδώλοισιν.

[45] *Il.* 3.39, 5.787, 10.316, 21.316; *Od.* 8.174, 17.454.

[46] Trans. West (1988).

[47] See above, pp. 37–8.

[48] Description of cosmogony can also be the description of art: see Wheeler (1995) on Ovid's cosmogony in *Metamorphoses* 1 as an artistic ekphrasis.

Cicero, translating the Aratean passage at *Aratea* 155–66, places more emphasis on the imagery of art, commenting on Aratus as well as translating him. Note especially 160–3:

> nam quae sideribus claris natura polivit
> et vario pinxit distinguens lumine formas,
> haec ille astrorum custos ratione notavit
> signaque dignavit caelestia nomine vero.

In Cicero it is nature who is the artist: she polished (*polivit*, 160) and painted (*pinxit*, 161) the *formae* (161) of the stars. By implication, the Namer engages in a two-layered act of mimesis, an artist copying art.

Who is this Namer? In Cicero's translation of *Phaenomena* 373, at *Aratea* 162, he is *ille astrorum custos.* But the Namers of Stars elsewhere in Cicero have a more specific identity. At *Aratea* 33, those who name the Pleiades are poets, maybe Homer and Hesiod:[49] *ut veteres statuere poetae, aeterno cunctas sane qui nomine dignant.* Aratus is one of the poets who name stars; as such he is like the primitive Namer who first constructed the Greek star map which filled the sky with named entities.

Like the poet, he 'shapes' (μορφόω) his world by naming things in it. Levitan expressed this as follows: 'As an individual or even as a teacher, Aratus remains like any other man, the exegete of the heavenly text. But as a didactic poet, he becomes responsible for a text of his own, Zeus-like in his own domain. His resources are a systematising intelligence and ultimately the system of his language. Of this he is well aware; understanding, for example, the ancient link between the recognition of pattern and the first act of language, the process of naming (as we see it in the passage on naming the stars).'[50]

This can be further illustrated with a passage which I believe to be a parallel expression of the daedalic act of the poet: Aratus' simile of the Craftsman at *Phaenomena* 529–33. This

[49] On Homeric and Hesiodic astrothesis, see Dicks (1970) chapter 1, Domenicucci (1996) 16.
[50] Levitan (1979) 64–5.

passage is preceded by what purports to be a first-hand description of the Celestial Circles (*Ph.* 462–8):

ἤτοι μὲν τά γε κεῖται ἀλίγκια δινωτοῖσι
τέσσαρα, τῶν κε μάλιστα ποθὴ ὄφελός τε γένοιτο
μέτρα περισκοπέοντι κατανομένων ἐνιαυτῶν.
σήματα δ' εὖ μάλα πᾶσιν ἐπιρρήδην περίκειται
πολλά τε καὶ σχεδόθεν πάντῃ συνεεργμένα πάντα·
αὐτοὶ δ' ἀπλατέες καὶ ἀρηρότες ἀλλήλοισι
πάντες· ἀτὰρ μέτρῳ γε δύω δυσὶν ἀντιφέρονται.

There are indeed these four circles set like wheels, for which there will be particular desire and need if you are studying the measurements of the self-fulfilling years. Many guide-stars lie along them all, to mark them, all bound closely together all the way; the circles themselves are without breadth and fastened all to each other, but in size are matched two with two.

The Celestial Circles are symbolic of the order of the poem itself, and their description contains the themes which are the basic elements of the poem; note words of symmetry, synchronicity, permanence, multitude. Κατανομένων ἐνιαυτῶν (464) may recall the theme of seasons in line 11 of the proem; the phrase looks forward to the 'whole year' with its 'fruitful seasons' (echoing in turn δεξιαὶ ὧραι in line 8 of the proem) at 550–2, which describes the circle of the zodiac:

ἐν τοῖς ἠέλιος φέρεται δυοκαίδεκα πᾶσι
πάντ' ἐνιαυτὸν ἄγων, καί οἱ περὶ τοῦτον ἰόντι
κύκλον ἀέξονται πᾶσαι ἐπικάρπιοι ὧραι.

Through all these twelve signs goes the sun as it brings the whole year to pass, and as it goes round this circle, all the fruitful seasons increase.

Ἀρηρότες at *Phaenomena* 467 brings to mind the passage in which Aratus first set out the dimensions of his universe: recall ἄξων αἰὲν ἄρηρεν (line 22). The participle also occurs in Aratus' 'Craftsman simile', συναρηρότα at line 532.

It is not surprising that Aratus should choose to stage his description of the Celestial Circles as a concentrated reiteration of the main motifs of the poem, since, like the passages we have studied above, this description comes at an important structural point in the poem, the transition from the mapping of stars to the measurement of time.[51] The basis of Aratus' description will be the system of the four circles drawn by mathematicians on the celestial sphere as points of reference for the position of the sun at various times of year: the Equator, the Tropics of Cancer and Capricorn, and the Ecliptic or Zodiac. This system of circles may have been introduced by Eudoxus, whose prose treatise Aratus is 'translating' in the *Phaenomena*, and to whom is attributed the manufacture of an armillary sphere.[52]

The circles are said at *Phaenomena* 462 to be 'like wheels'; the theme is developed at 529–33, in the simile itself:

> οὔ κεν Ἀθηναίης χειρῶν δεδιδαγμένος ἀνὴρ
> ἄλλῃ κολλήσαιτο κυλινδόμενα τροχάλεια
> τοῖά τε καὶ τόσα πάντα περὶ σφαιρηδὸν ἑλίσσων,
> ὡς τά γ' ἐναιθέρια πλαγίῳ συναρηρότα κύκλῳ
> ἐξ ἠοῦς ἐπὶ νύκτα διώκεται ἤματα πάντα.

In no other way would a man trained in the craftsmanship of Athene weld together revolving wheels in such a pattern and of such a size, rounding off the whole like a sphere, than the system of celestial circles, which, united by the oblique circle, speed from dawn to nightfall all the time.

The Celestial Circles have just been described in detail by the poet; now we look down on them synoptically, as on a spherical model, and find that (appropriately enough in the Stoic cosmos with its divine design) they are linked not otherwise than a skilled artisan would have joined them. Again we are made aware of the Aratean poetic by echoes of key expressions and ideas. The language of the simile is rich to the point of redundancy, seemingly because it strives to distil the linguistic and conceptual essence of the poem into a few lines. Note especially the emphasis on circularity and constancy in κυλινδόμενα ... | ... περισφαιρηδὸν ἑλίσσων (530–1), τοῖά τε καί τόσα πάντα (531), and ἐξ ἠοῦς ἐπὶ νύκτα ... ἤματα πάντα (533). The style and diction here are recognisably that which characterise the poem and are most concentrated at its defining points. Because of this, the Craftsman's act is

[51] See Kidd (1997) *ad loc.*

[52] Cicero *Rep.* 1.21–2. See below, pp. 96–100.

assimilated to the nature of the poem. The model made by the Craftsman is a figure for Aratus' poem, the Craftsman a figure for the poet, since both 'make' the world by their art.

The Craftsman simile is the realisation of the sculpture metaphor used earlier of the Namer of Stars. In the simile, the verb κολλάω in line 530 means 'to join one metal (or other substance) to another', and could be used in contexts of artisanship, as of a crown inlaid with gold and ivory, in Pindar, *Nemean* 7.78. In this case, the δεδιδαγμένος ἀνὴρ is like Plato's demiurge at *Timaeus* 75d, of whom the same verb is used.[53] The poet is also a modeller of the cosmos. The participle δεδιδαγμένος may even carry programmatic value, coming from the verb διδάσκω, 'teach' – which is what the didactic poet does.[54]

The system of the poem is presented in the simile as a means by which the universe may be perceived synoptically. The poem is parallel to a model made by a craftsman, which in turn is mimetic of the universe. If you reverse the analogy between art and the universe, the unity of the Stoic universe can become a metaphor for reading the *Phaenomena* as a work of art. The concluding lines of the poem are both about reading the signs of nature together, and about reading the poem as a unified entity:

> τῶν ἄμυδις πάντων ἐσκεμμένος εἰς ἐνιαυτὸν
> οὐδέποτε σχεδίως κεν ἐπ' αἰθέρι τεκμήραιο. (*Phaenomena* 1153–4)

Conclusion

In this chapter we have seen how the *Phaenomena* is a unified poem which reflects a system of physics, the central idea of which is a unified and divinely governed cosmos. It was nec-

[53] Of the making of mankind: τὰ δὲ νεῦρα διὰ ταῦτα καὶ οὕτως ὁ θεὸς ἐπ' ἐσχάτην τὴν κεφαλὴν περιστήσας κύκλῳ περὶ τὸν τράχηλον ἐκόλλησεν ὁμοιότητι ('It was on these grounds and in this way that God set the sinews at the bottom of the head round about the neck and glued them there symmetrically ...').

[54] The word διδάσκει, applied to Aratus himself, occurs throughout the Aratean scholia. The verb appears only thrice in the *Phaenomena* itself, used (apart from the Craftsman simile) of the moon (διδάσκει at 734 and διδάσκοι at 793).

essary to set up a way of reading the *Phaenomena* as a whole so that we can go on to explore its symbolic importance in Rome and its Roman metamorphosis at the hands of Ovid.

In Stoicism, the physical cosmos is also the λόγος: the world is also the word. The concept of a natural relation between language and the world was seen to work at every level in the *Phaenomena*: individual etymologies express the natural relationship between words and nature; the structure of the poem expresses the structure of the universe. 'In singing of the stars and of nature – for the Stoic a perfectly ordered *kosmos* – Aratus' poem is its own guarantee of truth.'[55]

Comparison of Ovid and Aratus in the next chapter will show that the issues of poetic order and universal truth are not as simple as that: Ovid can sing the universe (κόσμος); but nonetheless κόσμος ('order', in both the cosmic and poetic sense) can paradoxically be lacking. We shall now see what happens to the Aratean universe when it becomes part of the Julian year.

[55] Hunter (1995) 6.

CHAPTER 4

VESTA AND THE ARCHITECTURE OF THE *FASTI*

οὔ κεν Ἀθηναίης χειρῶν δεδιδαγμένος ἀνὴρ
ἄλλῃ κολλήσαιτο κυλινδόμενα τροχάλεια
τοῖά τε καὶ τόσα πάντα περὶ σφαιρηδὸν ἑλίσσων,
ὡς τά γ' ἐναιθέρια πλαγίῳ συναρηρότα κύκλῳ
ἐξ ἠοῦς ἐπὶ νύκτα διώκεται ἤματα πάντα.

(Aratus, *Phaenomena* 529–33)

In no other way would a man trained in the craftsmanship of Athene weld together revolving wheels in such a pattern and of such a size, rounding off the whole like a sphere, than the system of celestial circles, which, united by the oblique circle, speed from dawn to nightfall all the time.

arte Syracosia suspensus in aere clauso
stat globus, immensi parva figura poli

(Ovid, *Fasti* 6.277–8)

Introduction

The previous chapter explored Aratus' *Phaenomena*, showing how the philosophical background of the poem generates aesthetic unity. The unity of the Stoic universe becomes a metaphor for artistic unity: the word ἄμυδις at the close of the poem is both about reading the signs of nature together, and reading the poem as a unified entity. In the case of the *Phaenomena* it is unity – of the thematic elements in the poem and of its structural units – which conveys meaning.

What happens when the *Phaenomena* is transposed into the Roman calendar – and not just any Roman calendar, but Ovid's poetic version of it? An answer presents itself in abstract form in *Fasti* 6.249–460 (the Vestalia, celebrated on 9 June). Near the beginning of this passage, the temple of the Roman goddess Vesta is compared to an armillary sphere created by the third-century Syracusan mathematician Archimedes (*Fasti* 6.277–80). In addition, Hesiodic and Roman mythical elements are presented as relevant to the same festival. The Vestalia can illustrate Ovid's techniques of composition in the *Fasti*, with its juxtaposition of philosophical and mythical elements inside the framework provided by the Roman festivals. In addition, the Sphere of Archimedes, like Aratus' Craftsman simile (*Ph.* 529–33), presents us with a synoptic view of the world, an *imago mundi*,[1] which can also function as an image of Aratus' poem in the Roman context. Ovid lets us see Aratus' unified world briefly, at the same time placing it in the context of the Vestalia.

Critics have recognised Ovid's treatment of this festival as particularly capricious and disjunct. Franz Bömer speaks of its 'heterogene Elemente';[2] Alessandro Barchiesi describes Vesta as 'elusive and imageless, torn between incompatible representations'.[3] Elaine Fantham brought out the problems both of the Vestalia itself and of its structural place in the *Fasti*, in her discussion of the reduplication in *Fasti* 1 and 6 of the Priapus episode.[4] Gareth Williams showed how a conflict in the passage between Ovid's stance as inspired *vates* and the derivative, literary nature of his information, serves to destabilise the poet's narratorial position;[5] most recently Carole Newlands developed this reading to argue that the three incompatible views of Vesta that Ovid presents – rationalising, popular, and Augustan – are part of a cumulative destabilisation of the didactic intention of the *Fasti*.[6] The Vesta passage is representative on the small scale of the problems of the *Fasti* as a whole.

In particular, the issue of Vesta's etymology at *Fasti* 6.299–304 brings to light a *lack* of correlation between language and reality. Language becomes an arbitrary system of polysemic value rather than a true system of unitary meaning, as in Aratus. Issues of poetic structure will be seen to be involved here too, since the Ovidian etymology of Vesta, as well as the

[1] For the term see Hardie (1985a). [2] Bömer (1957–8) *ad Fasti* 6.249.
[3] Barchiesi (1997) 137. [4] Fantham (1983).
[5] Williams (1991). [6] Newlands (1995) 124–45.

relationship of the Vesta passage to the Janus episode of Book 1, may contribute to a structural openness which is one of the main ways in which the *Fasti* differs from the *Phaenomena*.

The Vesta passage is long, and composed of a series of false correlations and spurious progressions. Scribes have long attempted to sort out the episode by divisions in the manuscripts. For example, in one of the earlier manuscripts, Vaticanus Latinus 1604 (twelfth century), the episode is divided by marginal markings at 247, 348, 395, and 469 – an excessive number of divisions for a manuscript which is still close to the undivided state of earlier manuscripts such as the Ursinianus (Vaticanus Latinus 3262, eleventh century). By the fifteenth century, Vaticanus Latinus 3263 (copied by Pomponius Laetus) divides the passage in twenty-four places.[7]

The episode may be divided for our purposes as follows:

249–66	Invocation of Vesta, cultic setting, history of the temple
267–82	*Aition* for the shape of the temple – Vesta as the earth
283–94	*Aitia* for Vesta's virgin priestesses – fire
295–8	There is no image of Vesta, nor of fire
299–318	The etymology of Vesta (Ἑστία)
319–48	Vesta and Priapus
349–94	Jupiter Pistor
395–416	*Aition* for the Lacus Curtius
417–54	Metellus and the Palladium
455–60	Vesta at the present time.

We see that the passage falls into two parts, of which the first is predominantly rationalising, the second mythological. I intend to look in detail at the rationalising part, showing how its literary underlay provides a link with the Stoic tradition connected to Aratus.

The Stoic tradition

Here I aim to demonstrate that the literary history of the first part of the Vestalia (*Fasti* 6.267–318), which can be ascertained

[7] Interlinear headings or interstices occur at 249, 267, 283, 295, 299, 301, 303, 305, 311, 319, 349, 355, 375, 383, 387, 395, 401, 419, 427, 439, 445, 461, 465, and 489.

tained through the particular elements it contains and the way in which these elements are combined, ties it in with a Stoic (or Stoicising) tradition of cosmology and exegesis, including the exegesis of Aratus' *Phaenomena*.

In *Fasti* 6.267–88, three important elements occur: (a) a synoptic world picture (*Fasti* 6.267–76), (b) an analogy for this world-view, the Sphere of Archimedes (277–80), and (c) an allegorical explanation of the goddess through Hesiodic cosmogony (*Fasti* 6.285–8). The third element is expressed in a different idiom from the first two: the rational gives way to the mythical, the incorporeal to the anthropomorphic.

The *aition* for the shape of the temple from Vesta's identity as earth is not straightforward. The fundamental idea is that of sphericity: *terra pilae similis* (269), *orbem* (271), and *globus* (278), a term which is glossed by Cicero in *DND* 2.47 by the Greek σφαῖρα. The *forma rotunda* of the earth (280) is said to be the reason for the *forma templi* (265). But can a temple be spherical? Coins struck near the end of Tiberius' reign represent the Temple of Vesta as a circular structure with a conical roof.[8] The circular ground plan of the temple must somehow project a sphere in the round.[9]

The progression of the argument in lines 265–76 seems logical, as it is presented by the poet:

(i) Ovid's object is to explain the shape of the temple (265–6)
(ii) Vesta is the same as the earth (267–8)
(iii) The temple is round because the earth is round (269–70)
(iv) Lines 271–6 answer a question which is elided: 'But why is the earth round?'[10] The answer is, 'Because this is the shape that ensures its equidistance from every part of the heavens and dictates that it remain still (enabling Ovid to give the etymology *vi stando* in line 299) and in equipoise (*libratum*, line 271) at the centre of the universe.' Line 271 may be translated 'Its own rotundity keeps the globe in equilibrium.'

[8] Platner and Ashby (1929) 557–9.
[9] See below, p. 108.
[10] Lines 271–6 have been considered by some to be interpolated, since they do not appear in some of the best manuscripts, and have thus been excised from the text. However, as Postgate (1910) 198 pointed out, they are in the Ursinianus, which is the best authority; and as well as this the reason for their omission in the other manuscripts is obvious: the homoeoteleuton *onus*, which occurs in 270 and 276.

Having devised this progression, Ovid can now with no difficulty extrapolate to a geometrical model of the earth, the globe of Archimedes (277–80). The globe was an instrument of theoretical astronomy, enabling the observer to orient himself among the Celestial Circles, poles, and constellations. The three-dimensional *sphaira* is a better analogy for the world-view that Ovid has just presented than for the temple. In the progression of the argument as we have just seen it, the world-view becomes primary, the globe and temple parallel analogies for it.

Ovid's association of Vesta with the globe of Archimedes is unique. Why has he conceived of his *aition* for the temple as an image from astronomy? In attempting to answer this question, we shall see that the Sphere makes the passage both astronomical, since it is an abstract image of the geocentric universe, and Stoic, by the other literary contexts in which it appears.[11] The Stoic/astronomical equation can act as a starting-point from which to conceive the relationship between the Vesta passage and Aratus' poem.

The sphaira

arte Syracosia suspensus in aere clauso
 stat globus, immensi parva figura poli,
et quantum a summis, tantum secessit ab imis
 terra; quod ut fiat forma rotunda facit. (*Fasti* 6.277–80)

These lines refer to a globe made by the Syracusan mathematician Archimedes (*c.* 287–212 BC),[12] who was known to Livy as *unicus spectator caeli siderumque*.[13] The Sphere of Archimedes to which Ovid refers was brought back, with one other, by M. Claudius Marcellus after his sack of Syracuse in 212 BC,

[11] The Sphere of Archimedes occurs three times in literature before Ovid. All three occurrences are in the philosophical works of Cicero: *Rep.* 1.21–2, *Tusc.* 1.63, and *DND* 2.88.

[12] Bömer (1957–8) *ad loc.* On the globe of Archimedes, and ancient *planetaria* generally, see Pease (1955–8) *ad* Cicero, *DND* 2.88.

[13] Livy 24.34.2.

as Cicero tells us in *Republic* 1.21:[14]

nam memoria teneo C. Sulpicium Gallum, doctissimum, ut scitis, hominem, cum idem hoc visum diceretur et esset casu apud M. Marcellum, qui cum eo consul fuerat, sphaeram, quam M. Marcelli avus captis Syracusis ex urbe locupletissima atque ornatissima sustulisset, cum aliud nihil ex tanta praeda domum suam deportavisset, iussisse proferri...

For I remember an incident in the life of C. Sulpicius Gallus, a most learned man, as you know: at a time when a similar phenomenon was reported, and he happened to be at the house of Marcus Marcellus, his colleague in the consulship, he ordered the celestial globe to be brought out which the grandfather of Marcellus had carried off from Syracuse when that very rich and beautiful city was taken, though he took home with him nothing else out of the great store of booty captured...[15]

Cicero goes on to describe two types of model globes, solid and hollow. Archimedes made both kinds – a solid one, and a more complex armillary version, in which the revolutions of the different celestial circles and heavenly bodies were visible. Although the former, which was kept in the Temple of Virtue, was the more popular, the latter is the one Gallus expounds in *Republic* 1.21–2:[16]

[14] See also Plutarch, *Marc.* 14–19. The Sphere is mentioned at 19.6 in connection with Archimedes' death: καὶ τρίτος ἐστὶ λόγος, ὡς κομίζοντι πρὸς Μάρκελλον αὐτῷ τῶν μαθηματικῶν ὀργάνων σκιόθηρα καὶ σφαίρας καὶ γωνίας, αἷς ἐναρμόττει τὸ τοῦ ἡλίου μέγεθος πρὸς τὴν ὄψιν, στρατιῶται περιτυχόντες καὶ χρυσίον ἐν τῷ τεύχει δόξαντες φέρειν ἀπέκτειναν ('There is also a third story, that as Archimedes was carrying to Marcellus some of his mathematical instruments, such as sun-dials and spheres and quadrants, by means of which he made the magnitude of the sun appreciable to the eye, some soldiers fell in with him, and thinking that he was carrying gold in the box, slew him', trans. Perrin (1917)). On the passage of Cicero, see Haury (1964).

[15] Trans. Keyes (1928).

[16] Archimedes' globe was made of either glass (Claudian, *Carm. Min.* 51.1) or bronze (as here, *in aere illo*). It is not clear exactly what Ovid means by *in aëre clauso* (*Fasti* 6.277), 'in trapped air'. The poet is either visualising the Sphere as containing air trapped in glass; or perhaps *clauso* is better taken as 'defined' by the bronze bands which represented the Celestial Circles on an armillary sphere. The probability for bronze is increased by Propertius 4.1.76, where the astrologer Horus is not *nescius aerata signa movere pila*, 'not unversed in the art of moving the heavenly bodies around on a bronze planetarium'; and by the fact that it is hard to imagine that such a complex thing could have been achieved in ancient glass. A simple answer is that in his reading of this passage of Cicero, Ovid saw *in aere* (in bronze) and wrote *in aëre* (in air). Whatever the case, the phrase is primarily designed to strike an exact parallel between the globe and the earth itself, which in 270 was resting *aëre subiecto*.

cuius ego sphaerae cum persaepe propter Archimedi gloriam nomen audissem, speciem ipsam non sum tanto opere admiratus; erat enim illa venustior et nobilior in volgus, quam ab eodem Archimede factam posuerat in templo Virtutis Marcellus idem. sed posteaquam coepit rationem huius operis scientissime Gallus exponere, plus in illo Siculo ingenii, quam videretur natura humana ferre potuisse, iudicavi fuisse. dicebat enim Gallus sphaerae illius alterius solidae atque plenae vetus esse inventum, et eam a Thalete Milesio primum esse tornatam, post autem ab Eudoxo Cnidio, discipulo, ut ferebat, Platonis, eandem illam astris stellisque, quae caelo inhaererent, esse descriptam; cuius omnem ornatum et descriptionem sumptam ab Eudoxo multis annis post non astrologiae scientia, sed poetica quadam facultate versibus Aratum extulisse. hoc autem sphaerae genus, in quo solis et lunae motus inessent et earum quinque stellarum, quae errantes et quasi vagae nominarentur, in illa sphaera solida non potuisse finiri, atque in eo admirandum esse inventum Archimedi, quod excogitasset, quem ad modum in dissimillimis motibus inaequabiles et varios cursus servaret una conversio. hanc sphaeram Gallus cum moveret, fiebat, ut soli luna totidem conversionibus in aere illo, quot diebus in ipso caelo, succederet, ex quo et in sphaera solis fieret eadem illa defectio et incideret luna tum in eam metam, quae esset umbra terrae, cum sol e regione... (the text breaks off).

Though I had heard this globe mentioned quite frequently on account of the fame of Archimedes, when I actually saw it I did not particularly admire it; for that other celestial globe, also constructed by Archimedes, which the same Marcellus placed in the Temple of Virtue, is more beautiful as well as more widely known among the people. But when Gallus began to give a very learned explanation of the device, I concluded that the famous Sicilian had been endowed with greater genius than one would imagine it possible for a human being to possess. For Gallus told us that the other kind of celestial globe, which was solid and contained no hollow space, was a very early invention, the first one of that kind having been constructed by Thales of Miletus, and later marked by Eudoxus of Cnidus (a disciple of Plato, it was claimed) with the constellations and stars which are fixed in the sky. He also said that many years later Aratus, borrowing this whole arrangement and plan from Eudoxus, had described it in verse, without any knowledge of astronomy, but with considerable poetic talent. But this newer kind of globe, he said, on which were delineated the motions of the sun and moon and of those five stars which are called wanderers, or, as we might say, rovers, contained more than could be shown on the solid globe, and the invention of Archimedes deserved special admiration because he had thought out a way to represent accurately by a single device for turning the globe those various and divergent movements with their different rates of speed. And when Gallus moved the globe, it was actually true that the moon was always as many revolutions behind the sun on the bronze contrivance as would agree with the number of days it was behind in the sky. Thus the same eclipse of the sun happened on the globe as would actually happen, and the moon came to the point where the shadow of the earth was at the very time when the sun ... out of the region ...

The complex Sphere built by Archimedes supersedes the solid type used by Thales and Eudoxus.[17] The globe described by Ovid at *Fasti* 6.277–80 must have been of the more complex type, since only in this type would one have been able to gain a picture of the centrality of the earth inside the *mundus*. This type of globe is a model of the cosmos as we find it defined by the Syracusan himself at the beginning of his work, ὁ Ψαμμίτης, *The Sand-Reckoner*, an extended calculation of how many grains of sand would be required to fill the volume of the universe:

κατέχεις δὲ διότι καλεῖται κόσμος ὑπὸ μὲν τῶν πλείστων ἀστρολόγων ἁ σφαῖρα, ἇς ἐστι κέντρον μὲν τὸ τᾶς γᾶς κέντρον, ἁ δὲ ἐκ τοῦ κέντρου ἴσα τᾷ εὐθείᾳ τᾷ μεταξὺ τοῦ κέντρου τοῦ ἁλίου καὶ τοῦ κέντρου τᾶς γᾶς.[18]

Cosmos is the name given by most astronomers to the sphere whose centre is the centre of the earth and whose radius is equal to the distance between the centre of the sun and the centre of the earth.[19]

Another Ciceronian passage in which the Sphere of Archimedes occurs is *DND* 2.88. The context of the passage is an argument for the rationality of the universe (as evident primarily through astronomical phenomena), which for the Stoic speaker is analogous to the rationality displayed in art, one manifestation of which (a particularly appropriate one, since

[17] Kidd (1997) 17 comments on *Rep.* 1.22, 'The association of a globe also with Thales gives one little confidence in Gallus' authority, and indeed there is no evidence that such an artefact existed in the fourth century ... Eudoxus did not have a system of co-ordinates [invented by Hipparchus in the 2nd century BC], which would have been essential for any attempt to represent the fixed stars accurately on an artificial globe.' Hipparchus (who himself probably made the first accurate star globe) in his commentary on Eudoxus attributes to him no such globe. Kidd believes the globe of Archimedes mentioned at *Rep.* 1.22 was too early to have been a true armillary sphere, and was probably more like the Farnese globe, with the constellations represented by figures. Kidd does not, however, mention the second globe, with moving components, also described by Cicero. It would perhaps have been possible to make an approximate representation of this kind, even without co-ordinates.

[18] Text in Mugler (1970–2) vol. II, 135.

[19] Trans. Dijksterhuis (1987) 362.

it is in fact a microcosmic representation of the universe) is a *sphaira* made by Posidonius:[20]

quod si in Scythiam aut in Britanniam sphaeram aliquis tulerit hanc quam nuper familiaris noster effecit Posidonius, cuius singulae conversiones idem efficiunt in sole et in luna et in quinque stellis errantibus quod efficitur in caelo singulis diebus et noctibus, quis in illa barbaria dubitet quin ea sphaera sit perfecta ratione? hi autem dubitant de mundo, ex quo et oriuntur et fiunt omnia, casune ipse sit effectus aut necessitate aliqua an ratione ac mente divina, et Archimedem arbitrantur plus valuisse in imitandis sphaerae conversionibus quam naturam in efficiendis...

Our friend Posidonius has recently fashioned an orrery; each time it revolves, it makes the sun, moon and five planets reproduce the movements which they make over a day and a night in the heavens. Suppose someone carried this to Scythia or to Britain. Surely no one in those barbaric regions would doubt that the orrery had been constructed by a rational process? Yet our opponents here profess uncertainty whether the universe, from which all things take their rise, has come into existence by chance or some necessity, or by divine reason and intelligence. They believe that Archimedes was more successful in his working model of the heavenly revolutions than was nature who achieved them...

This passage is part of an explicitly Stoic argument for the rationality of the universe and its maker.[21] Ovid must surely be taking on Stoic baggage when he imports into his Vestalia the image of the Sphere of Archimedes. In the Ciceronian passage, Archimedes rather than Posidonius becomes the author of the *sphaira*: a kind of telescoping occurs, of the historical Posidonius, Cicero's Stoic source, into the quasi-legendary figure of Archimedes.

Ovid's intention here might be (such an argument can only be conjectural) to announce his affiliation to other literary contexts in which the *sphaira* occurs, namely philosophical writing, particularly Stoic or Stoicising. This argument can be supported by examination of the second element of the rationalising part of the Vestalia, the world picture.

[20] This passage is the only evidence for a sphere of Posidonius.

[21] Archimedes' own philosophical orientation is disputed. Scholars run the gamut of possibilities: Pythagorean, Democritean, Platonic, Aristotelian, or Stoic (Dijksterhuis (1987) 440).

The world picture

Vesta eadem est et terra: subest vigil ignis utrique:
significant sedem terra focusque suam.
terra pilae similis, nullo fulcimine nixa,
aere subiecto tam grave pendet onus:
ipsa volubilitas libratum sustinet orbem,
quique premat partes angulus omnis abest:
cumque sit in media rerum regione locata,
ut tangat nullum plusve minusve latus,
ni convexa foret, parti vicinior esset,
nec medium terram mundus haberet onus. (*Fasti* 6.267–276)

It is easier to think of Ovid's *sphaira* not so much as an analogy for the temple of Vesta, but as an analogy for the world-view he presents.[22] Compare these lines with Aratus' setting up of the structure of his world at *Phaenomena* 19–26, which orients the reader in the big picture, before the exposition of the stars in the rest of the poem:

οἱ [ἀστέρες] μὲν ὁμῶς πολέες τε καὶ ἄλλυδις ἄλλοι ἐόντες
οὐρανῷ ἕλκονται πάντ' ἤματα συνεχὲς αἰεί·
αὐτὰρ ὅ γ' οὐδ' ὀλίγον μετανίσσεται, ἀλλὰ μάλ' αὕτως
ἄξων αἰὲν ἄρηρεν, ἔχει δ' ἀτάλαντον ἁπάντη
μεσσηγὺς γαῖαν, περὶ δ' οὐρανὸν αὐτὸν ἀγινεῖ.
καί μιν πειραίνουσι δύω πόλοι ἀμφοτέρωθεν·
ἀλλ' ὁ μὲν οὐκ ἐπίοπτος, ὁ δ' ἀντίος ἐκ βορέαο
ὑψόθεν ὠκεανοῖο . . .

The numerous stars, scattered in different directions, sweep all alike across the sky continuously forever. The axis, however, does not move even slightly from its place, but just stays forever fixed, holds the earth in the centre evenly balanced, and rotates the sky itself. Two poles terminate it at the two ends; but one is not visible, while the opposite one in the North is high above the horizon.

This world-view is similar to that of Ovid in its description of the centrality, stability and equipoise of the earth. Aratus' ἀτάλαντον does the work of Ovid's *libratum* and *suspensus* (*Fasti* 6.271, 278) in expressing this. The same picture is implicit in Ovid's etymology of Vesta from *vi stando* at *Fasti*

[22] 'The sole point of the citation of Archimedes' model here is to illustrate the place of the *earth*' (Postgate (1910) 197).

6.299, dependent as it is on the idea of the earth's stability, generated by its equipoise.

One can compare Cicero's exposition of the structure of the universe at *DND* 2.115–18.[23] Here the *mundus* is *stabilis*, and *cohaeret ad permanendum*, the same idea as Aratus' ἄξων αἰὲν ἄρηρεν and ἀτάλαντον ἁπάντη (*Ph.* 22). All its parts strive equally towards the middle of the sphere: *omnes enim partes eius undique medium locum capessentes nituntur aequaliter* (*DND* 2.115). The same is the case with the earth (*DND* 2.116):

> si mundus globosus est ob eamque causam omnes eius partes undique aequabiles ipsae per se atque inter se continentur, contingere idem terrae necesse est, ut omnibus eius partibus in medium vergentibus (id autem medium infimum in sphaera est)...
>
> If, then, the universe is spherical, and if all its parts are balanced throughout and joined with each other of their own volition, it necessarily follows that the same is true of the earth; all its parts incline to the centre, the lowest point of the sphere.

Because Aratus' earth is seen to be stable and 'in the middle' (μεσσηγύς, *Ph.* 23), it can be said that his universe is implicitly round, like Cicero's *mundus globosus* (*DND* 2.116), in which all things are attracted towards the centre. And in fact the Aratean scholia on *Phaenomena* 22 say that the earth described in the *Phaenomena* is, like Cicero's, spherical (σφαιροειδής).

The elements of Cicero's world picture can also be paralleled from Ovid. Cicero's *medium locum carpessentes* is like *Fasti* 6.273 and 276; he uses *aequaliter*, *aequabiles*, and *aequabiliter* throughout *DND* 2.115–18 to convey the same idea as Ovid's absence of *anguli* (unequal protuberances) in *Fasti* 6.272, an absence which means that the earth is exactly central (*ut tangat nullum plusve minusve latus*, 274). Ovid's *volubilitas*, sphericity (*Fasti* 6.271), and *globus*, sphere, of the earth's model (278), are parallel to Cicero's *globosus*. The equilibrium of the earth is seen to be contingent upon this shape (*vol-*

[23] See also *DND* 2.54, 90, 98.

ubilitas, sphericity): *ipsa volubilitas libratum sustinet orbem* (*Fasti* 6.271).

Achilles, one of the Stoicising commentators on Aratus, in his introductory work, the so-called *Isagoge*, describes the cosmos as a series of concentric spherical shells (σφαιρικὸν σχῆμα ἔχοντα), of ether, air, water and earth.[24] Of these spheres, that of the earth alone stays still: καὶ τὰς μὲν ἄλλας τρεῖς σφαίρας ἢ τέσσαρας περιδινεῖσθαι, τὴν δὲ τῆς γῆς μόνην ἑστάναι. Ἑστάναι denotes the same idea of stability which gives rise to the etymology *vi stando* in *Fasti* 6.299.

There are further Stoic parallels for this passage of the *Fasti*, for example Aëtius, *Placitae* 2.2.1, οἱ μὲν Στωικοὶ σφαιροειδῆ τὸν κόσμον . . . ; *ibid.* 3.10.1, Θαλῆς καὶ οἱ Στωικοὶ καὶ οἱ ἀπ' αὐτῶν σφαιροειδῆ τὴν γῆν . . .[25] On the strength of comparative evidence, Postgate was unequivocal about the Stoic nature of the world picture in *Fasti* 6.269ff.: 'The comparison of the passages has now disclosed that Ovid was drawing from a Stoic source, another indication of which is his identification of Terra and Vesta and his insistence on the immobility of the earth as the centre of the universe,'[26] and again, 'In the whole passage Ovid is reproducing Stoic doctrine.'[27]

Through his use of a pre-existing identification of Vesta as the earth, and by his linking her in the *Fasti* to the kind of world picture exemplified in Aratus, the Aratean commentators, and the Stoic book of Cicero's *DND*, Ovid in the rationalising section of his Vestalia portrays the goddess as a kind of Stoic world deity, equivalent to the *volubilis et rotundus deus* whose nature, identical with the form of the spherical universe, is defended by Balbus at *DND* 2.45–6:

[24] Maass (1898) 32. Achilles was identified by Maass and by Neugebauer as a grammarian of the third century AD (Maass (1898) Proleg. xvi–xvii, Neugebauer (1975) 666). For identification of Achilles as belonging to a group of Stoicising commentators on Aratus, see Maass (1898) Proleg. xlix. The *Isagoge* is described by Neugebauer (1975) 951.

[25] Postgate (1914) 246–7; see also Diels (1929) 329 and 376.

[26] Postgate (1914) 247. He refers in the note to parallel Stoic influence on the cosmogony of Ovid, *Met.* 1.

[27] Postgate (1918) 139.

ad hanc praesensionem notionemque nostram nihil video quod potius accommodem quam ut primum hunc ipsum mundum quo nihil excellentius fieri potest animantem esse et deum iudicem. his quam volet Epicurus iocetur ... et dicat se non posse intellegere qualis sit volubilis et rotundus deus ...

... In my view nothing so aptly accords with this preconceived conviction as the conclusion that the universe first and foremost is alive and divine, for nothing more outstanding can exist. Epicurus can crack jokes at this if he likes ... he can say that he cannot envisage what a whirling, tubby god [*volubilis et rotundus deus*] is like ...

Vesta's temple is an *imago mundi* – a visual representation of an abstract philosophical picture of the universe – and is thus parallel to the Sphere of Archimedes.[28]

So far we have explored two of the elements in Ovid's *aition* of Vesta: a world picture which could be regarded as Stoic, and an analogy for this, the Sphere of Archimedes. The coincidence of these elements may support the view of a Stoic substratum to *Fasti* 6.267–82. In *DND* 2.88 the globe of Archimedes is assimilated to Cicero's Stoic source Posidonius, and thereby appropriated as an image of the Stoic cosmos; the Archimedean model is used to express the Stoic world picture. Both of these elements can be seen as recurring in Ovid. Stoic exegesis, as we find it in *DND*, could be seen as the precedent.

Theogony

ex Ope Iunonem memorant Cereremque creatas
  semine Saturni; tertia Vesta fuit.
utraque nupserunt, ambae peperisse feruntur;
  de tribus impatiens restitit una viri. (*Fasti* 6.285–8)

Ῥείη δὲ δμηθεῖσα Κρόνῳ τέκε φαίδιμα τέκνα,
Ἱστίην Δήμητρα καὶ Ἥρην χρυσοπέδιλον. (Hesiod, *Theogony* 453–4)

[28] Whether a statue of Vesta really did exist or not is uncertain. Cicero refers twice to a *simulacrum Vestae* (*De Orat.* 3.10, *DND* 3.80; cf. Frazer (1929) *ad Fasti* 6.295). Official calendars tell us that Augustus welcomed the arrival of a *signum* of Vesta into his house (see Barchiesi (1997) 206).

Rhea, surrendering to Kronos, bore resplendent children: Hestia, Demeter, and gold-sandalled Hera.[29]

We now reach the point where Ovid shifts from rationalising to mythical. The opposition between physics and myth is not a straightforward one, being partially resolvable through the interpretative technique of allegory. This brings us closer to the literary/philosophical genre which combines Archimedes and the world-view: Stoic or Stoicising exegesis.

We know that Hesiodic allegory was practised from the early Stoa onwards: Zeno, the founder of the school, is mentioned by name in the scholia on *Theogony* 117, 134 and 139, Chrysippus on 135 and 459; in *DND* Cicero has his Epicurean speaker describe the practice of allegorising by Zeno, Chrysippus and other Stoics.[30] Following a general Stoic interest in Hesiod, Aratus himself used Hesiodic language for his scientific didactic poem.[31] The commentators on the *Phaenomena* seem in turn to have followed an allegorising trend in Stoic scholarship.

Ovid's connection between Hesiod and the world picture may arise in an Aratean exegetical tradition similar to that of the writings collected by Ernst Maass, which may reflect an earlier body of work. 'Anonymus I', for example, begins his introductory section, Περὶ ἀρχῆς, with a cosmogony which emphasises the centrality and fixity of the earth, and the motion of the universe round it: τὴν γῆν οὖν οὖσαν βαρυτάτην μέσην συνέβη συναχθῆναι ... τὸ ⟨γὰρ⟩ πνεῦμα πανταχόθεν περιελάσαν αὐτὴν ἐν μέσῳ στῆναι τοῦ παντὸς φυσήματος συνέσχεν...[32] ('It therefore happened that the earth, being the heaviest, was brought together as the middle... For the πνεύμα, having pressed around it from all sides, held it together to stand in the middle of all the air'). He follows this with a quotation of the Hesiodic cosmogony of *Theogony* 116–17:

διὰ τοῦτο καὶ Ἡσίοδος τοῦτ' εἰδὼς φησιν·
 ἤτοι μὲν πρώτιστα χάος γένετ', αὐτὰρ ἔπειτα
 γαῖ' εὐρύστερνος, πάντων ἕδος ἀσφαλὲς αἰεί...

[29] Trans. West (1988). [30] *DND* 1.36–42. See also *DND* 2.63.
[31] On Aratus, Hesiod and allegory, see Hunter (1995). [32] Maass (1898) 90.

Therefore Hesiod also, knowing this, said, 'First came chaos, then broad-breasted Earth, secure seat forever of all . . .'

This is followed in turn by Aratus 22–3:

ὅτι δὲ καὶ μέση ἡ γῆ, μαρτυρεῖ Ἄρατος λέγων·

ἄξων αἰὲν ἄρηρεν, ἔχει δ' ἀτάλαντον ἁπάντη
μεσσηγὺς γαῖαν . . .

Aratus testifies that the earth is in the middle, saying, 'the axis stays forever fixed, and holds the earth in the centre evenly balanced . . .'

The Aratean scholia on line 22 of the *Phaenomena* expound a similar world-view, and follow it directly with another quotation from the *Theogony*:[33]

ἀτάλαντον ἁπάντη· ἴσην καὶ ὁμοίαν· καὶ αὐτὴ γὰρ σφαιροειδὴς καὶ ὁ οὐρανός. Ἡσίοδος·

γαῖα δέ τοι πρῶτον μὲν ἐγείνατο ἶσον ἑαυτῇ
οὐρανὸν ἀστερόεντα.

'Evenly balanced, forever': equal and the same: both the earth and the heaven are spherical. As Hesiod said: 'Earth bore first of all one equal to herself, starry Heaven.'

Here Hesiod is being used to say something about the form of the earth and of the heavens: a mythological and poetic *exemplum* for a philosophical point.

In both of these cases, some kind of allegorising or rationalising (the scientific explanation of myth, or the interpretation of myth as proto-science) is going on between the world-view and Hesiod. It is an idea of Ἡσίοδος φυσικευόμενος[34] – Hesiod as a practitioner of natural philosophy, explicable by allegory and hence able to be employed in a 'scientific' context.

The conjunction of the Sphere, the world picture, and Hesiodic myth in the first part of Ovid's Vestalia could support a hypothesis that Ovid was following not just the *DND*, which provides a precedent for the first two elements, but some kind of Stoicising commentary or collection of explicatory lem-

[33] Maass (1898) 341 gives the line-numbering of Hesiod as 124–5. In West (1966) these are lines 126–7.

[34] The phrase is from the so-called *Isagoga* ('Introduction to Aratus'): see Maass (1898) 319.

mata on the *Phaenomena*, much like what still exists in Maass' 1898 edition of the Aratean commentaries, which used Hesiod in an Aratean/Stoic context.[35]

If this is so, then Ovid's programme here is to show himself as working in the tradition of Hesiodic allegory as practised by the Stoics, including the commentators on Aratus. This technique represents a method of making a straightforward connection between mythology and physics, μῦθος and λόγος. Allegory and interpretative scholarship (such as the commentators on Aratus) mediate between these two different 'languages'. Ovid is discussing in the Vestalia not only the universe itself, but the different ways of talking about the universe which form part of his project in the *Fasti*. Involved in this is the further question of the status of the *Fasti* as a work of art in relation to Aratus' *Phaenomena*, a work which has been seen in the previous chapter as conveying cosmological truth (the λόγος of the poem mapping the λόγος of the universe).

Art, Aratus and the *Fasti*

The literary underlay to the first part of the Vestalia presents two different ways of discussing the universe, rationalising and mythological, and incorporates a tradition of scholarship which allows us to create a resolution between them. In a sense, then, the *sphaira* is a synoptic image of the literary background to the *Fasti*, as well as of the *mundus*.

The Sphere is an *imago mundi*, like Homer's Shield of

[35] Most of the material in Maass is late or undated. One can say that Ovid may have been using a similar collection of scholia and introductory works. There were many such commentaries on Aratus in existence, at least from the time of Hipparchus (*c.* 190 BC). Martin (1956a xi–xx, 1956b) believes it is likely that even some of the earliest manuscripts had an attached corpus of scholia. The theory that Ovid may have used such commentaries is made more plausible by the technique of his Aratean predecessor Cicero, who seems to have interpolated some material from the commentators into his translation of Aratus, the *Aratea* (Soubiran (1972) 93). The fact that Cicero could deploy his translation of Aratus as part of his exegesis in the Stoic book of the *DND* (see below p. 109), with transitional glosses binding the poem to its Stoic context, argues for the importance of the Stoic element in Roman readings of Aratus.

Achilles as interpreted by Hellenistic allegorisers.[36] Its circular shape can allude to a sphere, the shape of the universe.[37] The Shield of Achilles is a synopsis of elements of Homer's *Iliad*, such as peace and war. We saw in chapter 2 how Virgil's Shield of Aeneas likewise condenses the world of the epic. I would like now to consider whether Ovid's Temple of Vesta, which is an *imago mundi*, can also work as in some sense an image of the *Fasti*. We shall see that it can in fact represent a synoptic view of one strand of the *Fasti*, didactic. In this sense it is an imperfect image of the *Fasti*, since it is an image of only one of the manifold strands present in the poem. This is reflective of the problem of the mixing of genres in the *Fasti*. The mind's eye cannot visualise all the elements of the poem at once, but sees the work strand by strand. This results in an impression of a work which is lacking in unity when compared to Aratus' *Phaenomena*.

Nature and art share a rational basis. In Cicero, *DND* 2.88, Archimedes' Sphere is a result of its maker's *ratio* and *sollertia*. The world, elsewhere in *DND* 2, is the product of the same.[38] The universe and its model are parallel, art reflecting reality.[39] The parallelism is emphasised throughout Cicero's Stoic book. It is possible to see the following analogy as underlying all the philosophical argumentation in *DND* 2:

- God exists and his rationality is evident in the world.
- This may be proven by analogy with the rationality of man as illustrated in art (e.g. a model sphere).

One way of interpreting the structure of the whole second book of *DND* is to see it as a series of cumulative illustrations of this nature/art analogy, of which the *sphaira* is one.

36 See Hardie (1985a).

37 Hardie (1985a) 19: 'We remember that in Heraclitus (*Quaestiones Homericae* 43) the circular form of the Shield of Achilles alludes to the spherical universe.'

38 See *DND* 2.81, 85, 87, 128, 140, 142, 155. *Sollertia* and *ratio* are the two terms which recur most often in Cicero's descriptions of art, and of the ordering activity of a providential Nature.

39 Hardie (1985a) 17, n. 43: 'The assimilation of the heavens to a human artefact is very common in pre-scientific (and indeed scientific) thought; the allegorisation of the Shield, manufactured by the demiurge Hephaestus as an *imago mundi* can be understood as an inversion of this way of thinking.'

In *DND* 2.87, the conclusion of arguments in favour of divine providence does double duty as the proposition which leads to the Sphere of Archimedes: *si igitur meliora sunt ea quae natura quam illa quae arte perfecta sunt, nec ars efficit quicquam sine ratione, ne natura quidem rationis expers est habenda* ('If, then, nature's attainments transcend those achieved by human design, and if human skill achieves nothing without the application of reason, we must grant that nature too is not devoid of reason.'). The analogy between art and nature is made explicit here by the repetition of *ratio:* nature is also full of the kind of *ratio* that results in human art.

This proposition generates a series of *exempla* of human *ratio* as revealed by various arts. The Sphere comes at this point. After this, Balbus proceeds at *DND* 2.104–15 to quote the *Aratea*, Cicero's own translation of Aratus' *Phaenomena*. The metaphor for the *ordo* and *ratio* of the universe changes from its geometric modelling by art, as exemplified by the sphere, to its modelling in words, exemplified by Aratus (Latinised). Now the celestial order is encapsulated inside a poem in illustration of divine *ratio*, and the poem is thus, as it functions within the Stoic argument, parallel to the *sphaira*. Both, like Ovid's temple of Vesta, are images of the universe, art at the microcosmic level expressing the art of the macrocosm.

If we look again at Cicero's *Republic* we shall see that collapse of the distinction between the art of the universe and the art of the poem is already implicit in Aratus' *Phaenomena*. In *Republic* 1.22, Cicero's speaker seemed to be telling us that Aratus wrote a work which was a kind of poetic rendition of, or commentary on, a *model* globe made by Eudoxus:

dicebat enim Gallus sphaerae illius alterius solidae atque plenae vetus esse inventum, et eam a Thalete Milesio primum esse tornatam, post autem ab Eudoxo Cnidio, discipulo, ut ferebat, Platonis, eandem illam astris stellisque, quae caelo inhaererent, esse descriptam; cuius omnem ornatum et descriptionem sumptam ab Eudoxo multis annis post non astrologiae scientia, sed poetica quadam facultate versibus Aratum extulisse.

For Gallus told us that the other kind of celestial globe, which was solid and contained no hollow space, was a very early invention, the first one of that kind having been constructed by Thales of Miletus, and later marked by Eudoxus of Cnidus (a disciple of Plato, it was claimed) with the constellations and stars which are fixed in the sky. He also said that many years later Aratus, borrowing this whole arrangement and plan from Eudoxus, had described it in verse, without any knowledge of astronomy, but with considerable poetic talent.

Yet Aratus' extant work shows no outward sign of being a description of a work of art rather than of the universe itself. Modern commentators disagree among themselves: 'Aratus of Soli ... wrote a didactic poem on astronomy, entitled *Phaenomena* ... This does not, however, contain any description of the sphere in question.'[40] And conversely, 'The poem referred to is the *Phaenomena*, translated into Latin by Cicero in his youth.'[41] The problem is compounded by the fact that Cicero, *Republic* 1.22, is the only association of the *Sphaira* of *Eudoxus* with the poet Aratus.[42]

What are the possibilities? Firstly, that the description of Eudoxus' *Sphaira* occurred in one of Aratus' many works not now extant. Secondly, that in Cicero an assimilation may have taken place between Eudoxus' literary work as a source for Aratus and the idea of a model sphere as an aid to reading the work (just as in the manuscript tradition of certain astronomical works maps and drawings of the constellations are provided).[43]

The second hypothesis is rendered more plausible by the threefold meaning of the word σφαῖρα – the globe or sphere as a geometric figure, the starry sphere of the heavens, and a shorthand name for literary works describing this starry sphere. The Roman astrologer Nigidius Figulus (98–45 BC) wrote works entitled *Sphaera Graecanica* and *Sphaera Barbarica*.[44] Both of Eudoxus' literary works, the *Phaenomena* and the *Enoptron*, which the ancient biographies, introductory

40 Dijksterhuis (1987) 24 n. 2.
41 Keyes (1928) 42.
42 On Eudoxus and his sphere, see Dicks (1970) 151–89, Kidd (1997) 14–18.
43 The terms *descriptam* and *descriptionem*, used in *Rep.* 1.22 of the 'marking out' of constellations on the globe by Eudoxus, connote both visual representation and writing.
44 Servius *ad Georgics* 1.19, 43, 218.

treatises and commentaries cite as the model for Aratus' versification,[45] were such descriptions of the σφαῖρα, and may have gone by that nickname.

It is not impossible that confusion could have arisen from Cicero's reading of a collection of scholia and interpretative nuggets such we have in Maass' edition of 1898. Consider for example Achilles' initial description of Aratus' *Phaenomena*: τὴν δὲ τῶν Φαινομένων ἐξήγησιν πρῶτον μὲν ἑστώσης της σφαίρας, μετὰ δὲ ταῦτα κινουμένης ἐποιήσατο Ἄρατος[46] ('Aratus made the plot of the *Phaenomena* by describing the sphere, first at rest, then in motion'). This must refer to the first two parts of Aratus' description of the universe (σφαῖρα) in his *Phaenomena*, the so-called 'Phainomena' and the 'Sunanatolai': first he plots the stars and constellations in the sky, then he describes their risings and settings in relation to one another. But the words might equally be taken as referring to Aratus writing about a model globe, first as it stood, then as it was when moved. Literary work, universe and model globe could all be expressed by the same term: σφαῖρα (Sphere).

A French scholar of ancient astronomy, Germaine Aujac, resolves the problem in a different way, by taking the mapping in words of the artistic model of the universe a generation further back, to Eudoxus himself; she agrees with Cicero that Eudoxus was the first to represent the constellations on a solid ball which was a model of the starry sphere, and advances the theory that Eudoxus' *Phaenomena* was a description of his model globe: 'Eudoxus of Cnidos was the first, as Cicero tells us (*Republic* 1.21), to represent the constellations on a solid sphere, an image of the starry sphere. His work the *Phaenomena* was a kind of description of it.'[47] This is an attractive theory: Aratus' poem was a versification of a literary work by Eudoxus which itself described a model sphere.

[45] See Attalus, Maass (1898) 23–4; Achilles, Maass (1898) 77–8. Anonymus II, Maass (1898) 149, however, is clear about the literary nature of Aratus' source, referring to it as τὸ Εὐδόξου σύγγραμμα. On Aratus' reliance on Eudoxus, see Kidd (1997) 16–17.

[46] Maass (1898) 80.

[47] Aujac (1979) 38.

If, then, we read Aratus' work, the *Phaenomena*, as eliding the distinction between the literary and the artistic in such a way, this collapses the two poles of the Stoic argument for divine rationality, which, we recall, were as follows:

(i) God exists and his rationality is evident in the world
(ii) This must be so because the rationality of man as evident in art (one example of which is an armillary sphere) is indisputable.

The two arms of the analogy are now implicit in Aratus' work, rather than explicit: his description of the world as made by a rational divine creator is the same as his description of a work of art made by a rational craftsman (Eudoxus). The universe and its model are assimilated, rather than the second being used as an image for the first. Model globe and literary work are telescoped into one another.

Implicit in this is a congruent assimilation between the poem and the cosmos. If Aratus was mapping a model globe, or a previous literary work which itself mapped a model globe, this makes his world a poetic one. His poem is not directly reflective of the universe but can exist as a closed system, art relating to art, not to reality: a κόσμος ἐπέων (universe of words).[48]

Perhaps the Aratean scholiast saw this when he spoke of Homer's Shield of Achilles, on *Phaenomena* 26: παρηκολούθηκε δὲ [ὁ Ἄρατος] αὐτῷ [Ὁμήρῳ] εἰπόντι ὠκεανὸν τὸν ὁρίζοντα· δημιουργῷ γὰρ τῷ Ἡφαίστῳ χρησάμενος τῆς Ἀχιλλέως ἀσπίδος ταύτην ὑπέθετο κόσμου μίμημα, ὅπου δὴ τελευταῖον τὸν ὠκεανὸν ἐποίησεν: 'Aratus followed Homer, who called the horizon "Ocean". For using Hephaistos as demiurge of the Shield of Achilles he set this (the Shield) as a representation of the cosmos, wherein he made Ocean the outer edge.'[49]

Phaenomena 26 comes in the passage in which Aratus gave a synoptic image of the world.[50] The scholiast introduces his artistic image when he comments on the beginning of Aratus'

[48] The phrase is borrowed from Democritus fr. B21 Diels and Kranz (1951–2) vol. II, 147.
[49] Maass (1898) 343.
[50] See above, p. 101.

work. The circular Shield of Achilles stands in for the spherical model of the universe, in acting as its artistic analogue. And Aratus' poem bears the same relation to the universe as the Shield or the *sphaira*: the Shield of Homer and the poem of Aratus are parallel *imagines mundi*.

For the scholiast to quote Homer's Shield of Achilles at this point is for him to comment on the parallelism between art and nature. By referring to the Shield of Achilles, he gives us an artistic image of Aratus' astronomical poem, through the pre-existing analogy between Shield and universe.

In Aratus' poem, the artistic analogue briefly detaches itself from the purported first-hand description of the universe, in the Craftsman simile of *Phaenomena* 529–33:[51]

> οὔ κεν Ἀθηναίης χειρῶν δεδιδαγμένος ἀνὴρ
> ἄλλῃ κολλήσαιτο κυλινδόμενα τροχάλεια
> τοῖά τε καὶ τόσα πάντα περὶ σφαιρηδὸν ἑλίσσων,
> ὡς τά γ' ἐναιθέρια πλαγίῳ συναρηρότα κύκλῳ
> ἐξ ἠοῦς ἐπὶ νύκτα διώκεται ἤματα πάντα.

In no other way would a man trained in the craftsmanship of Athena weld together revolving wheels in such a pattern and of such a size, rounding off the whole like a sphere, than the system of celestial circles, which, united by the oblique circle, speed from dawn to nightfall all the time.

The activity of the δεδιδαγμένος ἀνήρ is parallel to the activity of the didactic poet in fashioning his *Phaenomena*, in the 'image' of Eudoxus' *Sphaira*, as a κοσμοῦ μίμημα. As in Cicero's *DND*, the poem is parallel with the sphere.

What if the δεδιδαγμένος ἀνήρ is a figure for Aratus' predecessor Eudoxus, maker of a model sphere which imitates in bronze 'wheels' the disposition of the Celestial Circles in the universe?[52] In that case, Aratus' metaphor of visual for poetic art takes on a new literary-historical significance. If Aratus' Craftsman meditates on the activity of translating Eudoxus, and ultimately on the ordering of the universe in poetry, then one might say that, in Ovid, the globe of Archimedes meditates

[51] See pp. 87–90 above.
[52] Kidd (1997) comments *ad Ph.* 530, 'A. seems to have an actual model in mind here, perhaps an armillary sphere' (see also Kidd (1997) *ad* 531).

on the act of translating Aratus. The fact that the sphere is embedded in the problematic context of the Vestalia might symbolise the difficulty in the part of Ovid's project that involves the 'translation' of Aratus into the Roman calendar.

Etymology and poetic structure

In the first part of the Vestalia, Ovid chooses to portray himself as working in the Stoic/Aratean scholarly tradition. Etymology is part of this tradition. However, Ovid should be contrasted rather than compared with Aratus, for while in Aratus etymology and poetic structure expressed cosmic unity, in Ovid they will be seen to entail a fluid relation between language and the world, in which multiple meanings can exist and compete. This kind of multiplicity is typical of Roman religious discourse; it may be problematic in relation to Augustus' streamlining of the cult of Vesta.[53] In Ovid, it may also generate problems of poetic structure.

The etymology of Vesta is discussed at *Fasti* 6.299–304:

> stat vi terra sua: vi stando Vesta vocatur;
>   causaque par Grai nominis esse potest.
> at focus a flammis et quod fovet omnia dictus;
>   qui tamen in primis aedibus ante fuit.
> hinc quoque vestibulum dici reor; inde precando
>   praefamur Vestam, quae loca prima tenet.

Language is involved here, just as in Aratus: *vocatur* (like Aratus' characteristic καλέονται, in *Ph.* 27, for example), *nominis*, *dictus*, *dici*. But one need only look at the problems that arise in these five lines to see how different is Ovid's etymologising from the theme of language in the *Phaenomena*.[54] The progression of Vesta's etymology is as follows:

(i) The earth stands by (its own) force (*vi stando*); Vesta is the earth, thus she is called Vesta

[53] For recent interpretations of the Vestalia which stress multiple aetiology, see Miller (1992), Barchiesi (1997) 205–10.

[54] See Barchiesi (1991) on the similar problems of the opening etymology of Book 5, and below pp. 143–4.

(ii) The reason for her Greek name (Hestia, 'Hearth') is the same
(iii) But 'hearth' in Latin (*focus*) is from *flamma* and *foveo*
(iv) Formerly the hearth stood in the first room of the house
(v) This is why it is called the *vestibulum*
(vi) Vesta is first in prayers because she is first in houses.

(i) and (ii) seem to pose a problem of identity for Vesta. In *Fasti* 6.267–90 we have been given two *aitia*, one for the shape of Vesta's temple (it is round because Vesta is the earth, which is round), one (a double one) for the virginity of her priestesses (Vesta the daughter of Saturn and Ops was a virgin / her sacred fire is non-procreative). Now it seems that two separate identities of the goddess herself rest on these two *aitia*: Vesta is the earth, which stands by its own force (299); Vesta is Hestia, the Hearth, that is, the goddess is *the same as* the sacred fire. This is what Ovid has said in 291, *nec tu aliud Vestam quam vivam intellege flammam*. It is not what he has said at 265, *Vesta eadem est et terra*. Vesta has 'a double and mysterious identity, as both earth and fire'.[55]

Can Vesta be fire and earth at the one time? Servius Auctus *ad Aeneid* 2.296 may resolve the difficulty of Vesta's double identity as earth and fire, since one is said to contain the other: *Vestam deam ignis, quae, ut supra diximus, terra est: quod in medio mundo librata vi sua stet et ignem intra se habeat. alii de igne divino hoc volunt dictum quod vi sua stet, inde Vestam.* This could provide a gloss on *Fasti* 6.267, *Vesta eadem est et terra: subest vigil ignis utrique*. The Servian etymology is the same as Ovid's *vi stando* (*Fasti* 6.299).[56]

Vesta's etymology is explained by a translation of the

[55] Barchiesi (1997) 205. As Barchiesi notes, there are additional problems with the double *aition* for Vesta's virgin priestesses. First, there is the difference between the explanatory levels, Vesta as a goddess in the Greek pantheon / Vesta as a natural element (virgin daughter of Saturn / fire which does not procreate). I have shown that there is a way of resolving this difficulty through Stoic allegory. More problematic is the question why, if Vesta is a sister of Juno and Ceres, she cannot have an image.

[56] According to Feeney (1998) 127–33, one of the most striking aspects of Roman exegesis is its multiple nature, particularly in aetiology, where competition between explanations is endemic to the system (in Callimachus multiple aetiologies are few and resolved by authorial verdict). Likewise Fantham (1998) *ad Fasti* 4.783–806: 'It is characteristic of Roman didactic poetry to exploit all possible accounts rather than suppress any by favouring one particular explanation.'

Greek word for hearth. Servius, *ad Aeneid* 1.292 can clarify: *Vesta autem dicta vel* ἀπὸ τῆς ἑστίας, *ut digammos sit adiecta*... (Vesta is so called either 'from the hearth', with a digamma added...). Ἱστίη in Homer is 'hearth' (a common noun); it is used first of a goddess at *Theogony* 453–4, the very passage Ovid has paraphrased in *Fasti* 6.285–8. Cicero, *DND* 2.67 is the earliest testimony to the Latin etymology which identified Vesta with Hestia: *iam Vestae nomen a Graecis; ea est enim quae ab illis* Ἑστία *dicitur*; *vis autem eius ad aras et focos pertinet:* in Cicero, Vesta's powers pertain to fire.[57]

The Greek name Hestia was said by scholars in antiquity to come from ἑστάναι (ἵστημι, Ovid's *stando*).[58] Other ancient etymologies derive Hestia from ἕζομαι. This is already implicit in *Homeric Hymn* 5.30, καί τε μέσῳ οἴκῳ κατ' ἄρ' ἕζετο πίαρ ἑλοῦσα. The trouble is, Ovid applies *vi stat* to the earth, while in the exegetical tradition it is usually attached to the hearth (presumably the flame, which 'stands up by itself').

Flamma and *foveo* as etymologies for Vesta rest on the understanding that Vesta is Ἑστία, who is the hearth, in Latin *focus*. Ovid assumes the reader will understand the bilingual etymology. A connection between Vesta and the hearth also inheres in the fact that both Vesta and the hearth are said to come first (and we remember that at 291 Vesta *is* the flame: *nec tu aliud Vestam quam vivam intellege flammam*). Cicero says that Vesta embraces (so to speak) the hearth – *cumque Vesta quasi focum urbis, ut Graeco nomine est appellata, quod nos prope idem Graecum, non interpretatum nomen tenemus, complexa sit, ei colendae virgines praesint* (*Leg.* 2.29) – but this does not make the Ovidian progression any more lucid in itself. Ovid's etymology of *focus* is Varronian;[59] and Varro would have provided him with a perfectly good etymology for Vesta as the earth without the complications attached to *vi stando*: *tellurem, inquit (Varro), putant esse ...Vestam, quod*

[57] Dumézil (1966) 317 tells us that the name of the goddess is from an IE root meaning 'to burn', which gives rise to the Greek εὕει, Latin *urit*.

[58] Cornutus, for example, derived it from ἑστάναι διὰ παντός (Lang (1881) 52).

[59] See Bömer (1957–8) *ad loc.*

vestiatur herbis.[60] Ovid did not, however, choose to follow Varro's etymology of Vesta as the earth.

Vestibulum is from Vesta, because Vesta and the hearth both stand in the first room of the house. Servius agrees with the derivation of *vestibulum*: *dictum autem vestibulum ... quoniam Vestae consecratum est.*[61] However, for Ovid to say that Vesta is first in prayers goes counter to Roman practice as we see it in Cicero, *DND* 2.67: *itaque in ea dea, quod est rerum custos intumarum, omnis et precatio et sacrificatio extrema est.* Ovid's precedent may have been Greek convention.[62]

We see that there are two main problems in Ovid's etymology of Vesta: firstly, what looks like an aetiology for Vesta's virgin priestesses by fire in *Fasti* 6.283–94 slides into fire as an identity of the goddess, causing Ovid's etymologising to waver between fire and earth, and secondly, the notion of primacy entailed in the derivation of *vestibulum* from Vesta is not appropriate to ordinary Roman practice.

The Vestalia is a conundrum. Barchiesi sums up the elements involved:

> Vesta is the earth itself; she is like the earthly globe; she is a virgin daughter of Saturn; she is simply the flame on the hearth; she has no form and no image; her name is that of the earth that supports itself by its own force (Vesta = *vi stat*) as it is also that of the hearth (Greek Hestia); she is the first divinity that we invoke in litanies and it is no accident that she is the god of vestibules, the first part, the entrance to every dwelling.[63]

Barchiesi observes too that in Roman practice, Vesta is *last* in prayers, stating in addition that it may be no accident that Janus dominates the first book of the *Fasti*, Vesta the last.[64]

[60] Varro *apud* Augustine, *Civ.* 7.24. See Maltby (1991) 'Vesta'.

[61] Servius, *ad Aen.* 2.469.

[62] See Pindar, *Nem.* 11.1–7, Plato, *Cra.* 401b and d. In *Homeric Hymn* 29 (to Hestia), lines 4–6, Hestia is both first and last:

> οὐ γὰρ ἄτερ σοῦ
> εἰλαπίναι θνητοῖσιν, ἵν᾽ ου᾽ πρώτῃ πυμάτῃ τε
> Ἑστίῃ ἀρχόμενος σπένδει μελιηδέα οἶνον ...

[63] Barchiesi (1997) 206.

[64] *Ibid.*

He does not elaborate. How are we to interpret the tension between Ovid's statement that Vesta is first, and the fact that in his work she is last?

The structure of Ovid's poem, appropriately for a Roman religious calendar, is like that of a Roman prayer: it begins with Janus (the main character of the first book), and ends with Vesta (the main character of the final book). The *Fasti* can be seen as one long invocation, reflective of the practice recorded by Cicero at *DND* 2.67 (which I now quote in fuller form):

cumque in omnibus rebus vim haberent maxumam prima et extrema, principem in sacrificando Ianum esse voluerunt, quod ab eundo nomen est ductum, ex quo transitiones perviae iani foresque in liminibus profanarum aedium ianuae nominantur. nam Vestae nomen a Graecis (ea est enim quae ab illis Ἑστία dicitur); vis autem eius ad aras et focos pertinet, itaque in ea dea, quod est rerum custos intumarum, omnis et precatio et sacrificatio extrema est.

In all matters, beginnings and ends are vital features. This is why they cite Janus first in sacrifices, for his name is derived from the verb *ire*, to go; hence the word *iani* for archways, and *ianuae* for the doors of secular buildings. As for Vesta, her name is adopted from the Greeks, being identical with their Hestia. Her province is altars and hearths, and this is why the goddess is invoked at the end of all prayers and sacrifices, because she guards the things deep within.

Vesta and Janus are an allegorical as well as a liturgical pair, representing between them the two aspects of a Stoicising cosmos, Vesta the earth, Janus the *mundus* encompassing it: πᾶς ὅδε κόσμος ἑλισσόμενος περὶ γαῖαν ('this entire heaven whirling around the earth', Cleanthes, *Hymn to Zeus*, line 7).[65] Janus is the *mundus* in Macrobius, *Saturnalia* 1.9.11: *alii mundum id est caelum esse voluerunt Ianumque ab eundo dictum, quod mundus semper eat, dum in orbem volvitur et ex se initium faciens in se refertur* ('Others hold that Janus is the universe, that is to say, the heavens, and that the name is derived from *eundo*, since the universe is always in motion, wheeling in a circle and returning to itself at the point where it

[65] The picture of Janus in *Fasti* 1.103 apparently goes back to a Chaos-cosmogony founded on Stoicism (Bömer (1957–8) *ad Fasti* 1.103).

began'[66]). Together Vesta and Janus act as a symbol of the universe, and lend an ostensible (but ultimately perhaps spurious) unity to the poem as a representation of the cosmos.

At *Fasti* 1.125–7, Janus is an allegorical figure of time, the personification of the subject of the *Fasti*:

> praesideo foribus caeli cum mitibus Horis
> (it, redit officio Iuppiter ipse meo):
> inde vocor Ianus...

In Macrobius, *Saturnalia* 1.9.9–10 he is the solar year (an appropriate figure to represent Ovid's Julian calendar, if the identification goes back that far):

> Ianum quidam solem demonstrari volunt, et ideo geminum quasi utriusque ianuae caelestis potentem, qui exoriens aperiat diem, occidens claudat: invocarique primum, cum alicui deo res divina celebratur, ut per eum pateat ad illum cui immolatur accessus, quasi preces supplicum per portas suas ad deos ipse transmittat. inde et simulacrum eius plerumque fingitur manu dextera trecentorum et sinistra sexaginta et quinque numerum tenens ad demonstrandam anni dimensionem, quae praecipua est solis potestas.

> Some are of the opinion that Janus represents the sun and that his two faces (*geminus*) suggest his lordship over each of the two heavenly gates, since the sun's rising opens and his setting closes the day. The fact that men call on the name Janus first when any god is worshipped is held to indicate that it is through him that access may be had to the god to whom the sacrifice is being made, and that it is as it were through his doors that he suffers the prayers of suppliants to pass to the gods. Again, it is as marking his connection with the sun that an image of Janus commonly shows him expressing the number three hundred with his right hand and sixty-five with his left; for these numbers point to the measure of a year, and it is a special function of the sun to determine this measure.

With Ovid's *foribus caeli*, Janus marks out the year by being at the gates of heaven. Macrobius defines these as the limits of day and night; they could also be the celestial tropics through which the sun passes on its annual course. This idea occurred to the renaissance annotator of Reginensis Latinus 1826 (a fifteenth-century manuscript), who glosses *foribus caeli* (*Fasti* 1.125) '*Cancro et Capricorno*', the tropics which mark the

[66] Trans. Davies (1969).

limits of the sun's movement across the ecliptic in the course of the solar year.

He is also a lot like Vesta. Note *praesideo foribus caeli*: *sedere* is what Vesta does in *Fasti* 6 (Hestia, according to one of the etymologies we have seen, being from ἕζω, to sit). Like Vesta, he 'sits in the first place' (*prae-sedeo*). In Ovid's poem he does indeed. On the other hand, *inde* (*Fasti* 1.127) may refer to *it* in the previous line: the etymology of Janus from *ire*. This etymology appears in Macrobius (*Saturnalia* 1.9.11, quoted above, p. 118).

We see from their etymologies that Janus and Vesta are complementary pairs in a Stoicising cosmology: Janus from *ire*, Vesta from ἕζω or ἵστημι; Janus as the heaven moves, Vesta as the earth stays. The etymology *vi stando* in *Fasti* 6.299, applied to the earth of the centripetal cosmos, serves to enable Vesta (as earth) to be placed in counterpoise to the heavenly Janus with whom the work began. At either end of the *Fasti* we have Janus as *caelum*, Vesta as *terra*. In the Stoic cosmos, the spherical shape of both allows the regular movements of the heavenly bodies. Like Vesta, Janus can be considered as an aspect of the world deity, since he represents the spherical heaven. In a sense, then, this is an abstract world setting through which all the astronomy in the *Fasti* can be read. Janus and Vesta are two components of the globe of Archimedes. The *Fasti* might be a kind of poetic version of this globe, framed by the components of the universe.

However, the problem of *vestibulum* may undercut the correlations between Vesta and Janus, directing the reader's attention towards structure. The *vestibulum* is where one enters a house, and this is why, according to Ovid, Vesta is first in prayers. This does not just reflect Greek practice, but destabilizes the ending of the poem in a more specific way than that articulated by scholars who have written on closure.[67] Instead of a beginning/end opposition between the Janus episode of Book 1 and Vesta in *Fasti* 6, we now have a beginning/

[67] See Newlands (1995) chapter 7, 'The Ending of Ovid's *Fasti*', and Barchiesi (1997) 259–72.

beginning correlation in the main episodes of the first and last books (since *ianuae* and *vestibula* are both places where one enters a house), and this may reflect the nature of the poem, obsessed with beginnings, and ambiguous in its finished/unfinished quality.

For Ovid to provide two conflicting structures for his poem – a 'liturgical' one based on a beginning/end opposition between the god and goddess predominant in its first and last books, and an etymological one giving a beginning/beginning correlation – and to situate an image of order (the Sphere of Archimedes) inside this problematic structure, is to undermine the Aratean relationship between art and the universe.

I do not intend to try to resolve the problems of etymology, aetiology, and structure which Ovid has created, but I shall leave them to compete in good Roman fashion, merely making an observation about them which relates to the difference between the Aratean cosmos and the Ovidian one. We saw in chapter 3 that when Aratus talks about language (as with the Namer of Stars) he is also talking about poetic programme. If Vesta and her etymology are similarly symbolic of how Ovid's poem works, then the figure of the goddess expresses the problematic nature of this aetiological poem when seen against a unitary background such as Stoic cosmology, as we have it in the *Phaenomena* of Aratus. In Ovid, polysemy has replaced the Aratean cosmos/language relation.[68]

Conclusion

We could stop here, having achieved the objective of seeing what happens to Aratus when placed inside the Roman calendar. But the Ovidian lack of a one-to-one correlation between language and the cosmos is not out of place in Roman aetiology. In the passages of Servius quoted above, for example, multiple aetiologies are often given, of which I have quoted

[68] In chapter 3 we saw, for example, how the linguistic relationship between Ἀητός and ἄηται in *Ph.* 313–15 expressed a true relationship between constellation and weather.

one part.[69] Denis Feeney notes that Plutarch's *Roman Questions* practically all have multiple explanations, the *Greek Questions* rarely.[70] He sees Ovid as reduplicating an established cultural pattern. He deploys not just many explanations, but many *types* of aetiological explanation, at the one time. For example, the Parilia of *Fasti* 4 carries seven possible explanations, coming from natural science (fire as a purifier), philosophy (fire and water as opposing elements), Roman custom, Greek myth, Roman myth, Roman history; 'The power of the passage comes from the attempt to harmonise its Roman totalising impetus (all explanations lead to Rome) with the fragmented and contradictory atmosphere created by the competition of frameworks (do a Greek cosmogony and a Greek myth have to lead to Rome? Maybe it was all just an accident?).'[71] This quotation could apply to the Vestalia as aptly as it does to the Parilia.

At the same time, it must be recognised that tension exists between the styles of exegesis.[72] As Feeney himself says, 'The "Greek" pentameter which supplements the very first hexameter of the poem is a dramatic declaration of intent, announcing that Ovid's treatment of Roman ritual will be in continual dialogue with another form of knowledge and another frame of reference.'[73] Thomas Habinek puts the opposition in a slightly different way, discussing the Speech of Anchises in *Aeneid* 6: according to him, science tends to be identified with the Greeks (the *alii*); but the union between science and tradition was a distinctive Roman achievement. At the same time, the union of science and tradition in Rome was never comfortable and the struggle between them never ceased.[74]

The *Fasti* is symptomatic of these tensions. On the one hand, Ovid's incorporation of Aratus chimes in with the

[69] See Habinek (1989) 248–51 on the Speech of Anchises in *Aeneid* 6, with particular reference to his comments on Cicero's *Republic*.

[70] Feeney (1998) 129–30.

[71] Feeney (1998) 131.

[72] See Beard (1987) 10

[73] Feeney (1998) 127.

[74] Habinek (1989) 251.

Roman tradition of synthesis of the traditional (religious) and scientific. But at the same time, in looking at the *Fasti* and the *Phaenomena* together, are we not (sanctioned by Ovid himself from his opening couplet on) comparing two essentially incompatible texts, one being a cartographic exegesis of celestial space, and the other a diachronic movement through Roman time? Could one not see this incompatibility as a result of the different conventions of Greek and Roman tradition, the Greek tending towards unity, the Roman towards plurality? It is this sense of irresolution which generates meaning when Ovid transposes Aratus into the Roman year.

Aratus is changed not only by the poetic context in which he is imitated, but by the political factors that provide a context for Ovid's imitation of him. Ovid's world is not the abstract geometrical one of the Sphere of Archimedes or the Aratean rendition of the *Sphaira* of Eudoxus; it is a world in which cosmology and astronomical myth are used to express a concrete reality which is political.

In Rome, the geometric sphere becomes the politicised globe, the cosmographic model carrying with it the potential to become a symbol of world rule.[75] The cosmographic vision of the world could be appropriated and subordinated. A triumphal statue-group on the Capitol erected in 46 BC, which is described by Dio, showed Caesar as a ἡμίθεος resting his feet on the globe.[76] Ovid's positioning of the Sphere of Archimedes inside the Vestalia, a Roman festival most important to the Julians after 12 BC, superimposes the presence of the ruler on the globe in an analogous fashion: 'If Vesta is the earth (267), then Augustus is its military master, and if the earth lies at the centre of the universe (269–76), then by implication Vesta's Roman hearth is the focal point of the universe.'[77]

[75] On the globe as a political symbol, see Weinstock (1971) 42–50 and Arnaud (1984). The cosmographic globe of Greek science became a Roman symbol in the late republic, and was adopted by Caesar as one of his personal images.

[76] . . . καὶ ἐπὶ εἰκόνα αὐτὸν τῆς οἰκουμένης χαλκοῦν ἐπιβιβασθῆναι, γραφὴν ἔχοντα ὅτι ἡμίθεός ἐστι . . . (Dio 43.14.6; also 43.21.2). See Weinstock (1971) 50.

[77] Williams (1991) 196. Ideas of οἰκουμένη and κόσμος are conflated, so the ruler of the former also dominates the latter.

At *Fasti* 3.419–26 Ovid had already brought Vesta's *ignes aeterni* and the *aeterni numina Caesaris* into relation with one another, commemorating Augustus' appointment as Pontifex Maximus on 6 March 12 BC:

> Caesaris innumeris, quos maluit ille mereri,
> accessit titulis pontificalis honor.
> ignibus aeternis aeterni numina praesunt
> Caesaris: imperii pignora iuncta vides.
> di veteris Troiae, dignissima praeda ferenti,
> qua gravis Aeneas tutus ab hoste fuit,
> ortus ab Aenea tangit cognata sacerdos
> numina: cognatum, Vesta, tuere caput.

The dedication of the new shrine of Vesta (in the House of Augustus on the Palatine) is commemorated at *Fasti* 4.949–50:[78]

> aufer, Vesta, diem: cognati Vesta recepta est
> limine; sic iusti constituere patres.

The theme of *cognatio* (*cognati*, *Fasti* 4.949) is important.[79] Vesta now becomes part of the family of her priests, so that only the Julians can rightly hold the office of Pontifex Maximus. At *Fasti* 5.573 Julius is called *Vestae sacerdos*: in effect a dynastic retrojection of the Augustan pontificate onto the Princeps' ancestor. Vesta is the agent of Julius Caesar's apotheosis at *Fasti* 3.701–4.[80] Vesta is also associated with

[78] On the various temples of Vesta, see Hill (1989) 23–4. The *Fasti Praenestini* record the consecration of the *aedicula* on 28 April (12 BC): *eo di⟨e aedicul⟩a et ⟨ara⟩ Vestae in domu Imp. Caes. Augu⟨sti po⟩ntif. Ma⟨x.⟩ dedicatast* (Mommsen (1863) 317). As Pontifex Maximus, Augustus should have lived in the Regia adjoining the Temple of Vesta and House of the Vestals near the Forum. Instead, he set aside one part of his own house on the Palatine as the residence of the Pontifex Maximus, and in another consecrated an *aedicula* of Vesta, which either replaced or duplicated the Forum cult. Feeney (1991) 215 points out the nature of the metamorphosis: 'It was an extraordinary transformation for *Vesta publica populi Romani Quiritum*, the guarantor of the city's identity and continuity, whose whole raison d'être consisted in remaining fixed in her *sedes*.'

[79] See below, pp. 158, 164–7.

[80] On the catasterism of Julius Caesar, which I shall discuss in chapter 6, see Taylor (1931) chs. 3–5, Weinstock (1971) 370–84, Domenicucci (1989), Galinsky (1996) 312–22, 'The Road to Divinity', Domenicucci (1996) and Ramsey and Licht (1997).

Augustus' star sign Capricorn at Manilius 2.445: *atque angusta fovet Capricorni sidera Vesta.*[81]

It is Barchiesi who is clearest on the effect of the plurality inherent in both Callimachean and Roman antiquarian writing in destabilising the cult of Vesta under Augustus: 'The dubious and fragmentary form that is typical of the Callimachean tradition, and the contradictions that are typical of antiquarian discourse, make up a picture in which the dominating notes are those of discontinuity and the difficulty of bringing the past to life.'[82] According to Barchiesi, Vesta is a household deity of Augustus, 'subjected to deconstruction'.[83] 'The poet participates with relish in the series of mediations which enable the prince to achieve a monopoly of a great traditional state cult, but at the same time he also takes pleasure in reentangling the problems that this process of appropriation has smoothed out.'[84] This is the effect of the clash of 'languages' (myth and physics) and of aetiologies and etymologies in Ovid's Vestalia.

[81] One might wish to see in Manilius' *fovet* a play on the etymology of *focus* from *flamma* and *foveo* that we have seen in *Fasti* 6.301. On Capricorn and Augustus, see below, pp. 138–42.

[82] Barchiesi (1997) 210.

[83] *Ibid.*, 137–8.

[84] *Ibid.*, 209.

CHAPTER 5

ROMAN ARATUS

Aratus' *Phaenomena* is a work which was translated by Cicero and Varro of Atax in the Republican period, and drawn upon by Cicero in his *Republic*; during the early imperial period it was adapted by Virgil in the first book of the *Georgics*, and translated by Germanicus and Ovid.[1] Aratus was a source for mythical as well as technical information. The mythical element in particular was expanded by the Latin Arateans, possibly under the influence of an Aratean scholiastic tradition,[2] but also incorporating material from Eratosthenes and other sources. The themes and phrases most commonly imitated by the Latin poets show a limited range of familiar passages and a concern with the mythology of the stars (in fact a relatively minor part of the original text): *Phaenomena* 1 (beginning with Zeus), 36–9 (the Great and Little Bears), 98–136 (the Golden Age), 164 (the Olenian Goat), 219–21 (Pegasus and Hippocrene).[3]

The *Phaenomena* is both a scientific text (which incorporates some mythical material), and a work commissioned by a Hellenistic monarchy. A monarchical framework for our reading of Aratus may prove helpful in the Roman context.[4] In this chapter we shall see how star myths in the *Fasti* may marry material from the *Phaenomena* with the imagery of Julian imperial panegyric.

The grammar of panegyric[5] functions by the incorporation

[1] On the Latin Aratean tradition, see Reeve (1983).
[2] Soubiran (1972) 93. On the scholiastic tradition as we have it, see Kidd (1997) 43–8.
[3] Kidd (1997) 41.
[4] See Introduction, p. 3 and chapter 3, pp. 66–70.
[5] The term is that of West (1995) 14–15, in the introduction to his edition of Horace, *Odes I*; the definition is mine.

of motifs, including those of both mythology and philosophical cosmology, into a didactic unity formed of a finite number of symbols, capable of being recombined and repeated. This is so in Augustan iconography, as, for example, on the Prima Porta statue of Augustus, where many small significant motifs are subordinated to the monumental figure of the ruler. It is equally so in Augustan literature. Astral myth may be involved. In this and the next chapter we shall see how the technique functions in the *Fasti*, and examine some of the factors behind Ovidian selection of motifs in astral myths.

Here we are concerned not so much with direct astral encomium, emperors turning into stars and suchlike (this will be the subject of chapter 6), but with the telling of astral myth in a way which ties it in with imperial concerns. The best example of this phenomenon is the myth of Capella at *Fasti* 5.111–28:

ab Iove surgat opus. prima mihi nocte videnda
  stella est in cunas officiosa Iovis:
nascitur Oleniae signum pluviale Capellae;
  illa dati caelum praemia lactis habet.
Nais Amalthea, Cretaea nobilis Ida,
  dicitur in silvis occuluisse Iovem.
huic fuit haedorum mater formosa duorum,
  inter Dictaeos conspicienda greges,
cornibus aeriis atque in sua terga recurvis,
  ubere, quod nutrix posset habere Iovis.
lac dabat illa deo; sed fregit in arbore cornu,
  truncaque dimidia parte decoris erat.
sustulit hoc nymphe cinxitque recentibus herbis,
  et plenum pomis ad Iovis ora tulit.
ille ubi res caeli tenuit solioque paterno
  sedit, et invicto nil Iove maius erat,
sidera nutricem, nutricis fertile cornu
  fecit, quod dominae nunc quoque nomen habet.

By studying the myth of Capella, the She-goat who became a star, I shall show how Ovid handles his Aratean material and his techniques of selection and combination with other models. The She-goat will show us how groups of images can intersect and be recombined, and how Ovid interpolates non-Aratean elements into his Aratean original, in order to favour particular connections. The passage illustrates the interlocking of astral myth and political imagery.

'Capella' designates the star α *Aurigae*, a bright yellow sun in Auriga (ἡνίοχος), the Charioteer. The temporal indications at *Fasti* 5.111–13 are three. Firstly, in the ancient edition, the poet's note of Capella would have followed seamlessly from the preceding etymology of the month, thus assuming the date of 1 May. Next, we have *prima nocte* in line 111; this expression can mean 'at nightfall', or 'on the first night (of the month of May)'. Thirdly, *nascitur* (113) must be construed as 'rises'. These three indications, taken together, mean that Ovid places the evening rising of Capella on 1 May.

Ovid seems to have confused the evening rising (if *prima nocte* means that the star rises just after the sun sets, i.e. its apparent evening rising[6]) with the apparent morning rising of Capella on this date, the nearest of any of the movements of that star to the date Ovid gives.[7] Even if the poet had referred to the morning rising of the star, rather than the evening one, he is still in error by more than a month, since in his time the morning rising of Capella took place in early April in the latitude of Rome. The evening rising of the star does not occur until 26 August.

Many authors refer, like Ovid at *Fasti* 5.113 (*signum pluviale Capellae*), to the raininess of Capella.[8] The evening rising of Capella on 15 September, and that of her adjacent stars, the Kids, on 28 September, brings the end of the sailing season.[9] The etymology of her Greek name may indicate the Goat's raininess.[10] In both passages in which he mentions the She-goat, Aratus issues a navigational warning:

[6] For the terms 'true' and 'apparent', see appendix 2.

[7] Ideler (1825) 143–4; Frazer (1929) *ad loc.*

[8] Columella, *DRR* 11.14.12, Lydus, *De Ostentis* 70.17 (Wachsmuth (1863), 153–4), Virgil, *Aen.* 9.668–9 with Servius *ad loc.*, Horace, *Odes* 3.7.6, scholia on Aratus 158 (Maass (1898) 367).

[9] See Kidd (1997) *ad Ph.* 157–8. Likewise Manilius' *Haedi claudentes sidere pontum*, *Ast.* 1.365.

[10] According to Le Boeuffle (1977) 109, the etymology of ἡ Αἴξ was from the verb ἀίσσω, 'to hurl, strike, raise a storm' ('Lancer, frapper, souffler en tempête', as he says).

καί τοι φάτις ἤλυθεν Αἰγὸς
αὐτῆς ἠδ' Ἐρίφων, οἵ τ' εἰν ἁλὶ πορφυρούσῃ
πολλάκις ἐσκέψαντο κεδαιομένους ἀνθρώπους ... (*Phaenomena* 157–9)

And [if] rumour has reached you of the Goat herself and the Kids, who have often looked down on men being tossed upon the heaving sea ...

ἀλλ' οὐχ Ἡνιόχῳ Ἔριφοι οὐδ' Ὠλενίη Αἴξ
εὐθὺς ἀπέρχονται· τὰ δέ οἱ μεγάλην ἀνὰ χεῖρα
λάμπονται, καί οἱ μελέων διακέκριται ἄλλων
κινῆσαι χειμῶνας ὅτ' ἠελίῳ συνίωσιν· (*Phaenomena* 679–82)

But in the Charioteer the Kids and the Olenian Goat do not immediately depart: along his great arm they still shine, and are distinguished from his other limbs in the raising of storms when they come together with the sun.

Ovid is partially wrong and partially right in his astronomical data; his *pluviale* reflects meteorological reality (or at least reality as handed down in Aratean meteorology), but the date he gives is inaccurate and the movement of the star to which he refers is in any case the incorrect one for that date. What is more important is the network of motifs which he uses to construct his astronomical entry.

Note first Ovid's echo of Aratus' Ὠλενίη Αἴξ (*Ph.* 679) at *Fasti* 5.113. This is one of the Aratean motifs most often imitated by the Romans, who seem to have seen it as a sort of Aratean 'signature'; Ovid is no exception.[11] This is also true of Ovid's Latinisation of the opening words of the *Phaenomena*, ἐκ Διὸς ἀρχώμεσθα, at *Fasti* 5.111, *ab Iove surgat opus*.[12] Aratus' initial invocation of Zeus has been displaced in the *Fasti* by the twin forces of Germanicus and Janus, who together stand in for the Zeus invoked at *Phaenomena* 1–18. The invocation of Zeus rests uneasily at *Fasti* 5.111 as the preface to the rising of the star Capella, the first astronomical entry of Book 5, but the beginning neither of the work (*opus*, 111) nor even of the book.

[11] See above, n. 3. Ὠλενίη (*Ph.* 164) occurs in Greek literature only in Aratus and Strabo. Ovid attaches the same adjective to Capella in the synoptic list of seafaring constellations at *Met.* 3.592–6.

[12] See Cicero, *Aratea* fr. 1.

The myth of Capella in Ovid is the same one that Aratus tells at *Phaenomena* 162–4:

σκαιῷ δ' ἐπελήλαται ὤμῳ
αἴξ ἱερή, τὴν μέν τε λόγος Διὶ μαζὸν ἐπισχεῖν·
'Ωλενίην δέ μιν Αἶγα Διὸς καλέουσ' ὑποφῆται.

Fastened to his [the Charioteer's] left shoulder is the sacred Goat, who is said to have tendered her breast to Zeus: the interpreters of Zeus call her the Olenian Goat.

As we see, Ovid's reference to the nurture of Jupiter (*in cunas officiosa Iovis*, 112) picks up *Phaenomena* 163–4. Other elements in the Ovidian passage can be seen to come from a different passage of Aratus, which refers to the Bears (*Ph.* 26–44). This passage is also prominent in the Roman tradition. Aratus gives a version of the Bears' catasterism in *Phaenomena* 30–5 which is different from the one Ovid gives in *Fasti* 2.153–92 (the myth of Callisto, which we shall examine in the next chapter), but which harmonises with Ovid's version of Capella. Aratus' story is that the Bears were the nurses of the young Zeus on Crete:

εἰ ἐτεὸν δή,
Κρήτηθεν κεῖναί γε Διὸς μεγάλου ἰότητι
οὐρανὸν εἰσανέβησαν, ὅ μιν τότε κουρίζοντα
Λύκτῳ[13] ἐν εὐώδει, ὄρεος σχεδὸν 'Ιδαίοιο,
ἄντρῳ ἔνι κατέθεντο καὶ ἔτρεφον εἰς ἐνιαυτόν,
Δικταῖοι Κοῦρητες ὅτε Κρόνον ἐψεύδοντο.

If the tale is true, these Bears ascended to the sky from Crete by the will of great Zeus, because when he was a child then in fragrant Lyctus near Mount Ida, they deposited him in a cave and tended him for the year, while the Curetes of Dicte kept Cronus deceived.

A false collocation of Ida and Dicte, places in Crete actually disjunct from one another,[14] occurs in *Phaenomena* 33 and 35, pertaining to the place in which the Bears nourished Zeus. In Ovid the same false collocation is used of the place where

[13] The manuscript tradition at line 33 has Δίκτῳ for Λύκτῳ, the latter a conjecture by Grotius, as well as the reference to Dicte at line 35; see Kidd (1997) *ad Ph.* 33.

[14] As Strabo tells us at *Geog.* 10.4.12 (but see Kidd (1997) *ad loc.* for alternative explanations of the topographical nomenclature).

the Goat fulfilled a rôle similar to that of Aratus' Bears (*Fasti* 5.115–18).[15]

Ovid's substitution of Capella for Aratus' Bears is an ingenious example of *variatio* of the Greek original. Ovid follows the invocation of Zeus with the tale of Capella, rather than that of the Bears. The link between the two is that both had a hand in Zeus' upbringing, and Ovid reinforces this link by imitating in connection with Capella Aratus' false collocation of Ida and Dicte. Both sets of stars are explained in Aratus by an aetiological myth (rare in that poet, who concentrates on spatial description).

Some of the elements in the Capella panel are non-Aratean:[16] the goat belonged to the Naiad Amalthea (*Fasti* 5.115); her horn became the Cornucopia (121–2); she (and possibly her horn, depending on one's reading of the Latin[17]) was made into a star by *Iuppiter invictus* after the war with the Titans (125–6).

We find the catasterism of the goat, the name Amalthea,[18] and the *Iuppiter Invictus* motif in the epitome of Eratosthenes *Catasterismoi* 13,[19] in which version (said to be from Musaeus)

[15] The same collocation occurs twice in Callimachus' first hymn, to Zeus (Δικταῖον in line 4 is followed by Ἰδαίοισιν ἐν οὔρεσι in line 6, Δικταῖαι Μέλιαι in line 47 by Ἰδαίοις ἐν ὄρεσσι, 51). Ida is important in Hellenistic poetry: according to Griffiths (1979) 73, on Theocritus, *Idyll* 17 (on which see below, pp. 148–54), Mt Ida is a point of intersection between the divine and mortal spheres, 'a permeable boundary which suggests that certain privileged natures can pass from one realm to the other'.

[16] For some other versions, see Kidd (1997) *ad Ph.* 163.

[17] The interpretation of this last point depends on whether one takes *fertile* as the attribute or complement of *cornu*. The final couplet could mean either, 'He made his nurse, and the fertile horn of his nurse, into stars', or 'He made his nurse into a star and the horn of his nurse fertile'. The latter is more probable: there is no evidence elsewhere for a star or constellation which might represent a catasterised cornucopia (although this would not be the first time Ovid has created a new constellation; he manufactures the Kite at *Fasti* 3.794). The awkwardness of the *asyndeton bimembre* in line 127, upon which the first reading depends, also makes the second more likely.

[18] For the name, see also Pherecydes, fr. 42 Jacoby (1923–58) vol. 1 no. 3, Callimachus, *Hymn to Zeus* 48, Servius *ad Aen.* 9.665, and the scholia on Aratus 161, citing Nicander as a source.

[19] See Robert (1878) 98–105. On the authenticity of the *Catasterismoi* ascribed to Eratosthenes, see Robert (1878) 29–35. Eratosthenes may have written a work of this name (as Suidas records), but the work which survives may not be by him. The material is nonetheless evidence for the existence of a body of astral mythography.

Rhea gave the infant Zeus to Themis to be nurtured, and Themis passed him on to the Nymph Amalthea, who had a goat with whose milk she fed the baby. This goat was the daughter of Helios, and so fearful in aspect that the Titans were frightened by her appearance and asked their mother Earth to hide her in one of the caves on Crete. Earth agreed to this, and gave her to Amalthea, who then reared Zeus with her milk. When Zeus grew up and wanted to fight the Titans, but had no weapons to hand, he received oracular instructions to use the goat's hide as a weapon because she was invulnerable and fearful and had a Gorgon's head in the middle of her back(!). After the war with the Titans, Zeus re-upholstered the bones of the goat with another skin, brought her back to life and gave her (astral[20]) immortality.

We have in Eratosthenes the catasterism of the Goat for the donation of her skin to Zeus' war-effort against the Titans, as well as for the nurture of Jupiter, which was the reason for her installation in heaven in Aratus. Ovid may hint at a familiarity with the Eratosthenic story as well as the Aratean one, by his allusion to the battle between Zeus and the Giants or Titans. *Fasti* 5.125–6 is the point of connection:

> ille [Iuppiter] ubi res caeli tenuit solioque paterno
> sedit, et invicto nil Iove maius erat ...

The connection with Jupiter and the war with the Titans is accentuated in Manilius' version of the tale (*Astronomica* 1.365–70), contemporary with or slightly later than Ovid:

> hunc [Heniochum] subeunt Haedi claudentes sidere pontum,
> nobilis et mundi nutrito rege Capella,
> cuius ab uberibus magnum ille ascendit Olympum
> lacte fero crescens ad fulmina vimque tonandi.
> hanc ergo aeternis merito sacravit in astris
> Iuppiter et caeli caelum mercede rependit.

You would think that goats' milk was pretty tame, but this goat's milk is the right food for the thundering Jupiter to

[20] Robert's text of 'Eratosthenes' has been restored at this point, on the analogy of the parallel scholia to Germanicus, as ἄστρον οὐράνιον κατασκευάσαι.

grow up on and defeat the Titans. Manilius' *lacte fero crescens ad fulmina vimque tonandi* is explained by Eratosthenes' story. Because the Eratosthenic Capella is herself so frightening (a fact no doubt related to the first magnitude of her star, α *Aurigae*), her milk was fitting nourishment for the future Jupiter Tonans.[21]

Anthologia Graeca 9.224, an epigram by Crinagoras, an Augustan successor of the Ptolemaic court poets, mentions a goat whose milk was particularly appreciated by Augustus.[22] Crinagoras celebrates the Princeps by the assimilation of the animal to the star Capella, who was catasterised for being the nurse of Zeus:

Αἶγά με τὴν εὔθηλον, ὅσων ἐκένωσεν ἀμολγεὺς
  οὔθατα πασάων πουλυγαλακτοτάτην,
γευσάμενος, μελιηδὲς ἐπεί τ' ἐφράσσατο πῖαρ
  Καῖσαρ, κἠν νηυσὶν σύμπλοον εἰργάσατο.
ἥξω δ' αὐτίκα που καὶ ἐς ἀστέρας· ᾧ γὰρ ἐπέσχον
  μαζὸν ἐμόν, μείων οὐδ' ὅσον Αἰγιόχου.

I am the good milch-goat with udders yielding more than any the milk-pan ever drained, and Caesar, when he had tasted the richness of my milk, sweet as honey, took me with him even on the ship to be his fellow-voyager. Some day I think I shall even reach the stars, for he to whom I gave suck from my breast is by no means inferior to the Aegis-bearer.[23]

We see that a contemporary of Ovid also used the myth of the She-goat, tying it into a panegyrical tradition in which the ruler is compared to Zeus. We shall explore this further shortly.

What about the cornucopia, which is nowhere in either Aratus or Eratosthenes? Its earliest appearance in literature is in a fragment of Pherecydes, who tells us that the Horn of

[21] Cf. *Aen.* 11.571, where Camilla is nursed *lacte ferino* (a *topos* denoting strength or fierceness).

[22] See Domenicucci (1996) 141, Williams (1978) 52–101, 'Ovid: the Poet and Politics'. Williams discusses the epigrams of Crinagoras (90–1, and also 135–7). He sees little difference between the panegyrics of Crinagoras and Ovid's panegyrical passages. Both mould 'a frivolous and trivial subject to carry a seriously meant compliment' (90). In both, a context is created 'in which...the rule of Augustus could be equated (by literary echo) with that of Zeus' (137).

[23] Trans. Paton (1925).

Amalthea, the daughter of Haemonius with a single bull's horn on her head, had the capacity to produce food and drink without ceasing: Ἀμάλθεια δὲ ἦν Αἱμονίου θυγάτηρ, ἣ κέρας εἶχε ταύρου. τοῦτο δέ, ὡς Φερεκύδης λέγει, δύναμιν εἶχε τοιαύτην ὥστε βρωτὸν ἢ ποτόν, ὅπερ ⟨ἂν⟩ εὔξαιτό τις, παρέχειν ἄφθονον.[24] Here the cornucopia is linked with a version of the *aition* of the Horn which Ovid uses in the *Metamorphoses* but not in the *Fasti*.[25]

The Horn of Amalthea is associated with the constellation ἡ Αἴξ (the asterism formed by the Goat and the Kids together[26]) in the Aratean scholia on *Phaenomena* 156:

ὁ δὲ μῦθος οὕτως ἔχει, ὅτι ἡ Αἴξ αὕτη γυνὴ ἦν Ἀρκαδιή, ἥτις ἀνέθρεψε τὸν Δία. καί φασιν, ὅτι μετὰ θάνατον λαβὼν αὐτῆς τὸ δέρμα κατὰ τὴν συνείλησιν περιέθετο καὶ αὐτὴν κατηστέρισεν. διὸ Αἰγίοχος κικλήσκεται ἀνθρώποισιν. ταύτην δὲ καλοῦσι καὶ Ἀμάλθειαν, καὶ Ἀμαλθείας κέρας τὸ τῆς Αἰγός.[27]

The story goes that Aix herself was an Arcadian woman who nourished Zeus. They say that after her death, taking her skin, he put it around himself as a covering and turned her into a star. On this account Zeus is called by mankind Aigiochus; she, on the other hand, is called Amalthea, and Aix' horn the Horn of Amalthea.

Whatever the scholiast is driving at here, the Horn of Amalthea is associated with Capella in her Greek guise as ἡ Αἴξ, the constellation of the Goat. The scholiast seems to have conflated two versions of the story, one in which Aix was an Arcadian woman, one in which she was a goat; the detail of the skin fits the latter. It is not stated that the Horn of Amalthea is the Horn of Plenty, although we can surmise this from our knowledge of the tradition recorded by Pherecydes, where, however, the Horn of Plenty is attached to a different story of Amalthea.

Ovid may have been drawing selectively on his own *corpus* of astronomical myth, combining details from two or more

[24] Jacoby (1923–58) vol. 1 no. 3, fr. 42 = Apollodorus, *Bibl.* 2.148.
[25] See *Met.* 9.85–8.
[26] See Kidd (1997) *ad Ph.* 157.
[27] Maass (1898) 367. The Arcadian setting finds an equivalent in neither Ovid nor Aratus; however, it provides an alternative setting for the youth of Zeus in Callimachus, *Hymn to Zeus* 4–7, and is associated with one version of the myth of the Bears, on which see chapter 6 below.

different versions in order to associate the star with the Horn of Plenty; it is equally possible that Ovid is the first to associate the star Capella with the cornucopia, and that his reasons for doing so had as much to do with Augustan Rome as with Aratean astral myth. The cornucopia is a leitmotif in Augustan literature and iconography.[28] It is a Hellenistic motif, a symbol of royalty in Ptolemaic Egypt.[29]

The image of the cornucopia is used throughout the Augustan Principate.[30] It can be associated with the *Ludi Saeculares*, as in Horace, *Carmen Saeculare* 57–60, where the horn belongs to an allegorical figure of Abundance:

> iam Fides et Pax et Honos Pudorque
> priscus et neglecta redire Virtus
> audet apparetque beata pleno
> Copia cornu.

On the cuirass of the Prima Porta Augustus (Figure 1) it is connected with the return of the Parthian Standards. The reclining figure in the bottom field of the cuirass is Copia, Tellus, or a similar figure of abundance; she holds a large cornucopia. The return of the Parthian standards is the scene in the centrepiece of the cuirass. Paul Zanker explains: 'On the cuirass relief the victory over the Parthians is celebrated as the culmination of a perfect world-order. Mother Earth reclines beneath the central scene, her attributes essentially the same as those of Pax on the Ara Pacis. Both goddesses stand for the *Aurea Copia* of the New Age.'[31] Karl Galinsky's reading of the Prima Porta cuirass is similar: 'Fruitfulness and prosperity

[28] Galinsky (1996) 106: 'Augustan culture uses traditional chiffers, such as the cornucopia, and invests them with contemporary meanings.'

[29] It occurs on coins (*ibid.*, 114); a Ptolemaic cameo of *c.* 30 BC shows Octavian as the successor of the Ptolemaic god-kings (*ibid.*, fig. 51). He holds a double cornucopia, symbolic in Ptolemiac art of the blessings dispensed by the royal brother and sister.

[30] See Galinsky (1996) 106–21, 'The Representation of the Golden Age in Art'. Shortly after 41 BC it appears with Fortuna on the reverse of a *denarius* of Octavian carrying the legend DIVI FILIVS; after AD 14 it is found on an altar of the deified Augustus: Galinsky (1996) figs. 50 and 240.

[31] Zanker (1988) 189.

Fig. 1

are not simply handed down by the gods. Instead, they are a result of Rome's dominance.'[32]

The fact that Mother Earth (as the reclining figure at the bottom of the cuirass is also identified by Galinsky[33]) is pendant to the main scene of Parthian conquest on the Prima Porta statue, is a sign that peace and prosperity are a result of Rome's dominance because of war: a connection between plenty and military might.[34] Likewise, Parthian conquest is associated with the cornucopia by Horace in *Epistles* 1.12.27–9:[35]

ius imperiumque Phraates
Caesaris accepit genibus minor; aurea fruges
Italiae pleno defudit Copia cornu.

As Galinsky puts it, 'The nexus between conquest and *pax* is a constant refrain.'[36] The Golden Age as contingent on Roman military might was a concept which found expression in the prophetic passages of the *Aeneid*, such as *Aeneid* 6.789–97 (Anchises' speech):

hic Caesar et omnis Iuli
progenies magnum caeli ventura sub axem.
hic vir, hic est, tibi quem promitti saepius audis,
Augustus Caesar, divi genus, aurea condet
saecula qui rursus Latio regnata per arva
Saturno quondam, super et Garamantas et Indos
proferet imperium; iacet extra sidera tellus,
extra anni solisque vias, ubi caelifer Atlas
axem umero torquet stellis ardentibus aptum.

Here the *aurea saecula* (lines 792–3) rest upon the extent of *imperium* (795), expressed in the language of time as driven by the heavenly bodies (*extra anni solisque vias*, 796), as well as space (*iacet extra sidera tellus*, 795).

Often in Augustan art the cornucopia is connected with

[32] Galinksy (1996) 107.
[33] *Ibid.*
[34] The same connection between war and peace is expressed by the cornucopiae on the shoulder-straps of the cult-statue of Mars from the Forum Augustum: see Galinsky (1996) fig. 46.
[35] See also *Odes* 1.17.14–16.
[36] Galinsky (1996) 107.

Capricorn, the Princeps' favoured sign.[37] Four examples of Augustan coinage show how these motifs can be combined (Figures 2a, b, c, d).[38] On a *denarius* of 12–11 BC, from Lugdunum (Figure 2a), Capricorn (on the reverse) is associated with Augustus, whose head appears on the obverse, and with world empire, since Capricorn holds a globe between his forefeet: here is the Romanised version of the Sphere of Archimedes, a symbol of universal domination, clasped between the cloven hooves of Augustus' favourite constellation.[39]

On an *aureus* of c20 BC from the East (Figure 2b), the head of Augustus on the obverse is again accompanied by Capricorn on the reverse, framed by the legend SIGNIS RECEPTIS.[40] A *denarius* of 19–16/15 BC from Spain (Figure 2c) has the profile of the Princeps on the obverse, accompanied on the reverse by the globe and cornucopia and the name AVGVSTVS.[41] Here is the motif of peace and prosperity after Parthian conquest.

On a *denarius* of 28 BC from the East (Figure 2d), Capricorn appears to be associated with Actium (in the guise of the conquest of Egypt), if the obverse, with a head of Augustus accompanied by a small Capricorn, is taken closely with the reverse, where there is a crocodile with the inscription AEGVPTO CAPTA.[42] Here victory in *civil* war (Actium), and the acquisition of territory (Egypt), are equated, and are both associated with Augustus' sign.[43]

[37] Augustus published his horoscope with Capricorn as his natal sign in 11 BC and issued coins with Capricorn (Suetonius, *Aug.* 94.12). On Capricorn and its significance for Augustus, see Housman (1903–30) *ad* Manilius 4.776, *id.* (1913), Bayet (1939) 152–5, Hölscher (1965), Kraft (1967), Dwyer (1973), Abry (1988), Brugnoli (1989), Barton (1994a) 39–41, (1994b) 40–7 and (1995).

[38] See also Barton (1994a) fig. 5.

[39] BMC 465, reproduced by permission of the British Museum (= Mattingly (1923) pl. 11.13).

[40] BMC 680 (Mattingly (1923) pl. 17.2).

[41] BMC 345 (Mattingly (1923) pl. 7.2). Compare a coin from Pergamum dated 27/26 BC, on which a rampant Capricorn, framed by the laurel wreath of Apollo (Augustus), carries a cornucopia (Zanker (1988) fig. 36a). A coin which dates to the time of the *Ludi Saeculares* combines the globe, rudder, cornucopia and Capricorn, symbols of empire and of the Golden Age (Galinsky (1996) fig. 53).

[42] BMC 653 (Mattingly (1923) pl. 16.3).

[43] The equation involved in Ovid's description of the temple of Mars Ultor, commemorated at *Fasti* 5.545–98, is perhaps a similar one: Mars Ultor was both the Avenger against the Parthians (a foreign enemy), and the god of Octavian as avenger of Caesar's murder (civil war).

Fig. 2a

Fig. 2b

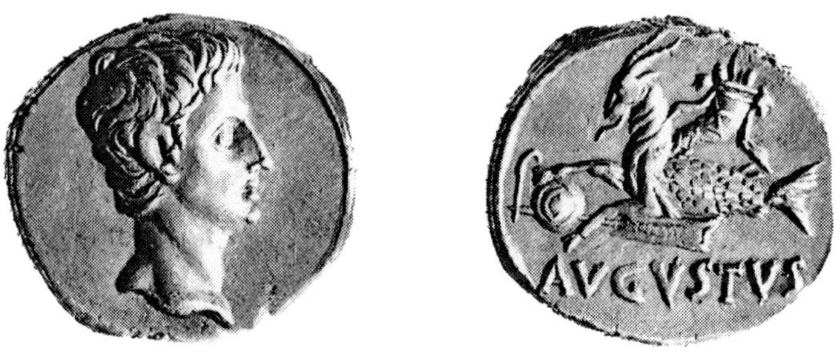

Fig. 2c

On the Gemma Augustea (Figure 3), dating from the closing years of the Augustan Principate, another element occurs. Capricorn and the cornucopia appear in the top register of this piece, juxtaposed with Augustus enthroned as

Fig. 2d

Jupiter.[44] The Gemma Augustea gives us an association in art of Capricorn, the cornucopia, and the grown-up Jupiter. Ovid in *Fasti* 5 gives us a parallel association: Capella, the cornucopia, and the baby Jupiter. Celestial goats (Capricorn and Capella are both constellations with goats' horns, *Capri-cornu*), the cornucopia, and Jupiter fit the same theme: the development and consolidation of Augustan power.

Scholars have explored the astrological connotations of Capricorn in looking for a reason for his adoption by Augustus;[45] perhaps there is a simple mythological reason to be

[44] Germanicus, writing *circa* AD 14, associates Capricorn with Augustus' apotheosis:

> cochlidis inventor, cuius Titania flatu
> proelia commisit divorum laetior aetas,
> bellantem comitata Iovem, pietatis honorem
> ut fuerat, geminus forma, sic sidere, cepit.
> hic, Auguste, tuum genitali corpore numen
> attonitas inter gentis patriamque paventem
> in caelum tulit et maternis reddidit astris. (*Phaenomena* 554–60)

Germanicus' *cochlidis inventor* comes from Eratosthenes, *Catasterismoi* 27, in which Capricorn found a conch to scare off the Titans; *divorum laetior aetas* refers to the Age of Jupiter after the battle of the gods and giants. These motifs are not in Aratus' text: Germanicus interpolates triumphal post-Titanic mythology into his Aratean original. Germanicus superimposes the apotheosised Augustus onto the constellation Capricorn, Augustus' birth sign (*maternis astris*). Unlike Julius, who became a new star, Augustus appears in Germanicus to be conjoined with his natal star. By the complex set of mythic associations of the Augustan period, at the same time as the Princeps is projected onto the Aratean star map, he is identified with the head of the Olympian pantheon. On Augustus' apotheosis, see Domenicucci (1996) 101–38.

[45] See n. 37 above.

Fig. 3

found in the allegorisation in Augustan literature of the civil wars (in particular the battle of Actium) by the battle of the gods and giants.[46] The Eratosthenic version of the myth of Capricorn was that Capricorn was the son of Pan and a she-goat, and the ally of Zeus in the war with the Titans, routing the enemy with the sound of a conch.[47] The conch discovered by Capricorn has the same function as the skin of the She-goat in the Eratosthenic battle with the Titans: protection of Jupiter. Capricorn is thus an appropriate tutelary sign for Augustus, the human equivalent of Jupiter. Its use in iconography may commemorate the Princeps' rise to power. The cornucopia associated with him denotes the peace and prosperity of this second Golden Age after military struggle.

The occurrence of the cornucopia in Ovid's Capella panel enables us to connect Aratean astral myth with some of the prevailing motifs of the Augustan Principate. But the image of peace after military endeavour is a slightly tricky one: it can mean both external conquest and conquest in civil war. Ovid's Capella carries the same set of associations as Capricorn, but is one step removed from civil war and its propaganda, a demilitarised form of Capricorn, pertaining more to the youth of Jupiter than to his *fulmina*.[48] The young Jupiter she nurtured could represent the Princeps in his capacity as Rome's second founder and the author of the new *saeculum* without emphasis on violence.

We have already seen in chapter 2 how Ovid expresses the nexus between conquest and *pax* in the story of Numa in *Fasti* 3: it seems to me that Capella belongs in the same thematic bracket, the dominant one in the *Fasti*. Ovid works with a disarmed version of Jupiter to express this theme; we saw this in his Veiovis passage, discussed in chapter 2, and we see it again here: the young Jupiter is an earlier, pacific form of the fierce grown-up Jupiter with his thunderbolts. Using the story

[46] As on Virgil's Shield of Aeneas, where the description of Actium exploits gigantomachic elements: see above, pp. 54–7.

[47] Eratosthenes, *Catasterismoi* 27, Hyginus, *Astr.* 2.28.

[48] See above, p. 38.

of the youth of Jupiter, Ovid alludes simultaneously to the theme of origins and to the theme of peace.

Involved in this, it seems to me, is a mythical meditation on the question of how Augustus came to be what he was. Note the phrasing of Ovid's reference to Jupiter at *Fasti* 5.126: *et invicto nil Iove maius erat*. The word *maius* is important in the Muses' debate about origins, those of the month of May (the etymology of *Maius*), and those of Rome, which is now *maior* than before, under Augustus (who is *maior* than everyone else). There is a triple pun at *Fasti* 5.126: on the month, on the idea of greatness, and on the name of the Princeps, since his name comes from *augere*, 'to augment', 'to increase'. The wordplay here helps us to associate Augustus, Jupiter, and the growth of Rome.

At the beginning of *Fasti* 5, three etymologies of *Maius* are given, which, characteristically, compete with one another and are left unresolved. The etymologies incorporate the three main aspects of the *Fasti*: the name is said to be from *Maiestas*, or *maiores*, or Maia: an imperial explanation (*Maiestas*, the greatness of the imperial family and a concept beloved of Tiberius[49]), a traditional explanation (the ancestors), and a legendary explanation which involves astronomy (Maia is one of the Pleiades).[50]

The third etymology of *Maius* brings in the early Roman tableau which we have already seen in the Carmentis scene of *Fasti* 1, in Propertius 4.1, and in *Aeneid* 8:[51]

> hic, ubi nunc Roma est, orbis caput, arbor et herbae
>   et paucae pecudes et casa rara fuit:
> quo postquam ventum est, 'consistite', praescia mater
>   'nam locus imperii rus erit istud' ait. (*Fasti* 5.93–6)

This is the Propertian proto-Rome tableau, linked with the Augustan *topos* of world rule. Thus the third explanation for

49 On *Maiestas*, see Mackie (1992).
50 On this passage, see Barchiesi (1991).
51 Above, pp. 25–7 and 35–7. On the relationship between Calliope's speech and Propertius' aetiological elegy, see Barchiesi (1991) 12.

Maius involves the growth of Rome, Ovid's aetiological theme. At *Fasti* 5.99–104 we have a description of one of the sacred rites that Evander shows Aeneas in *Aeneid* 8, the Lupercalia:

> sacraque multa quidem, sed Fauni prima bicornis
> has docuit gentes alipedisque dei.
> semicaper, coleris cinctutis, Faune, Lupercis,
> cum lustrant celebres verbera secta vias;
> at tu materno donasti nomine mensem,
> inventor curvae, furibus apte, fidis.

The golden age theme is involved here too, as we have seen it to be in the Capella passage which follows the etymology of *Maius.* Virgil began his golden age *Eclogue*, *paulo maiora canamus* (*Ecl.* 4.1). The hero of this *Eclogue* is a *parvus puer* (*Ecl.* 4.60, 62). Barchiesi believes Ovid's etymology of *Maius* in *Fasti* 5 to be a response to Virgil's golden age *Eclogue*, and that *Maiestas* 'is an augmented version of the *puer*: one is reminded that by a regressive historical perspective the *puer* is a prefiguration of that Increasing Man, Aug-ustus'.[52]

Augustus is going to prove greater than all the things which were described by the Muses as 'greater', superseding all other origins of Rome. His name reflects this, being connected, as Ovid tells us, with *augere*, a verb which signalled the divinely bestowed power to foster growth, increase in the sense of plenty:[53]

> huius et augurium dependet origine verbi
> et quodcumque sua Iuppiter auget ope.
> augeat imperium nostri ducis, augeat annos,
> protegat et vestras querna corona fores:
> auspicibusque deis tanti cognominis heres
> omine suscipiat, quo pater, orbis onus. (*Fasti* 1.611–16)

Thus the image of the cornucopia is an appropriate one, because *Aug*ustus, like Aratus' Zeus in *Phaenomena* 13, can cause things to increase (*augere*). He also gets bigger. He is

[52] Barchiesi (1991) 9.
[53] On the derivation, see Galinsky (1996) 315.

not only *pater patriae*, but also *pater orbis*, as Ovid tells us at *Fasti* 2.130. His *auctoritas* fills the world.[54]

Augustus even has the power to make heaven greater, as Manilius tells us at *Astronomica* 4.933–5:

> ne dubites homini divinos credere visus,
> iam facit ipse deos mittitque ad sidera numen,
> maius et Augusto crescet sub principe caelum.

He can do this by making gods: Manilius must be alluding to the deification of Caesar.[55] Manilius puns on the derivation of Augustus' name from *augere*, with *maius* and *crescet*. Housman's explanation of the passage signals the pun: *caelum, quod socio Tonante per signa recturum Augustum dixerat 1.800, nunc sub rectore eo* ***auctum iri*** *dicit posteris eius deinceps in deorum numerum succedentibus*.[56] Being bigger thus ties in with Julian catasterism. The heavens will increase because Caesar, Augustus, and their successors become gods.[57] This may remind us of Virgil's invocation of Octavian at *Georgics* 1.32–5, where Scorpio moves over, leaving the generalissimo more than his fair share of the sky:[58]

> anne novum tardis sidus te mensibus addas,
> qua locus Erigonen inter Chelasque sequentis
> panditur (ipse tibi iam bracchia contrahit ardens
> Scorpius et caeli iusta plus parte reliquit).

[54] At *Fasti* 1.603–4, Pompey is *magnus*, but Augustus is *maior* in terms of his name, since his name is the greatest of all, having not only quantitative connotations, but religious importance:

> Magne, tuum nomen rerum est mensura tuarum:
> sed qui te vicit nomine maior erat.

[55] Domenicucci (1996) 62–3 links this passage with *Fasti* 2.144, *caelestem fecit te [Romulum] pater, ille patrem [Caesarem]*, and Manilius, *Ast.* 1.9, *concessumque patri mundum deus ipse [Auguste] mereris.*

[56] Housman (1903–30) *ad Ast.* 4.935.

[57] On 17 September AD 14 the Senate declared Augustus a god. The *Fasti Amiternini* for that date are inscribed DIVO AVGVSTO HONORES CAELESTES A SENATV DECRETI (Mommsen (1863) 324). See also Dio 56.46.1–2.

[58] Although here he is assimilated by Virgil to Libra (*Chelae*), the foundation sign of Rome, rather than to Capricorn as in Germanicus (above, n. 44). For Libra as the foundation sign of Rome, see Manilius, *Ast.* 4.773 with Housman (1903–30). On Virgil's invocation of Octavian and the question of assimilation to Libra and Capricorn, see Bayet (1939) and Barton (1995).

All this alerts us to the encomiastic background behind Ovid's Capella passage. The phrase *nil maius* (*Fasti* 5.126) turns out to be a cliché of Augustan panegyric. It often seems to signal an assimilation of Augustus and Jupiter. For example, Horace says of Jupiter at *Odes* 1.12.17, *nil maius generatur ipso. Odes* 1.12 is primarily about creating parallels betwen Augustus and Jupiter. The parallel is exploited by Ovid himself in the *Fasti*:

hoc tu per terras, quod in aethere Iuppiter alto,
nomen habes: hominum tu pater, ille deum. (*Fasti* 2.131–2)

It is also found in the *Metamorphoses*:

Iuppiter arces
temperat aetherias et mundi regna triformis,
terra sub Augusto est; pater est et rector uterque.
di, precor, Aeneae comites, quibus ensis et ignis
cesserunt, dique Indigetes genitorque Quirine
urbis et invicti genitor Gradive Quirini
Vestaque Caesareos inter sacrata Penates
et cum Caesarea tu, Pheobe domestice, Vesta,
quique tenes altus Tarpeias Iuppiter arces,
quosque alios vati fas appellare piumque est:
tarda sit illa dies et nostro serior aevo,
qua caput Augustum, quem temperat, orbe relicto,
accedat caelo faveatque precantibus absens![59] (*Metamorphoses* 15.858–70)

It also occurs in the exile poetry, as at *Tristia* 2.33–40:[60]

si, quotiens peccant homines, sua fulmina mittat
Iuppiter, exiguo tempore inermis erit;
nunc ubi detonuit strepituque exterruit orbem,
purum discussis aera reddit aquis.
iure igitur genitorque deum rectorque vocatur,
iure capax mundus **nil Iove maius** habet.
tu [Auguste] quoque, cum patriae rector dicare paterque,
utere more dei nomen habentis idem.

[59] Ovid's *absens* could be a play on Horace, *Odes* 3.5.1–4:

caelo tonantem credidimus Iovem
regnare; *praesens* divus habebitur
Augustus adiectis Britannis
imperio gravibusque Persis.

[60] Galinsky (1996) 318: 'The Greeks constantly identified Augustus with Zeus/Jupiter, and so did Ovid, even if mostly from exile.'

This is the big Jupiter, who appears in his re-armed guise especially in Ovid's exile poetry, but only intrudes into the Capella passage at *Fasti* 5.126, with the *nil maius* theme.

This kind of panegyric is close to its Hellenistic roots. It is here that Aratus' invocation of Zeus is important. Horace paraphrases Aratus' invocation of Zeus at *Odes* 1.12.13–16 to express identification of Augustus with the Stoic Zeus:

> quid prius dicam solitis parentis
> laudibus, qui res hominum ac deorum,
> qui mare et terras variisque mundum
> temperat horis?

One can see the similarity of these lines with Aratus' opening 'Hymn to Zeus'. *Horis*, seasons, are Aratus' δεξιαὶ ὧραι, *Phaenomena* line 8. Horace places Aratus' invocation, and the philosophical baggage it carries, in the frame of imperial panegyric. The opening motto of the *Phaenomena* now refers to the ruler, who is identified with the providential Zeus of Aratus' proem, the god who set up the stars as a sign of his beneficence.

Horace's *temperat* (*Odes* 1.12.16) reinforces the association with Aratus' Zeus. Nisbet and Hubbard tell us that *temperat* means 'regulates' (in the sense of κεραννύναι), with just the right mixture of elements, commenting, 'The idea of a universe in equilibrium was particularly Stoic.'[61]

This might support a grand encomiastic interpretation of Ovid's Capella passage above, which begins with the Aratean *exordium* (*ab Iove surgat opus*, *Fasti* 5.111). Augustus is Jupiter, who placed Capella among the stars (recall Crinagoras' use of the same *topos*[62]).

There are precedents for this use of the invocation of Zeus. Theocritus' Encomium of Ptolemy (*Idyll* 17) is one. It opens with a straightforward parallel between Zeus and Ptolemy, beginning with Zeus:

[61] Nisbet and Hubbard (1970–8) *ad Odes* 1.12.16. [62] Above, p. 133.

ἐκ Διὸς ἀρχώμεσθα καὶ ἐς Δία λήγετε Μοῖσαι,
ἀθανάτων τὸν ἄριστον ἐπὴν †ἀείδωμεν ἀοιδαῖς·
ἀνδρῶν δ' αὖ Πτολεμαῖος ἐνὶ πρώτοισι λεγέσθω
καὶ πύματος καὶ μέσσος· ὃ γὰρ προφερέστατος ἀνδρῶν. (*Idyll* 17.1–4)

With Zeus let us begin, and with Zeus in our poems, Muse, let us make an end, for of immortals he is best; but of men let Ptolemy be named, first, last and in the midst, for of men he is most excellent.[63]

Cicero provides the Roman precedent. The Aratean motto forms Scipio's *exordium* to his disquisition on kingship in *Republic* 1.56:

S. Imitemur ergo Aratum, qui magnis de rebus dicere exordiens a Iove incipiendum putat.
L. Quo Iove? aut quid habet illius carminis simile haec oratio?
S. Tantum, inquit, ut rite ab eo dicendi principia capiamus, quem unum omnium deorum et hominum regem esse omnes docti indoctique pariter consentiunt.

It is clear that the Romans recognised Aratus' invocation as a political formula almost from the moment it was Latinised.[64] It pertains to rulership of the state and of the world. Cicero in the *Republic* applied it to the beginnings of the Roman state; Horace and Ovid apply it to Augustus, who is close to the Zeus of Aratus' proem.

'Big Jupiter', then, appears in two places in *Fasti* 5.111–28: in line 111 (*ab Iove surgat opus*), and in 126 (*et invicto nil Iove maius erat*). Elsewhere in *Fasti* 5.111–28, the connection between Augustus and Jupiter is expressed allusively, even playfully, and concentrates on 'small Jupiter'. This too derives from Hellenistic precedents, particularly Theocritus' seventeenth *Idyll* and Callimachus' *Hymn to Zeus*. Both of these combine the youth of Jupiter with kingship theory. The latter is closest to the indirect or allusive panegyric we are dealing with in *Fasti* 5.111–28; the former, while it contains both direct and allusive panegyric, leans towards the direct.

The whole of Callimachus' first *Hymn* (to Zeus) might be

[63] Text and trans. Gow (1950–2). On Theocritus 17, see Meincke (1965), Cairns (1972) 100–20, Griffiths (1979) 71–82, Hunter (1996) 79–82.
[64] The earliest instance of its Latinisation is probably Cicero, *Aratea* fr. 1.

taken as allegorical encomium of the Ptolemies.[65] Callimachus uses the youth of Zeus theme to refer allegorically to the youth of Ptolemy II, in the same way that Ovid alludes to Augustus in *Fasti* 5.111–28. Like Theocritus, Callimachus begins his ritual fiction with Zeus:

> Ζηνὸς ἔοι τί κεν ἄλλο παρὰ σπονδῇσιν ἀείδειν
> λώιον ἢ θεὸν αὐτόν, ἀεὶ μέγαν, αἰὲν ἄνακτα;
> (Callimachus, *Hymn to Zeus* 1–2)

At libations to Zeus, what else should rather be sung than the god himself, mighty forever, king for evermore?[66]

Note the affinity of this with Aratus' opening 'hymn', especially in its theme of permanence (ἀεί). At *Hymn to Zeus* 78–9 Callimachus uses the ἐκ Διός tag:

> ἐκ δὲ Διὸς βασιλῆες, ἐπεὶ Διὸς οὐδὲν ἀνάκτων
> θειότερον.

But from Zeus come kings: for nothing is diviner than the kings of Zeus.

Ἐκ δὲ Διὸς βασιλῆες is a quotation of Hesiod, *Theogony* 96. Likewise Theocritus, as Richard Hunter points out, 'stretches' the phrase around the proem of *Idyll* 17, ἐκ Διὸς . . . βασιλήων, as well as beginning with the Aratean ἐκ Διὸς ἀρχώμεσθα.[67] Aratus, Callimachus and Theocritus go back to a common source, a passage of Hesiod (*Theogony* 68–103) which sets up a close relationship between Zeus and just kings.[68] At *Theogony* 71–4 and 84–7, for example, the king's acts on earth mirror those of Zeus in heaven. At *Theogony* 91 a just king is said to be looked to by the citizens 'like a god'. McLennan comments: 'The propaganda value of Hesiod's famous hemistich was particularly useful to a Hellenistic court poet.'[69]

The assimilation of Zeus and the monarch may be present in varying degrees of explicitness. We have seen how

[65] McLennan (1977) *ad* Call. *Hymn* 1.61. The poem contains allusions to Ptolemy I Soter and Ptolemy II Philadelphos. On Callimachus' *Hymn to Zeus*, see also Hopkinson (1984) and (1988) 121–31.
[66] Trans. Mair and Mair (1921).
[67] Hunter (1996) 80–1.
[68] See Bing (1988) 76–83.
[69] McLennan (1977) *ad* Call. *Hymn* 1.79.

Theocritus' seventeenth *Idyll* begins with an initiatory formula similar to that of Aratus; but its application to the poet's sovereign is made more explicit than in Callimachus.[70] The relationship between Theocritus, *Idyll* 17 and Callimachus' first *Hymn* is particularly clear at *Idyll* 17.53–76, where Theocritus strikes up the 'youth of Zeus' theme which Callimachus had treated in his *Hymn*, but applies its motifs to king Ptolemy's youth on Cos.[71] This is the panegyrical background to Ovid's use of the same theme in *Fasti* 5.

Again, lines 59–66 of Callimachus' *Hymn* may allude to the territorial hegemony of the Ptolemies:[72]

> δηναιοὶ δ' οὐ πάμπαν ἀληθέες ἦσαν ἀοιδοί·
> φάντο πάλον Κρονίδῃσι διάτριχα δώματα νεῖμαι·
> τίς δέ κ' ἐπ' Οὐλύμπῳ τε καὶ Ἄϊδι κλῆρον ἐρύσσαι,
> ὃς μάλα μὴ νενίηλος; ἐπ' ἰσαίῃ γὰρ ἔοικε
> πήλασθαι· τὰ δὲ τόσσον ὅσον διὰ πλεῖστον ἔχουσι.
> ψευδοίμην ἀίοντος ἅ κεν πεπίθοιεν ἀκουήν.
> οὔ σε θεῶν ἐσσῆνα πάλοι θέσαν, ἔργα δὲ χειρῶν,
> σή τε βίη τό τε κάρτος, ὃ καὶ πέλας εἵσαο δίφρου.

The ancient poets spake not altogether truly. For they said that the lot assigned to the sons of Cronus their three several abodes. But who would draw lots for Olympus and for Hades – save a very fool? for equal chances should one cast lots; but these are the wide world apart. When I speak fiction, be it such fiction as persuades the listener's ear! Thou wert made sovereign of the gods not by casting of lots but by the deeds of thy hands, thy might and the strength which thou hast set beside thy throne.

This must be a reference to the prowess of Zeus in the wars against the Titans. The seizure of power by Zeus in Callimachus' *Hymn* can be read allegorically, as an allusion to the gaining of power by Ptolemy Philadelphus over his elder brothers. So also in Ovid, Jupiter victorious after the battle with the giants (*Fasti* 5.125–6) can represent Augustus victorious after the civil wars.

Theocritus' praise of the extent of Ptolemy's territory at

[70] For the similarities between Theocritus, *Idyll* 17 and Callimachus, *Hymn to Zeus*, see Gow (1950–2) 325.

[71] See Gow (1950–2) *ad loc.*

[72] According to McLennan (1977) 99 *ad loc.*

Idyll 17.85–90 again acts to render explicit Callimachus' oblique reference:

τῶν πάντων Πτολεμαῖος ἀγήνωρ ἐμβασιλεύει.
καὶ μὴν Φοινίκας ἀποτέμνεται Ἀρραβίας τε
καὶ Συρίας Λιβύας τε κελαινῶν τ' Αἰθιοπήων·
Παμφύλοισί τε πᾶσι καὶ αἰχμηταῖς Κιλίκεσσι
σαμαίνει, Λυκίοις τε φιλοπτολέμοισί τε Καρσί
καὶ νάσοις Κυκλάδεσσιν ...

Of all Lord Ptolemy is king. Aye, and of Phoenicia he takes himself a part, and of Arabia, and Syria and Libya and of the swart Ethiopians. In all Pamphylia his word is law, and with the spearmen of Cilicia, the Lycians and the warlike Carians; in the isles of the Cyclades also ...

Theocritus' mapping of the extent of Ptolemy's territory is like Horace's mapping of the Empire in the closing lines of *Odes* 1.12:[73]

ille [Caesar] seu Parthos Latio imminentes
egerit iusto domitos triumpho,
sive subiectos Orientis orae
    Seras et Indos,

te [Iove] minor latum reget aequus orbem:
tu gravi curru quaties Olympum,
tu parum castis inimica mittes
    fulmina lucis. (Horace, *Odes* 1.12.53–60)

– and like *Georgics* 4.560–2, where, like the god, Augustus hurls thunderbolts (*fulminat*) over his conquered territory:

Caesar dum magnus ad altum
fulminat Euphraten bello victorque volentis
per populos dat iura viamque adfectat Olympo.

At the end of *Odes* 1.12 Jupiter's thunderbolts take on an additional moral function, smiting the impure. This may be an allusion to the civil wars or to the avenging of Caesar's murder.[74] If so, we again see that civil war and foreign

[73] See also Horace, *Odes* 3.5.1–4, where Augustus as lord of the οἰκουμένη is likened by implication to omnipotent Jove.

[74] 'These stanzas belong to a different sphere of ideas, the speculations of Hellenistic philosophers on the nature of kingship and its relation to divinity', as Nisbet and Hubbard (1970–8) vol. 1, 145 comment.

conquest had the potential to be conflated in Augustan literary encomium. David West asks (speaking of the closing stanzas of Horace, *Odes* 1.12), 'Was Augustus going to yield to the example of the dynasties of the Greek East and allow himself to be hailed as a god? The answer was not simple and in the beginning when Augustus was feeling his way to an ideology of power, Virgil and Horace were feeling their way to a grammar of panegyric.'[75]

Ovid too, perhaps, was treading a tricky path. In the *Fasti*, his praise of Augustus cannot be said to be non-military (take the temple of Mars Ultor, *Fasti* 5.545–98 as a military example); however, in the *Fasti*, as we have seen, Ovid often chooses to emphasise Zeus' youth over his maturity. It is perhaps significant that, on the whole, Ovid reserves his direct praise of Augustus as analogue of the mature Jupiter for the *Metamorphoses* and the exile poetry;[76] the example of panegyric we have seen from the *Fasti* belongs to the genre of allusive encomium, more like Callimachus' first *Hymn* than Theocritus' seventeenth *Idyll*, and deals with the origin of Jupiter: appropriate for a poem on origins, but also appropriate for a poem in which the *Pax Augusta* is strongly alluded to in various ways.

It can be said that Ovid's use of the Aratean exordium at *Fasti* 5.111 is really about the ruler, about the use of astral myth in a political context, and about Hellenistic kingship in Augustan Rome. We have examined the precedents for this. Ovid's innovation is to attach his youth of Zeus theme to a specifically astral myth.

Capella, no less than the more prominent Capricorn, fits into a system of expression of Augustus' rise to and maintenance of power through a collection of connected and inter-

[75] West (1995) 14–15.

[76] The very first of the exile poems uses this *topos* in connection with Ovid's exile (*Tristia* 1.1.81–2):

> me quoque, quae sensi, fateor Iovis arma timere:
> me reor infesto, cum tonat, igne peti.

changeable mythic elements.[77] The cornucopia in Augustan imagery is associated with Capricorn rather than Capella: Capricorn and the cornucopia, read in conjunction, might be read as saying that *Pax* (the Horn) is contingent on military conquest by the ruler (the war with the Titans). Ovid seems to have substituted Capella for Capricorn in connection with the cornucopia and the 'youth of Zeus' theme. Capella is the 'disarmed' version of Capricorn.[78]

In the Capella passage, as in the Numa passage discussed in chapter 2, it is fair to say that peace is emphasised over war. This does not have to be 'subversive' of the Principate: Galinsky points out that in the later Principate pacific imagery is expressed as much as military.[79] The civil wars had given way to the *Pax Augusta*. Thus a young Jupiter and a demilitarised Capricorn may be an appropriate strategy of praise.

The stars in the *Fasti* can show *the same* patterns as 'official discourse', and can be *integrated into* the Julian calendar with its political corollary. An individual astronomical reference such as Capella can mediate between astral myth and Augustan panegyric; it could be argued that the stars are there in the *Fasti* to bridge the gap between Hellenistic kingship and Augustan Rome.

[77] I do not mean to imply that I think that such a system was designed as a whole by Augustus as a system of propaganda; Galinsky (1996) in particular has developed the idea of an Augustan 'evolution', where certain mythic or iconographical elements could be favoured over certain others, and their components became part of a common pool of political imagery capable of evolving over time.

[78] Disarming is the preoccupation of Hinds (1992).

[79] Galinsky (1996) 36.

CHAPTER 6

THE METAMORPHOSIS OF TIME

Introduction

Theocritus' identification of the ruler with Zeus in *Idyll* 17 runs alongside a second kind of encomium: praise of the ruler through his divine ancestors, granted apotheosis for their great deeds. Ptolemy's deified father sits on a throne beside Alexander in heaven (16–19):

τῆνον καὶ μακάρεσσι πατὴρ ὁμότιμον ἔθηκεν
ἀθανάτοις, καί οἱ χρύσεος θρόνος ἐν Διὸς οἴκῳ
δέδμηται· παρὰ δ' αὐτὸν Ἀλέξανδρος φίλα εἰδώς
ἑδριάει, Πέρσαισι βαρὺς θεὸς αἰολομίτρας.

Him the father made of equal honour even with the blessed immortals, and for him is fixed in Zeus' halls a golden throne; and by his side in friendship sits Alexander, god of the gay diadem, the Persians' bane.[1]

Near Ptolemy Soter and Alexander is Heracles, the πρόγονος of the Macedonian kings (20–7). Like Horace's Augustus, Hercules and Pollux in *Odes* 3.3.9–12, Ptolemy's ancestors sip nectar. Ptolemy Philadelphos' mother too is deified (34–50).[2] Like Aratus' Zeus (in *Ph.* line 5) she is gentle to mortals (ἤπιος βροτοῖς, line 51).

Hellenistic praise poetry of this kind is what Horace modelled his list of divine heroes on in *Odes* 1.12.36–48,[3] a list which included Caesar and his comet:

[1] Trans. Gow (1950–2).
[2] This is Berenice I, the mother of Magas of Cyrene by her first husband. She married Ptolemy Soter in 317 BC. The Berenice about whose lock Callimachus wrote his poem is Berenice II, the daughter of Magas, born *c.* 273 BC, who married Ptolemy III Euergetes in 247.
[3] See also Horace, *Epistles* 2.1.

Regulum et Scauros animaeque magnae
prodigum Paulum superante Poeno
gratus insigni referam camena
Fabriciumque.

hunc et incomptis Curium capillis
utilem bello tulit et Camillum
saeva paupertas et avitus apto
cum lare fundus.

crescit occulto velut arbor aevo
fama Marcelli; micat inter omnis
Iulium sidus velut inter ignes
luna minores.

This poem of Horace displays the characteristic of Hellenistic panegyric we are interested in here, namely reference to astral divinisation in a dynastic context. Horace begins by praising Jupiter, as we have seen in chapter 5. Then other gods – Athena, Bacchus and Diana – are praised (*Odes* 1.12.19–24). Kings and heroes follow (25–48). Horace's list of apotheosised heroes includes Castor and Pollux, who are a constellation (*stella*, 28).[4] It ends with the Star of Caesar. This may be taken (despite some objections[5]) as a reference to the comet which appeared during Caesar's funeral games in 44 BC.

This kind of poetry is the model for encomiastic passages of the *Fasti* which exploit the dynastic motif. Note *Fasti* 1.527–36 (part of the prophecy of Carmentis, the mother of Evander):

iam pius Aeneas sacra et, sacra altera, patrem
adferet: Iliacos accipe, Vesta, deos.
tempus erit cum vos orbemque tuebitur idem,
et fient ipso sacra colente deo,
et penes Augustos patriae tutela manebit:
hanc fas imperii frena tenere domum.

[4] I take this to be the constellation Gemini, but for a different view (as St Elmo's fire) see West (1995) 58.

[5] Nisbet and Hubbard (1970–8) *ad loc.* take it metaphorically – 'Star (i.e. greatest member) of the Julian clan'. Ramsey and Licht (1997) 172, however, list it among literary allusions to the *sidus Iulium*. West (1995) 59 also takes it as referring literally to the comet which appeared at the funeral games of Caesar in 44 BC.

inde nepos natusque dei, licet ipse recuset,
pondera caelesti mente paterna feret,
utque ego perpetuis olim sacrabor in aris,
sic Augusta novum Iulia numen erit.

Here, Tiberius as *nepos natusque dei* is equivalent to Theocritus' Ptolemy; the *deus* his grandfather must be Julius, the *deus* his father, Augustus. *Caelesti mente* denotes both his superhuman powers and his own future status as a god. His mother Livia (Augusta) will also be, like Ptolemy's mother Berenice at *Idyll* 17.34–50, a *novum numen*.[6] 'Ovid has elevated Livia's rank from the chaste, obedient wife of the ruler to incipient goddess and head of the Augustan dynasty.'[7]

Elaine Fantham says: 'This is the exiled Ovid writing, at least the last few lines when Tiberius and Livia have outlived Augustus. But the orthodoxy of his tone and the authority of his speaker soften the shocking novelty of the imperial deification here sanctified by Carmenta's prophecy.'[8] However, it is possible to say, looking at the Hellenistic literature of praise, that imperial deification was only a 'shocking novelty' in Rome; and Roman authors had a wide base of literary precedents on which to draw in their Romanisation of the concept.

The three works of Ovid with which we are concerned here all have Hellenistic precedents. Bömer links the *Fasti*, the *Metamorphoses*, and Ovid's translation of Aratus, the *Phaenomena*, advancing the theory that they were all composed at around the same time in the poet's career, and that the roots of all three lie in Hellenistic aetiological literature.[9] They deal respectively with the causes of time, of natural phenomena,

6 See also *Fasti* 1.649–50, *Ex Pont.* 2.8.1–10, 3.1.117–18. Livia in fact took a while to get off the ground – she died in AD 29 but was subject to *damnatio memoriae* and ascended to heaven in AD 41.

7 Herbert-Brown (1994) 160. We know this passage must be post-AD 14 because Augustus' will gave Livia the right to the title Julia Augusta (Tac. *Ann.* 1.8, Suet. *Aug.* 101). Tiberius was given the title Augustus at this time, but refused to use it (Dio 57.2.1), as he in fact refused the honours for his mother which Ovid unwisely dwells on here.

8 Fantham (1995) 57–8.

9 Bömer (1957–8) vol. 1, 14. For discussion of the date of Ovid's *Phaenomena*, see above, pp. 68–70.

and of the stars. Their aetiological predecessors are Callimachus, Nicander, and Aratus.

If, as Bömer suggested, Ovid's *Fasti*, *Metamorphoses*, and *Phaenomena* were composed contemporaneously, it would seem reasonable to assume a particularly strong interest in astronomy on Ovid's part in the early years of the common era, since all three deal with the myths of the stars, with varying degrees of prominence. Tamsyn Barton provides a link based on this criterion: 'Germanicus in his Latin version of Aratus refers to Capricorn's taking Augustus up to heaven. Ovid follows suit, and it is in his *Metamorphoses* and *Fasti* most of all that catasterism becomes the natural end to many a legend ... Aratus of Soli, who in about 280 BC composed the *Phaenomena* ... was of course the ultimate Alexandrian model for writing about the stars.'[10] Here the link between the *Fasti*, the *Metamorphoses*, and the *Phaenomena* (whether in Aratus' own version or in a Roman translation such as Germanicus' or Ovid's own) is catasterism. Surely some of the impetus for Ovid's interest in the stars must lie in the importance of the politics of catasterism during the later Principate of Augustus. The evidence for Caesar's divinity had been plain to see with the appearance of a comet at his funeral games in 44 BC; how would Augustus choose to follow him? The stars are an area both of panegyric and of anxiety for a poet writing in the early years of the first century AD.

We must be clear about definitions here. Barton as quoted above does not make clear the difference between Aratus and Ovid. There is no explicit reference to *ruler*-catasterism in Aratus, although, as I have mentioned in the previous chapter, the circumstances of the composition of the *Phaenomena* might suggest assimilation of the ruler to the Zeus of the proem.[11] However, in the *Fasti*, the *Metamorphoses*, and his own translation of Aratus, Ovid has the benefit of hindsight in relation to the enstarment of Julius Caesar (as no doubt did Germanicus in his translation of Aratus). A distinction can be made between the star myths which appear in Aratus'

[10] Barton (1994b) 48. [11] See above, pp. 3, 147.

Phaenomena, which belong to the same genre of astral aetiology as was practised by Eratosthenes in the *Catasterismoi*, and the stars in the *Fasti*, which, while equally belonging to this genre, are also likely to host catasterised emperors. At the same time, this distinction is never clear in practice.

In Augustan Rome, the stars could be used dynastically. We see this in Ovid's references to Julius Caesar's catasterism, to be studied below, where the *sidera* are *cognata* – 'relatives' of the Julian family. But the point is that Caesar's family are not just catasterised rulers but also the characters of celestial mythology, like Capella, Ariadne, and Callisto. Julius Caesar *is* Aratean in a certain sense: he can be mapped onto the Aratean sky, and is near constellations whose myths are told by Aratus. In the previous chapter we have seen how Aratean star myths may be the stuff of panegyric; now we shall see how they may modify panegyric if mythological considerations are allowed to dominate.

Caesar the god

The main source for Caesar's catasterism, apart from allusions in Horace, Virgil[12] and Ovid (whom we shall deal with in a moment), is Pliny, *Naturalis Historia* 2.93–4, an account which purportedly comes from Augustus' own memoirs (composed *c.* 23 BC):[13]

cometes in uno totius orbis loco colitur in templo Romae, admodum faustus divo Augusto iudicatus ab ipso, qui incipiente eo apparuit ludis quos faciebat Veneri Genetrici non multo post obitum patris Caesaris in collegio ab eo instituto. namque his verbis id gaudium prodit: 'iis ipsis ludorum meorum diebus sidus crinitum per septem dies in regione caeli quae sub septentrionibus est conspectum est. id oriebatur circa undecimam horam diei clarumque et omnibus e terris conspicuum fuit. eo sidere significari volgus credidit Caesaris animam inter deorum immortalium numina receptam, quo nomine id insigne simulacro capitis eius, quod mox in foro consecravimus, adiectum est.' haec ille in publicum; interiore gaudio sibi illum natum seque in eo nasci interpretatus est; et, si verum fatemur, salutare id terris fuit.

[12] There are at least six sightings of the star in the *Aeneid*: see West (1993). See also Domenicucci (1996) 39–41.

[13] See Malcovati (1928) fr. 167.

The only place in the whole world where a comet is the object of worship is a temple at Rome. His late majesty Augustus had deemed this comet very propitious to himself; as it had appeared at the beginning of his rule, at some games which, not long after the decease of his father Caesar, as a member of the college founded by him he was celebrating in honour of Mother Venus. In fact he made public the joy it gave him in these words: 'On the very days of my games a comet was visible for seven days in the Northern part of the sky. It was rising about an hour before sunset, and was a bright star, visible from all lands. The common people believed that this star signified the soul of Caesar received among the spirits of the immortal gods, and on this account the emblem of a star was added to the bust of Caesar that we shortly afterwards dedicated in the forum.' This was his public utterance, but privately he interpreted the comet as having been born for his own sake and as containing his own birth within it; and to confess the truth, it did have a healthgiving influence over the world.[14]

The dynastic implications of the comet come out clearly from Pliny's description of events: the games were those of Venus Genetrix, ancestress of the Julians;[15] Caesar is Octavian's 'father'; Octavian took his genesis from it in some way.[16] Pliny's *uno* pertains not only to geographical location (Rome being the one place in the world where a comet is revered) but to an unusual interpretation of the comet, since, for the Romans, comets were previously portents of evil significance, as Pliny himself made clear in his preceding section.[17] The change must be a result of application to the comet of ideas of astral immortality as a reward for great deeds.[18]

A comet is *ex officio* both unpredictable (since the ancients had no grasp of periodicity) and ephemeral. It is something of a paradox that Caesar's astral apotheosis, the blueprint for Roman imperial catasterism, was linked with the transient

[14] Trans. Rackham (1950).

[15] On the games and their significance for the propagation of the *Sidus Iulium*, see Domenicucci (1996) 31–3, Ramsey and Licht (1997) 19–57.

[16] Servius, *ad Aen.* 8.681 tells us that Augustus also wore a star on his head: *ipse vero Augustus in honorem patris stellam in galea coepit habere depictam.* A star was already the symbol of the divine ruler, appearing, for example, over the head of Antiochus IV on coins (Weinstock (1971) pl. 28.1). In this respect the comet was only confirmation of an existing phenomenon.

[17] Pliny, *NH* 2.92. Comets are portents of civil war in Virgil, *Geo.* 1.487–92, Manilius, *Ast.* 1.906–22, and Lucan 1.526–9. Similar prodigies preceded Caesar's death in Ovid, *Met.* 15.783–98. See Ramsey and Licht (1997) 135–55, 'The Interpretation of Caesar's Comet as a Positive Omen', Domenicucci (1996) 38 n. 35, 79.

[18] See Weinstock (1971) 373.

phenomenon of the comet.[19] The solution was to turn the comet into a star.[20] Once this was done, the comet was open to Stoicising ideas of astral immortality, by which the souls of virtuous men become stars. It was also open to astrological interpretation. One can see in the comet a process of propagandistic negotiation between Octavian and his opponents played out on the astrological field.

In Virgil's fifth *Eclogue*, the source closest to the time of Caesar, the *star* of Daphnis (an allegorical figure representing Caesar, according to Servius[21]) is the harbinger of the Golden Age:

Me. Daphninque tuum tollemus ad astra,
Daphnin ad astra feremus; amavit nos quoque Daphnis.
Mo. an quicquam nobis tali sit munere maius?
et puer ipse fuit cantari dignus et ista
iam pridem Stimichon laudavit carmina nobis.
Me. candidus insuetum miratur limen Olympi
sub pedibusque videt nubes et sidera Daphnis.
ergo alacris silvas et cetera rura voluptas
Panaque pastoresque tenet Dryadasque puellas.
nec lupus insidias pecori nec retia cervis
ulla dolum meditantur; amat bonus otia Daphnis. (*Eclogue* 5.51–61)

The Golden Age is suggested by the inversions of the natural order which Daphnis' catasterism brings about (lines 60–1). Likewise, in *Eclogue* 9.46–9 the *Sidus Iulium* is identified with the Star of Venus, the bringer of plenty:

Daphni, quid antiquos signorum suspicis ortus?
ecce Dionaei processit Caesaris astrum,
astrum quo segetes gauderent frugibus et quo
duceret apricis in collibus uva colorem.

19 For the sole attestation (Pliny's, at *NH* 2.178) of the identification of the catasterised Caesar with a constellation called *Caesaris Thronus*, see Domenicucci (1996) 66–70. This is likely to be a fantasy of Pliny's.

20 Ramsey and Licht (1997) 144–5 observe that when literary references are to the apotheosis of Caesar, a star is spoken of, rather than a comet; when Caesar's death is mourned, comets prevail. For example, Virgil talks of a star at *Ecl.* 9.47 (see below) and *Aen.* 8.681 (the *patrium sidus*) but of *cometae* at *Geo.* 1.487–8.

21 Servius Auctus *ad Ecl.* 5.56: *et quibusdam videtur per allegoriam Caesarem dicere, qui primus divinos honores meruit et divus appellatus est.* On Caesar and the Daphnis allegory, see Domenicucci (1996) 163.

The comet seems from iconographical evidence to have become connected with the *Ludi Saeculares* in 17 BC.[22] It can therefore be associated with ideas of the Augustan Golden Age and the new *saeculum*.[23] We should recall Capella, Capricorn and the Golden Age *topos* discussed in the previous chapter. It seems that the *Sidus Iulium* may be part of this same complex of astral imagery.[24]

Indeed, Capricorn itself may be connected with the *Sidus Iulium*, if Ramsey and Licht are right: 'Capricorn was in the ascendant during the hour when the comet rose in July 44. In our view, this circumstance provides a new and promising explanation of Octavian's enigmatic remark which interprets the comet as a sign closely linked with his own birth.'[25] The astrology applied to the comet belongs, in this view, to Octavian's rhetoric of dynasty. Because this astrological interpretation involves Octavian's birth sign, it explains Pliny's *sibi illum natum seque in eo nasci*.[26]

The comet was considered a sign of Octavian's divine election (his 'political horoscope') as much as it was a sign of Caesar's apotheosis. Pliny's *incipiente eo* therefore signifies an astrological interpretation specific to one person; at the same time this is not incompatible with *salutare terris*, an 'ecumenical' interpretation of the comet. Augustus is the point where the two intersect: Capricorn and the *Sidus Iulium* are connected with his horoscope; Capricorn and the *Sidus Iulium* bring peace and prosperity.

In the *Fasti*, Ovid does not refer directly to the *Sidus Iulium*.

22 At this date the moneyer M. Sanquinius issued coins connecting the *Sidus Iulium* with the *Ludi Saeculares*, for example, a coin with Julius Caesar and his comet on the reverse, and the messenger of the games on the obverse carrying a starred shield and encircled by the legend AVGVST[VS] DIVI F[ILIVS] LVDOS SAE[CVLARES] (Galinsky (1996) 105–6 and fig. 40). See also Weinstock (1971) 379 and pl. 28.8.

23 Cf. Ramsey and Licht (1997) 140.

24 Domenicucci (1996) 47–60, 'Un acrostico sulla cometa in Virgilio?' notes an acrostic in Virgil, *Ecl.* 9.39–51, HAEDO, which he takes to refer to the spatial position of the comet near the 'Kid'. Thus it may be spatially conjunct with the constellations studied in the previous chapter.

25 Ramsey and Licht (1997) 15; cf. 147–53.

26 Cf. Servius Auctus *ad Ecl.* 9.46: *quam (stellam) quidam ad inlustrandam gloriam Caesaris iuvenis pertinere existimabant.*

For whatever reason, Ovid merely alludes twice to Caesar's deification, in *Fasti* 3.155–64, and in *Fasti*. 3.697–710. The former passage is about calendrical reform:[27]

> sed tamen errabant etiam nunc tempora, donec
> Caesaris in multis haec quoque cura fuit.
> non haec ille deus tantaeque propaginis auctor
> credidit officiis esse minora suis,
> promissumque sibi voluit praenoscere caelum
> nec deus ignotas hospes inire domos.
> ille moras solis, quibus in sua signa rediret,
> traditur exactis disposuisse notis;
> is decies senos ter centum et quinque diebus
> iunxit et a pleno tempora quinta die.

Caesar had to reform the calendar, because of his future divinity. Ovid's logic in tying calendrical reform and astral apotheosis together should now be clear. Because the dictator is to be akin to the stars, he has to know about the stars. By both calendrical reform and astral apotheosis, the ruler takes his place in the cycles of time. Calendrical reform – the control of time as well as space – is part of world empire: the natural year is now identical with the Roman year and its Julian festivals. The Julian family, whose festivals were grafted into the Roman year, is now part of the cycles of astronomically driven time. In astral apotheosis, the presence of the ruler is superimposed on the *mundus*, so that he participates in time as one of the heavenly bodies.

In this passage of the *Fasti*, Ovid asks us to think of Caesar's catasterism in terms of calendrical reform. The *Fasti* is calendrical (like Hesiod's *Works and Days*), so in it Caesar's apotheosis is to be understood primarily in the light of the calendar. However, a dynastic element enters into the second allusion to Caesar's apotheosis in the *Fasti* (3.697–710), where Augustus' avenging acts are *prima elementa Caesaris*, in the same way that Pliny's comet occurs *incipiente eo*. In this passage there may be an allusion to the literary ancestry of Caesar's catasterism too: *Fasti* 3.703, *ille quidem caelo positus*

[27] See above, p. 16.

Iovis atria vidit may remind us of Virgil, *Eclogue* 5.56–7, *candidus insuetum miratur limen Olympi | sub pedibusque videt nubes et sidera Daphnis.*

The dynastic element is awarded greater prominence at the end of the *Metamorphoses*, where Caesar had to become a god so that his son could be great. The *Metamorphoses* is a genealogical poem along the lines of Hesiod's *Theogony* – thus it is natural that in it the dynastic facet of Caesar's catasterism should be emphasised. Indeed, Ovid gives Caesar's comet a full and explicit treatment in *Metamorphoses* 15, as opposed to the skeletal references in the *Fasti*. Let us consider first *Metamorphoses* 15.745–61. It begins with a comparison between the god Aesculapius and the god Caesar:

> hic tamen accessit delubris advena nostris:
> Caesar in urbe sua deus est; quem Marte togaque
> praecipuum non bella magis finita triumphis
> resque domi gestae properataque gloria rerum
> in sidus vertere novum stellamque comantem,
> quam sua progenies. neque enim de Caesaris actis
> ullum maius opus quam quod pater exstitit huius.
> scilicet aequoreos plus est domuisse Britannos
> perque papyriferi septemflua flumina Nili
> victrices egisse rates Numidasque rebelles
> Cinyphiumque Iubam Mithridateisque tumentem
> nominibus Pontum populo adiecisse Quirini
> et multos meruisse, aliquos egisse triumphos,
> quam tantum genuisse virum? quo praeside rerum,
> humano generi, superi, favistis abunde.
> ne foret hic igitur mortali semine cretus,
> ille deus faciendus erat.

The convention of apotheosis for great deeds is here appropriated, and given a twist. As in the panegyrical passages seen in chapter 5, here too we have wars, triumphs, even civil achievements (*bella … finita triumphis | resque domi gestae*); in lines 752–6 we have all manner of distant Eastern and Western peoples added to the stock of Quirinus, after the manner of the closing stanzas of Horace, *Odes* 1.12. Such are Caesar's achievements: enough, one would have thought, to win him catasterism. Indeed, Karl Galinsky comments on the

Sidus Iulium: 'Extraordinary as such a cult was in Rome, it was based on the idea that men could become divine because of their great deeds. Caesar's had been primarily military, and to the poets, therefore, his deification could connote Rome's supremacy in the world.'[28] But Ovid adds another tier to the *topos*. These achievements are placed in a series of negatives and comparisons. ***Non** bella magis finita triumphis ... quam sua progenies*; ***neque** enim de Caesaris actis | ullum maius opus, quam quod pater exstitit huius*; *scilicet aequoreos **plus est** domuisse Britannos ... **quam** tantum genuisse virum*? The climax comes in 760–1: Caesar had to be made a god, lest Augustus remain created only from mortal seed.[29] The reason for Caesar's catasterism is not military; it is dynastic.

Note how Ovid has harnessed the *maius* theme to dynastic encomium.[30] Now territorial possessions are subordinated to the theme of Augustus' inherited status as *deus*, as a reason for astral apotheosis. The theme of *cognatio* – relationship – is the dominant one in the remainder of Ovid's panegyric at the end of *Metamorphoses* 15. Note especially lines 839–51:

'aetherias sedes cognataque sidera tanget [Augustus].
hanc animam interea caeso de corpore raptam
fac iubar, ut semper Capitolia nostra forumque
divus ab excelsa prospectet Iulius aede.'
vix ea fatus erat, media cum sede senatus
constitit alma Venus nulli cernenda suique
Caesaris eripuit membris nec in aëra solvi
passa recentem animam caelestibus intulit astris,
dumque tulit, lumen capere atque ignescere sensit
emisitque sinu: luna volat altius illa
flammeriferumque trahens spatioso limite crinem
stella micat natique videns bene facta fatetur
esse suis maiora et vinci gaudet ab illo.

Again note the panegyrical formula of *maiora* with the ablative of comparison. The deeds of the son are greater than those of

[28] Galinsky (1996) 17–18. On Augustus and Caesar, see White (1988).
[29] Compare Velleius Paterculus' comment on Tiberius' deification of Augustus, 2.126.1: *sacravit parentem suum Caesar non imperio, sed religione, non appellavit eum, sed fecit deum*.
[30] On this theme, see pp. 143–7 above.

the father. Everything will be greater than before, once the Augustan pinnacle has been reached. In this development of *Aeneid* 8, the Capitol and forum are actualised, fully post-Evandrian, with Caesar looking down from his own temple.

The subject of *tanget* is Augustus, but the *hanc animam* which follows is that of Caesar, which has to be snatched up to heaven before Augustus can touch his *cognata sidera*. The first step in Octavian's own deification was to establish his identity as the *Divi Filius;* in this the appearance of the comet in 44 BC was a fortunate co-incidence. The catasterism of the founding member of the Julian dynasty after his assassination in 44 BC meant that his successor was literally akin to the stars (*Met.* 15.839). This is where the theme of *cognatio* widens to embrace apotheosis.

Cognatio of a kind is essential to catasterism. Pliny says of Hipparchus, the commentator on Aratus, that he was *numquam satis laudatus, ut quo nemo magis adprobaverit cognationem cum homine siderum animasque nostras partem esse caeli.*[31] *Cognatio cum homine siderum* is the channel through which translation to the stars takes place.

In Cicero's *Republic*, the human soul is cognate with the stars, since both are composed out of πῦρ τεχνικόν:[32]

> homines enim sunt hac lege generati, qui tuerentur illum globum, quem in hoc templo medium vides, quae terra dicitur, hisque animus datus est ex illis sempiternis ignibus, quae sidera et stellas vocatis, quae globosae et rotundae, divinis animatae mentibus, circulos suos orbesque conficiunt celeritate mirabili. (*Republic* 6.15)

For man was given life that he might inhabit that sphere called Earth, which you see in the centre of this temple; and he has been given a soul out of

[31] *NH* 2.95.

[32] 'Cicero takes advantage of the resources of native Latin religious and poetic language to convey what was originally a Greek philosophical idea' (Powell (1990) 155). For the fiery soul as Stoic, see Cicero, *Tusc.* 1.19: *Zenoni Stoico animus ignis videtur*. A Roman source for this Stoic concept is the second Book of Cicero's *De Natura Deorum*. See, for example, *DND* 2.39: *atque hac mundi divinitate perspecta tribuenda est sideribus eadem divinitas, quae ex mobilissima purissimaque aetheris parte gignuntur neque ulla praeterea sunt admixta natura totaque sunt calida atque perlucida, ut ea quoque rectissime et animantia esse et sentire atque intellegere dicantur*; *DND* 2.42: *in deorum numero astra esse ducenda.*

those eternal fires which you call stars and planets, which, being round and globular bodies animated by divine intelligences, circle about in their fixed orbits with marvellous speed.

This idea has its origin in Plato, for whom the stars are divine (ὅσ' ἀπλανῆ τῶν ἄστρων ζῷα θεῖα ὄντα, *Timaeus* 40b[33]). For the Stoics, the stars were the souls of heroes divinised by their virtues in life.[34] The scholiast on Lucan quotes Varro's *Antiquitates Rerum Divinarum* Book 1 on this point:

mixtum dogma cum Platonico Stoicum. qui virorum fortium animas existimant in modum siderum vagari in aere et esse sic immortales, ut non moriantur sed resolvantur, secundum Platonem ⟨ne⟩ resolvantur quidem. quas 'semideos manes' dixit, quoniam Graece ἥρωες ἡμίθεοι vocantur id est semidei.[35]

A statue of Caesar with his feet on the globe is described by Dio (43.14.6): its inscription was 'ἡμίθεος'.

It is important, I think, that this kind of *cognatio* is already linked by Cicero to the Roman concept of *pietas*. Cicero continues, *Republic* 6.16:

sed sic, Scipio, ut avus hic tuus, ut ego qui te genui, iustitiam cole et pietatem, quae cum magna in parentibus et propinquis, tum in patria maxima est; ea vita via est in caelum et in hunc coetum eorum, qui iam vixerunt et corpore laxati illum incolunt locum, quem vides (erat autem is splendidissimo candore inter flammas circus elucens) quem vos, ut a Grais accepistis, orbem lacteum nuncupatis.

But, Scipio, imitate your grandfather here; imitate me, your father; love justice and duty, which are indeed strictly due to parents and kinsmen, but most of all to the fatherland. Such a life is the road to the skies, to that gathering of those who have completed their earthly lives and been relieved of the body, and live in yonder place which you now see (it was the circle of light which blazed most brightly among the other fires), and which you on earth, borrowing a Greek term, call the 'Milky Circle'.

[33] See also *Timaeus* 38e, 39e, etc. In *Fasti* 3.111–12 Ovid parodies this concept: *libera currebant et inobservata per annum | sidera; constabat sed tamen esse deos.*

[34] Cicero, *DND* 2.62: *utilitatum igitur magnitudine constituti sunt ei di qui utilitates quasque gignebant, atque his quidem nominibus quae paulo ante dicta sunt quae vis sit in quoque declaratur deo. suscepit autem vita hominum consuetudoque communis ut beneficiis excellentis viros in caelum fama ac voluntate tollerent.*

[35] *Scholia Bernensia* ed. Usener (1869) *ad* Lucan 9.6 (= Varro, *Ant. Rer. Div.* 1, fr. 25a ed. Agahd (1898) 154). On the attribution to Varro see Agahd (1898) 112–13.

Pietas here denotes behaviour according to one's 'kinship' with the fiery world soul, as well as behaviour befitting one's kinship with the illustrious ancestors. This Roman virtue is now one of the prerequisites for catasterism. Even in the Republican period the Milky Way is populated with virtuous Romans.[36]

The fact that Cicero provides, in the *Republic* and in the second book of *DND*, a body of theory on the subject of catasterism (derived from Greek sources), shows that the stars, which functioned in the early Empire as an area of dialogue between Greece and Rome, were already in the late Republic a tool in the articulation of the hereditary power of the Roman nobility. In the decade before Ovid's birth, when the philosophical works of Cicero were being written, Greek astral philosophy, with its encomiastic potential, was finding a place in Rome. In the Augustan period this concept was pressed into the service of dynasty.

Augustus is related to Julius; the Julians are also cognate with the heavens in the sense that they are related to the gods. The dynastic theme in the *Metamorphoses* is accentuated by the fact that it is Venus who carries Caesar to heaven. Again Caesar's genealogy is emphasised, his descent from Venus being mirrored in his ascent to heaven. This theme may go back to the origin of the *Sidus Iulium*, since it appears in our earliest source, Virgil's *Eclogues*:

> Daphni, quid antiquos signorum suspicis ortus?
> ecce Dionaei processit Caesaris astrum ... (*Eclogue* 9.46–7)

Here Caesar is described with an epithet which pertains to his divine ancestry, *Dionaei*, 'descendant of Venus'. Servius explains: *cum Augustus Caesar ludos funebres patri celebraret, die medio stella apparuit. ille eam esse confirmavit parentis sui: unde sunt versus isti compositi. 'Dionaei' autem longe repetitum est, a matre Veneris Diona* (Servius *ad Ecl.* 9.46).[37] Dionaei may also be an allusion to the appearance of the star at the

[36] Manilius develops this idea in *Ast.* 1.777–804 (an astral version of Virgil's Catalogue of Heroes at *Aen.* 6.756–892).

[37] On Caesar and Venus see Feeney (1991) 212–13.

Games of Venus Genetrix, which had been instituted by Caesar in 45 BC.[38] In 48 BC Caesar had issued coins carrying the star of Venus, and so apparently adopted the star of his ancestress while still alive.[39] Venus appears in Augustan iconography with similar effect. Galinsky says of the Belvedere altar, which carries the scene of Caesar's apotheosis, 'The dynastic element is enhanced by Venus, the ancestress of both the Julii and their descendants Gaius and Lucius Caesar.'[40]

Venus brings us into another area of ancestry: the literary ancestry of Ovid's panegyrical passages. We remember the dynastic associations of Aphrodite in Theocritus, *Idyll* 17; Venus' role is similar in the *Metamorphoses*, and takes us back into the realm of Hellenistic praise poetry. Venus is associated with Caesar's catasterism at *Metamorphoses* 15.843–8; he has this in common with Catullus' *Lock of Berenice*:

> isque per aetherias me tollens avolat umbras
> et Veneris casto collocat in gremio. (Catullus 66.55–6)

In background this poem is fully Alexandrian and monarchical. Its direct model is, of course, Callimachus' court poem (fr. 110). Berenice married Ptolemy III Euergetes in 247 BC, and shortly afterwards vowed to dedicate a lock of her hair for his safe return from the Syrian wars; the lock disappeared from the Alexandrian Pantheon, and was spotted by the court astronomer Conon in the northern region of the sky. Callimachus' *Lock of Berenice* functions both as astral encomium and as astral aetiology.

Ovid's representation of the apotheosis of Caesar employs many of the devices used in Callimachus' court poem.[41] *Metamorphoses* 15.848 (*emisitque sinu: luna volat altius illa*) recasts two images from Callimachus, Κύπρ]ιδος εἰς κόλ[πους ἔθηκε (fr. 110.56), or as rendered by Catullus, *et Veneris casto collocat in gremio*, 66.56, and in the second half of the verse a

[38] Domenicucci (1996) 41.
[39] Weinstock (1971) 376–7.
[40] Galinsky (1996) 321 (see fig. 151). Ovid's entry on the day of Augustus' election as Pontifex Maximus (*Fasti* 3.415–28) summarises the main themes of the Belvedere altar: the chariot of Phoebus, Venus, Vesta, the *numina* of the eternal Caesar.
[41] See Knox (1986) 76–8.

detail from Callimachus, fr. 228, on the apotheosis of Arsinoë, when she is imagined soaring past the full moon, κλεπτομέν]α παρέθει σελάνᾳ (228.6).[42] *Metamorphoses* 15.749, *in sidus vertere novum stellamque comantem,* contains a clear verbal echo of the Catullan *Lock of Berenice*: (*me | sidus in antiquis diva novum posuit*, Cat. 66.63–4). The participle *comans* occurs only here in Ovid, exploiting the etymological connection between *coma* and *cometes* (see Pliny, *NH* 2.89, Seneca, *Quaestiones Naturales* 7.6.1). Ovid's use of *comans* as an epithet for a celestial body is unique, and has the specific purpose of recalling the catasterism of the *coma*.

It seems that Catullus' translation of the *Lock of Berenice* not only provides a general precedent for panegyrical astronomy in Latin elegiacs, and thus for this aspect of the *Fasti*, but also gives later poets the concepts and even the language with which to express imperial catasterism. Virgil quotes Catullus 66.64 in his description of Octavian's prospective catasterism at *Georgics* 1.32, *anne* ***novum*** *tardis* ***sidus*** *te mensibus addas*. This is a Roman model for Caesar at the end of the *Metamorphoses*.

Literary proximity and topographical proximity are connected. Thomas, commenting on the *Georgics*, maps Octavian's star, noting not only its literary ancestry, but its proximity to the *Coma Berenices* in celestial space: 'Octavian's sign is to be between Virgo and Scorpio; on the other side of Virgo, between her and Leo, is the constellation Coma Berenices, discovered and named by Conon, friend and contemporary of Callimachus – whose playful but encomiastic account of the lock's catasterism provides the final episode of the *Aetia*.'[43]

Note the spatial position of the Lock of Berenice, as given by Catullus, 66.65–70:

> Virginis et saevi contingens namque Leonis
>   lumina, Callisto iuncta Lycaoniae,
> vertor in occasum, tardum dux ante Booten,
>   qui vix sero alto mergitur Oceano.
> sed quamquam me nocte premunt vestigia divum,
>   lux autem canae Tethyi restituit . . .

[42] See below, pp. 171–2. [43] Thomas (1988) *ad Geo.* 1.32–5.

This is Aratean celestial cartography, and announces itself as such by its similarities to the diction of the *Phaenomena*. *Vestigia divum* in line 69 recalls *Phaenomena* 359, θεῶν ὑπὸ ποσσί. *Tardum Booten* (line 67) is a *topos* found at *Phaenomena* 585 (ὀψὲ δύοντι).[44] Bootes is *tardum* because he is close to the Bears (Aratus, *Phaenomena* 721–3), which never set in the northern hemisphere. The Lock does set (Catullus 66.70 emphasises this fact), although it is *Callisto iuncta Lycaoniae* (line 66). This is the kind of mapping that Virgil inherited in his praise of Octavian in *Georgics* 1.32–5.

Appropriately, the Lock is near the Crown of Ariadne:

ὄφρα δὲ] μὴ νύμφης Μινωΐδος ο[
 . . . . .]ος ἀνθρώποις μοῦνον ἐπὶ.[
φάεσ]ιν ἐν πολέεσσιν ἀρίθμιος ἀλλ[ὰ γένωμαι
 καὶ Βερ]ενίκειος καλὸς ἐγὼ πλόκαμ[ος
ὕδασι] λουόμενόν με παρ' ἀθα[νάτους ἀνιόντα
 Κύπρι]ς ἐν ἀρχαίοις ἄστρον [ἔθηκε νέον. (Callimachus, fr. 110.59–64)

And so that not only the . . . of the Minoan bride . . . should [cast its light] on men, but I too, the beautiful lock of Berenice, be counted among the many stars. Washed in the waters [of the ocean], and rising close to the immortals, Cypris set me to be a new star among the ancient ones . . .

vario ne solum in lumine caeli
ex Ariadneis aurea temporibus
fixa corona foret . . . (Catullus 66.59–61)

Aratus gave the *aition* of the Crown of Ariadne at *Phaenomena* 71–3: it was the result of the love of Dionysus for Ariadne. Like the Crown, the Lock of Berenice is the result of love, that of the queen for her husband in his absence, described by Catullus at Poem 66.15–32.

Caesar can also be mapped topographically. Let us see what his celestial surroundings look like. According to Pliny in the passage we examined earlier, the region of sky where Caesar's comet was seen was the north (*sub Septentrionibus*). The maps of the comet's probable position in Ramsey and

[44] See also *Fasti* 3.405.

Licht (1997, figs. 3 and 4) show the Coma Berenices, the Charioteer, the Crown of Ariadne,[45] and the Bears, all inhabitants of the same northern region. Julius Caesar's topographical closeness to these constellations is a way of putting in visual terms the closeness of the catasterised Caesar in Ovid to the court poetry of Callimachus; both belong to what could be called an elegiac subgenre of astral panegyric.

The *Lock of Berenice* is a case of the appearance of a new star. Alexandrian court poetry provides us with an example of another kind of astral apotheosis, assimilation to an existing constellation. Arsinoë II, the sister and wife of Theocritus' Ptolemy, was elevated on her death in 270 to the constellation Ursa Minor.[46] P. M. Fraser has described this poem on the deification of Arsinoë as a 'laureate poem'.[47] Again it belongs fully to the Hellenistic monarchical setting. The poem itself is fragmentary, but a summary can be found in *Diegesis* 10.10, where it is said that Arsinoë was snatched up by the Dioscuri and a shrine set up for her near the Emporium.[48] The Dioscuri take Arsinoë to heaven, in the same way that Venus does Caesar.

We have already seen that *Metamorphoses* 15.848 is a combination of motifs from the *Lock of Berenice* and the *Apotheosis of Arsinoë*. In addition, the dialogue between Arsinoe's already-deified sister Philoteris, and Charis, in fr. 228.47–51, might underlie the dialogue between Venus and Jupiter in *Metamorphoses* 15.761–842.[49]

In Callimachus, fr. 228 there is an intriguing reference to Arsinoë's spatial position (line 5):

νύμφα, σὺ μὲν ἀστερίαν ὑπ' ἄμαξαν ἤδη

[45] The Crown of Ariadne is not far from the catasterised Caesar in the topography of *Fasti* 3; Ariadne comes at *Fasti* 3.459–516, Caesar at *Fasti* 3.697–710.

[46] Pfeiffer (1949–53) vol. I fr. 228. On her deification and cult see Macurdy (1932) 126–9.

[47] Fraser (1972) vol. I, 729. On details of dating, see vol. II, 937 n. 415. On its content see vol. I, 668–9 and 729–30.

[48] Pfeiffer (1949–53) vol. I, 218.

[49] Knox (1986) 77.

She is 'beneath the starry Wagon', that is, The Bear. This is the kind of precision in the mapping of a catasterised ruler that we find in Virgil, *Georgics* 1.32–5 or Germanicus, *Phaenomena* 554–60. Likewise, we recall that, according to Pliny (*NH* 2.94), the *Sidus Iulium* appeared *sub Septentrionibus* – either 'in the northern sky' or specifically 'in the vicinity of the Bears'.[50] Caesar's catasterism begins with Arsinoë's. He added his *numen* to a part of the sky already settled by Hellenistic rulers and their accoutrements, including Arsinoë, and the Lock of Berenice, which, we remember, was *Callisto iuncta Lycaoniae* (Catullus 66.66).

Caesar too is conjunct with the Great Bear. This is confirmed by Servius Auctus *ad Aeneid* 10.272, in a passage which is part of an extended disquisition on different types of comets and their astrological effects, culminating with the beneficial effects of Caesar's comet:

est etiam alter cometes, qui vere cometes appellatur; nam comis hinc inde cingitur. hic blandus esse dicitur. qui si orientem attenderit, laetas res ipsi parti significat; si meridiem, Africae aut Aegypto gaudia; si occidentem inspexerit, terra Italia voti sui compos erit. hic dicitur apparuisse eo tempore quo est Augustus sortitus imperium: tunc denique gaudia omnibus gentibus futura sunt nuntiata. si septentrionem attenderit, prospera universa significat.

In the intricate hermeneutical baggage attached to ancient astrological interpretation of comets, they can be bad or good depending on the celestial bodies in the part of the sky where they appear.[51] Thus Servius *ad Aeneid* 10.272: if a comet accompanies the Great Bear (*Septentrionem*), it means universal good things. Hence also the comet in Pliny is *salutare terris*. Of course the comet of Caesar, as Pliny tells us, did accompany the Great Bear, and the reason for this, in addition, was

[50] For the name, see Le Boeuffle (1977) 87–9. A detailed discussion of Pliny's *sub Septentrionibus* and its parallels in other sources for the *Sidus Iulium* is to be found in Ramsey and Licht (1997) 86–90.
[51] See Domenicucci (1996) 78.

that the Septentriones were deputed in astral panegyric to host catasterised emperors.[52]

The *Sidus Iulium* shows how astrology could be manipulated for dynastic ends. Consideration of Ovidian reference to it, and of Pliny, whose report of the comet claims to emanate from 'official' readings, has shown how Ovid uses the stars and astral panegyric to align himself with the language (in the broadest sense of the word) of Julian dynasty. But the location of Caesar means that he takes his place in a world populated by the figures of myth. Some of these mythic figures – such as Capella and even the Lock of Berenice – may be consonant with the mythic elements that prevailed in the iconography and literature of the Augustan Golden Age; others can be construed otherwise.

Caesar is *sub Septentrionibus*, 'in the region of the Bears', where rulers should be; on the other hand, Catullus names the Great Bear at Poem 66.66: she was the nymph Callisto, raped by Zeus, turned into a Bear, and catasterised. The topographical and literary proximity of Caesar to Callisto may bring us from imperial panegyric into the murky world of the *Metamorphoses*, and, through the *aition* of the constellation, to the implications of the affiliation of imperial catasterism and apotheosis with star myths. Ovid might be seen as undermining the Stoic/didactic affiliation he gains from Aratus, by the affinity of the *Fasti* to the *Metamorphoses*, where the world-view is 'profoundly ... destabilised by constant mutability'.[53] The effect of this is not limited to the fragmentation and mutation of the Aratean model; it may carry political

[52] For the Bears as a location for catasterised royalty, see (apart from Callimachus, fr. 228, discussed above) Martial, *Epigrams* 4.3, with Domenicucci (1996) 173–7. The young dead son of Domitian was located near the Bears. There is numismatic evidence to this effect, namely *aurei* and *denarii* of Domitia Augusta with a baby seated on a globe, surrounded by the seven stars of Ursa Major (the *Septentriones*). A coin of Trajan from Crete shows the baby Jupiter on a globe surrounded by seven stars (schematic representation of Ursa Major) with the goat Amalthea beside him, which, because of its astral context, probably alludes to the star Capella (Domenicucci (1996) 177).

[53] Myers (1994) 25.

implications. Let us now examine the myth of Callisto and its treatments by Ovid, in order to suggest ways that the stars in the *Fasti* might pull against the prevailing range of ideas and images in the Augustan repertoire.

Callisto (*Fasti* 2.153–192, *Metamorphoses* 2.401–530)

Some scholars have questioned whether the astronomical reference to Aquarius at 145–6, joined originally to the preceding praise of Augustus as *pater patriae* (*Fasti* 2.131–40) without any dividing mark, can be read subversively.[54] The appearance of the constellation is natural for the beginning of February; not so natural is the identification of the constellation with Ganymede, the *puer Idaeus* (*Fasti* 2.145) who was snatched up to heaven to slake the desires of Jupiter.

Newlands has linked the astronomical material in *Fasti* 1.651–4 with the preceding encomiastic passage (1.649–50) in which Augustus is hailed as Jove, via Livia, who alone is 'found worthy of the bed of great Jupiter' (*sola toro magni digna reperta Iovis*).[55] In the following lines, 651–2, Ovid refers to Phoebus (the sun) passing from Capricorn to Aquarius:

> haec ubi transierint, Capricorno, Phoebe, relicto
> per iuvenis curres signa regentis aquam.

Newlands notes that the god and constellation were both associated with Augustus: 'Hence the astronomical observation can be read as forming a subtle complement to the imperial panegyric. This is not the end of the matter, however. The reference to Aquarius (652) offers the possibility of a subversive reading of this encomium.'[56]

In *Fasti* 1.650 Ovid's praise of Livia was as consort of Jove; in the astronomical reference which follows Newlands sees an allusion to one of the god's extra-marital exploits, which pro-

[54] See Barchiesi (1997) 81–3.
[55] Newlands (1995) 46–7.
[56] Newlands (1995) 46.

vides a counter effect to Ovid's praise of Jupiter-Augustus.[57] Newlands is perhaps suggesting that the move of the sun, Apollo, from Capricorn to Ganymede in *Fasti* 1.651–2 signals a move from astral encomium to astral subversion. She continues: 'Even brief astronomical notices can encode mythical allusions that serve either to complement or subvert the official concept of *Romanitas* – or indeed they may offer the possibility of both readings.'[58]

Let us explore the astral myth of Callisto, bearing in mind both sides of the argument.[59] Here we will develop our discussion of Capella in the previous chapter by looking at a star myth in which similar motifs are subjected to different treatment. This discussion will involve a reading of the same myth across Ovid's two long works, the *Fasti* and the *Metamorphoses*.

In the *Fasti*, Ovid disperses material from the same Aratean passage (*Ph.* 26–44) across several different entries. Paradoxically, such fragmentation of this particular literary model is a symptom of Ovid's calendrical structure. Writing a history of calendrical reform in *Fasti* 3, Ovid paraphrases Aratus in a polemical passage directed against the ignorance of the early Romans, *Fasti* 3.105–10:

> quis tunc aut Hyadas aut Pliadas Atlanteas
>   senserat, aut geminos esse sub axe polos,
> esse duas Arctos, quarum Cynosura petatur
>   Sidoniis, Helicen Graia carina notet,
> signaque quae longo frater percenseat anno,
>   ire per haec uno mense sororis equos?

[57] Newlands (1995) 46–7. Cf. Fantham (1995) 53–4: 'It is surely unnecessary to infer from Ovid's parallel between the father of gods and men, honouring the *pater patriae* in *Fasti* 2.131–44, that the astronomical notice which follows, identifying Aquarius as the Idaean youth (that is, Ganymede), if it is intended to reflect on Jupiter as a seducer, is also intended to reflect on Augustus.'

[58] Likewise Boyle (1997) 9, on the juxtaposition of Jupiter-Augustus, Ganymede and Callisto in *Fasti* 2: 'Throughout the *Fasti* the politics of *Roma* and *amor* are juxtaposed; imperial patriotism, militarism and public virtue with mythological desire, pleasure, joy and rape. Often the violent dimensions of the latter do not simply reflect upon but impregnate the former.'

[59] On Callisto see Newlands (1995) 157–9, and 47 nn. 53 and 54. Her treatment of the episode is tangential.

Here Ovid abbreviates *Phaenomena* 19–39, the passage of transition between Aratus' opening 'hymn to Zeus' and his first constellations,[60] at the same time injecting a note of polemic against the rusticity of the early Romans.

At *Fasti* 2.153–92, Ovid tells the Bear's myth of catasterism. This story, the pretext for which is the partial rising of Bootes (Arctophylax), seems to be deliberate *variatio* on Aratus, *Phaenomena* 19–48. Ovid tells a myth of the Bear, but a myth different from the Aratean λόγος of the nurture of Zeus (*Ph.* 30–5), which Ovid saw fit to transfer to Capella.[61] The alternative story, that of Callisto's rape and catasterism, may be seen as an extended aetiology of an Aratean motif, Ἄρκτοι, κυανέου πεφυλαγμέναι ὠκεανοῖο (*Phaenomena* 48). This motif is based on the astronomical fact that the Bears, being the most northern of all constellations, never set for an observer in the northern hemisphere, but merely chase each other in a circle around the celestial pole, almost directly overhead. Like so much Roman astronomy, this is a theme already Romanised by Virgil in *Georgics* 1: *Arctos Oceani metuentis aequore tingi* (*Georgics* 1.246). Ovid uses it as the closing motif of his tale:

> saevit adhuc canamque rogat Saturnia Tethyn
> Maenaliam tactis ne lavet Arcton aquis. (*Fasti* 2.191–2)

This is pure astral aetiology along the lines of Aratus and Eratosthenes, but here embedded in the Julian calendar.

We see that Ovid has fragmented material from one passage in Aratus, *Phaenomena* 19–48, across three astronomical entries of the *Fasti*, the story of Callisto at *Fasti* 2.153–92, the rhetorical list of constellations at *Fasti* 3.105–10, and the description of Capella (5.111–28). He has also given in *Fasti* 2 an alternative myth of catasterism to that which is told by Aratus, a device replicated in certain other astral myths.[62]

[60] *Fasti* 3.106 is parallel to *Ph.* 24, *Fasti* 3.107–8 to *Ph.* 37–39.
[61] See chapter 5, p. 130.
[62] See appendix 1.

This kind of fragmentation and mutation is what happens when Aratus is placed inside the Roman year.[63]

Ovid tells the tale of Callisto in the *Fasti* and the *Metamorphoses*. In both cases, the mythical material Ovid adds diverges widely from Aratus' version of the Bears. In Aratus and associated texts, the Bears, like Capella, are the nurses of the baby Zeus on Crete: the scholia to Germanicus, for example, have *Aratus Cynosuram et Helicen Cretenses Iovis nutrices fuisse dicit, ob quod sunt caelesti honore donatae.*[64] Although Aratus' tale is set in Crete, εἰ ἐτεὸν δή in line 30 intimates, with characteristic economy, that there may be other traditions. Aratus does not elaborate, but his readers may adduce Callimachus, *Hymn to Zeus* 6–8:

Ζεῦ, σὲ μὲν Ἰδαίοισιν ἐν οὔρεσί φασι γενέσθαι,
Ζεῦ, σὲ δ' ἐν Ἀρκαδίῃ· πότεροι, πάτερ, ἐψεύσαντο;
'Κρῆτες ἀεὶ ψεῦσται.'

O Zeus, some say that thou wert born on the hills of Ida; others, O Zeus, say in Arcadia; did these or those, O Father, lie? 'Cretans are ever liars'.

We saw in chapter 5 that there are in fact two traditions of the 'Youth of Zeus' Cycle (to which the Bears belong in Aratus and Callimachus), one set in Crete, one in Arcadia; Callimachus in his *Hymn to Zeus* has the latter setting, Aratus the former.

In crafting the *aition* of the Bear, the first choice Ovid would have made was to use a version of the myth in which the bears were *ferae* (see for example Germanicus, *Ph.* 28) rather than wagons.[65] His next choice would have been to

[63] It is significant that Ovid should single out the Bears, since in Aratus the Arktoi are the first (northernmost) constellation. As such, they become the index for all other constellations, the point around which the reader must orient himself, just as the sailor uses them as a fixed point for navigational star-gazing. Their body parts act as a measure of the spatial position of other constellations throughout Aratus' poem (see *Ph.* 45–60, 137–46, 182–5, 227). Ovid has chosen to disperse material from Aratus' description of those very constellations which provide a basis for the perception of all others in the *Phaenomena*. Is he aware of their initiatory status (and etymology) in the *Phaenomena*, which begins (the verb is ἀρχεῖν) with the Ἄρκτοι? Could one see a bilingual etymology in ***prior** est quam dicimus **Arcton*** (*Fasti* 2.189)?

[64] Robert (1878) 58.

[65] *Fasti* 2.179. See also *Tristia* 4.3.1, *magna minorque ferae*.

reject the version in which the Bears were the nurses of Zeus, found in Aratus and Callimachus, in favour of the tale of Callisto's rape found in Eratosthenes, Hyginus, and the scholia on Aratus.[66] He retained Callimachus' Arcadian setting in *Metamorphoses* 2.405 and *Fasti* 2.192, in which Zeus was born on Mount Lycaeon, and rejected Aratus' Cretan one, which appears in the myth of Capella instead. But while the setting here is the same as that of Callimachus, the tale Ovid tells is different from the 'Youth of Zeus' cycle of either Callimachus or Aratus.

In *Fasti* 2, the story of the Bear (Callisto) is presented as part of the *aition* for the constellation Arctophylax, the Bearward (Ovid latinises it as *custos Ursae* at *Fasti* 2.153). The story is as follows. Callisto was part of the woodland band that follows Diana (155–6). She swore that she would guard her virginity always, and in return, Diana said that she would remain *princeps* among her comrades (157–60). She would have kept her vows, but for the fact she was beautiful: she guarded against mortals, but her downfall came from Jove (*de Iove crimen habet*, 162). Her guilt, in the form of her tumescent womb, was discovered in due course, and she was driven out of Diana's throng and away from the sacred waters in which they bathed (163–74). When ten lunations had passed, she became a mother (175–6). Juno, furious at her rival, changed her form (*formam mutatque puellae*, 177). Juno's *paelex* was now a *fera* (179), and as a bear, she who was recently desired by Jupiter wandered the woods, until she encountered her son, who was now fifteen years old (181–4). She attempted (in vain, as do the characters in Ovid's *Metamorphoses*) to speak, and the *puer ignarus* would have fixed her

[66] For this version of the tale, see the Aratean scholia *ad Ph.* 27, Maass (1898) 344 (possibly following Hesiod, *Astronomia*, Rzach (1913) fr. 181/Merkelbach and West (1967) fr. 163). Apollodorus, *Bibl.* 3.8.2 gives a similar version of the tale. See also Eratosthenes, *Catast.* 1 and 2, Robert (1878) 50–3 and Robert (1878) 56–9; Hyginus, *Astr.* 2.1, Viré (1992) 15–17 (multiple versions); Hyginus, *Fabulae* 177, Marshall (1993) 147–8, with Courtney (1993) 457–8; Germanicus, *Ph.* 24–38 with Gain (1976) *ad loc.*, scholia on Germanicus 58, 64. Kidd (1997) *ad Ph.* 26–44 lists the various myths of the Bears.

with his spear, had they not been snatched – just in time – into the heavenly realm (185–8). The configuration of the Bear and Arctophylax in the heavens represents Callisto and Arcas as they were just before being snatched up to heaven, one pursuing the other. As she was banned from the waters in which she was washing when the infringement of her vow of chastity was discovered by Diana, so in her astral state Callisto does not bathe in Ocean.

This is a bare-bones rendering of the astronomical aition of the Bear: the story is told in a straightforward form, and does double duty as an *aition* for the celestial cartography of the Bear and the Bear-ward, and for the fact that the circumpolar stars do not set. Callisto in the *Fasti* has as her literary background two Hellenistic models, Aratus and Callimachus. At *Fasti* 2.189–90, Ovid gives us Aratean celestial cartography, at 191–2 astral aetiology:

> signa propinqua micant: prior est, quam dicimus Arcton,
> Arctophylax formam terga sequentis habet.
> saevit adhuc canamque rogat Saturnia Tethyn
> Maenaliam tactis ne lavet Arcton aquis.

We remember that Catullus' Lock of Berenice was near Arctophylax (Poem 66.67–8), whose late setting had formed a *topos* in poetry since Aratus. We are reminded of Catullus too by Callisto's patronymic *Lycaonia* (*Fasti* 2.173). In Catullus 66.66, the Lock of Berenice was *Callisto iuncta Lycaoniae*. The epithet in Ovid serves to place the episode in Arcadia – the Callimachean rather than the Aratean setting (note Λυκαονίης ἄρκτοιο at Callimachus, *Hymn* 1.41).[67] As an erotic tale, the myth of Callisto is more closely linked to Callimachus and the *Lock of Berenice* than to Aratus; *eros*, although a negative force in *Fasti* 2.153–92, is the ultimate cause of Callisto's catasterism, as it was in its positive manifestation for that of the Lock.

We should not forget that Caesar and the Lock also have a

[67] Ovid deploys the patronymic at *Fasti* 2.173 (*Lycaoni*), 3.793 (*Lycaoniam*), and 6.235 (*Lycaona*, of Bootes). At *Met.* 2.496 Arcas is *Lycaoniae proles . . . parentis.*

lot in common. Caesar and Callisto in the *Fasti* also have things in common: Caesar at *Fasti* 3.160 is heading for *nec … ignotas domos*, the same *superas … domos* that Callisto and Arcas had gone to at *Fasti* 2.188. Vesta says of Caesar at *Fasti* 3.701 *ipsa virum rapui*; at *Fasti* 2.188, Callisto and Arcas are *raptus uterque*.

The gentle irony present in the catasterism of the Lock, as we saw it in Callimachus and Catullus, is developed by Ovid in his tale of Callisto into a point of tension – is catasterism a punishment or a reward? Might this affect how we interpret the material which surrounds the episode of Callisto, particularly in relation to the *topos* of Augustus as Jupiter which we examined in the previous chapter? Callisto in the *Fasti* is preceded by a passage in which Ovid hails Augustus as *Pater Patriae* on the anniversary of his accession to that title. Ovid exploits the same Jupiter/Augustus correlation as we have seen in Horace *Odes* 1.12 or at the end of the *Metamorphoses* in *Fasti* 2.127–32:

sancte pater patriae, tibi plebs, tibi curia nomen
hoc dedit, hoc dedimus nos tibi nomen, eques.
res tamen ante dedit: sero quoque vera tulisti
nomina, iam pridem tu pater orbis eras.
hoc tu per terras, quod in aethere Iuppiter alto,
nomen habes: hominum tu pater, ille deum.

In between the episode which celebrates Augustus as *Pater Patriae*, and the story of Callisto at *Fasti* 2.153ff., we have the reference to the rising of the *puer Idaeus*, *Fasti* 2.145–6:

iam puer Idaeus media tenus eminet alvo,
et liquidas mixto nectare fundit aquas.

The *puer Idaeus* of line 145 is Ganymede. The father of the gods (the correlative of Augustus as father of his country) is an erotic predator, since he snatched Ganymede up to heaven. This is followed by another of Jupiter's catasterisms – that of Callisto.

While we may not wish to construct an out-and-out subversive reading, it is nonetheless interesting to consider the progression of this part of *Fasti* 2 in the light of the theme of power.[68] Jupiter is *omnipotens*, and exercises that power in manifold ways. In the *Fasti*, Ovid's only protest against Jupiter's injustice is brief: *quid facis? invito est pectore passa Iovem* – 'What are you doing? – She suffered Jupiter against her will' (*Fasti* 2.178). We shall see the more developed form of the same theme – that of *arbitrary* power – in the *Metamorphoses*.

Ovid presents Callisto in the *Fasti* as a myth of metamorphosis: note *formam mutatque puellae, Fasti* 2.177. This ties her in with the *Metamorphoses*. The myth of Callisto is told at *Metamorphoses* 2.401–530. As in the *Fasti*, the tale combines astrothesis with astral aetiology. However, in the *Metamorphoses* there is a greater element of cosmographic parody. The idea of *sidera propinqua micant*, *Fasti* 2.189, is found in more developed form in the celestial mapping at *Metamorphoses* 2.505–7:

> arcuit omnipotens pariterque ipsosque nefasque
> sustulit et pariter raptos per inania vento
> imposuit caelo vicinaque sidera fecit.

In both the *Metamorphoses* and the *Fasti* there is a play on the kind of pinpointing of celestial location for catasterised characters we have seen in Catullus' *Lock* or Virgil's description of Octavian's celestial location. This sort of thing is fully in the Aratean tradition, but also has a history as part of astral encomium.

The language of catasterism does not itself escape unscathed in the *Metamorphoses*. When Jupiter raises Callisto and Arcas to heaven at *Metamorphoses* 2.505–6, one could be excused for thinking he is getting rid of the evidence of his adultery: *pariterque ipsosque nefasque sustulit*. But the verb *tollo* is also one that is used to describe 'straightforward' catasterism. When at *DND* 2.62 men 'raise their benefactors to the sky', the verb is *tollo*: *suscepit autem vita hominum consuetudoque communis ut beneficiis excellentis viros in caelum fama ac voluntate tollerent.* The same verb is used of Romulus'

[68] A *caveat* from Kennedy (1992) 35: 'Important as the term is, it is equally important to be aware of the dangers of integrating, or collapsing, everything into a single master discourse, the discourse of "power".'

apotheosis in Ennius' *Annales*,[69] quoted by Ovid in *Metamorphoses* 14.814 and *Fasti* 2.487, *unus erit quem tu tolles in caerula caeli.*[70]

Imposuit caelo in *Metamorphoses* 2.507 may echo one of the fragments of Ovid's own *Phaenomena*: *tot numero talique deus simulacra figura | imposuit caelo . . .* (quoted by Lactantius at *Inst.* 2.5.24). In the *Phaenomena*, the expression refers to the action of the demiurge in setting out the configuration of the fixed stars which the poet maps. In the *Metamorphoses*, the imposition of Callisto on the heavens is the solution to impending matricide.

Raptus (*Met.* 2.506, *Fasti* 2.188) also belongs to the terminology of serious catasterism. Ovid gives the participle to Hercules at his apotheosis, *Metamorphoses* 9.271–2:

> quem pater omnipotens inter cava nubila raptum
> quadriiugo curru radiantibus intulit astris.

At Manilius, *Astronomica* 2.29 Callisto is described as *raptam Lycaone natam*. This passage of Manilius gives us pause. Let us consider it for a moment. At this point in the *Astronomica*, Manilius justifies his choice of writing indigestible technical astrology rather than tractable and familiar astral aetiology:

> astrorum quidam varias dixere figuras,
> signaque diffuso passim labentia caelo
> in proprium cuiusque genus causasque tulere;
> Persea et Andromedan poena matremque dolentem
> solventemque patrem, raptamque Lycaone natam,
> officioque Iovis Cynosuram, lacte Capellam
> et furto Cycnum, pietate ad sidera ductam
> Erigonen ictuque Nepam spolioque Leonem
> et morsu Cancrum, Pisces Cythereide versa,
> Lanigerum victo ducentem sidera ponto,
> ceteraque ex variis pendentia casibus astra
> aethera per summum voluerunt fixa revolvi.
> quorum carminibus nihil est nisi fabula caelum
> terraque composuit mundum quae pendet ab illo. (*Astronomica* 2.25–38)

[69] *Annales* 1.54–5 ed. Skutsch (1985).

[70] In the natural sequence of reading the *Fasti*, Romulus would be encountered after the Callisto episode. What effect does Callisto have on Romulus, especially when Romulus is considered as a precedent for Augustus?

Here we have, among others, our old friend Capella, raised to the stars on account of her *lac* (line 30). This is the context for Callisto, the *raptam Lycaone natam*. The meaning of the participle in this context must be closer to 'raped' than 'snatched (up to the stars)'. Callisto's rape stands alongside the *officium* of the Great Bear (Cynosura[71]) and the *lac* of Capella as a cause for catasterism. Callisto found her way to the stars by rape rather than by *virtus*. Line 31 ridicules ideas of catasterism as a reward for *pietas* (in this case that of Virgo). *Pietas*, as we saw it in Cicero, *Republic* 6.15–16, is now placed on an equal footing with Callisto's rape, Cancer's bite, and so on.

For Manilius star myths are paradoxical: they superimpose the earth on the heavens (lines 37–8); in reality it is the heavens after which the earth is modelled:

> hic igitur deus et ratio, quae cuncta gubernat,
> ducit ab aetheriis terrena animalia signis (*Astronomica* 2.82–3)

Star myths are in fact a reversal of the natural order.[72]

Consider in this light Juno's request to Tethys, her former

[71] In most sources, the mythology of the two Bears is confused. In Aratus, they are both the nurses of Zeus. Manilius separates them, making Cynosura the nurse of Zeus and Helice Callisto.

[72] *nihil est nisi fabula caelum* (*Ast.* 2.37) reminds us of Cicero, *DND* 2.63–70, where the Olympian pantheon supplies poets with tales which are false unless expounded allegorically: *alia quoque ex ratione et quidem physica magna fluxit multitudo deorum, qui induti specie humana* ***fabulas poetis suppeditaverunt***, *hominum autem vitam superstitione omni referserunt ... nam vetus haec opinio Graeciam opplevit, esse exsectum Caelum a filio Saturno, vinctum autem Saturnum ipsum a filio Iove; physica ratio non inelegans inclusa est in impias fabulas ... videtisne igitur ut a physicis rebus bene atque utiliter inventis tracta ratio sit ad commenticios et fictos deos?* ('Another line of thought which derives from the world of nature has given rise to numerous gods. These have been clothed in human form and have provided fables for poets, cramming our lives with every kind of superstition ... To offer an example: there was an ancient belief pervading Greece that Caelus was mutilated by his son Saturn, who was himself clapped in irons by his son Jupiter. Behind these sacrilegious fables lies a scientific explanation which is quite sophisticated ... So do you now realise how the admirable and useful discoveries about the natural world have resulted in the creation of false and fictitious deities?') The Ovidian technique, particularly in the *Metamorphoses*, is the opposite of the allegorical method: a de-rationalisation or re-mythologisation of the gods. This runs counter to Manilius and Lucan. At the end of Manilius 4, men had the power to make gods (see above, p. 145). At *Pharsalia* 7.454–9, Lucan makes explicit the fallacy of catasterism: the creation of gods is a debasement in the divine order (below, p. 190).

nurse, to prevent the constellation of the Bear from bathing in Ocean:

'Quaeritis, aetheriis quare regina deorum
sedibus hic adsim? pro me tenet altera caelum.
mentior, obscurum nisi nox cum fecerit orbem,
nuper honoratas summo, mea volnera, caelo
videritis stellas illic, ubi circulus axem
ultimus extremum spatioque brevissimus ambit.
est vero cur quis Iunonem laedere nolit
offensamque tremat, quae prosum sola nocendo?
o ego quantum egi! quam vasta potentia nostra est!
esse hominem vetui: facta est dea. sic ego poenas
sontibus inpono, sic est mea magna potestas!' (*Metamorphoses* 2.512–22)

These lines of the *Metamorphoses* correspond to the cartography of *Fasti* 2.189–90 and the astral aetiology of *Fasti* 2.191–2. Note particularly the parody of cosmography at *Metamorphoses* 2.516–17. Here we see transferred to an erotic context the technical language of didactic astronomy. We may compare Manilius 1.589–90, describing the Arctic circle:

unus ab his superest extremo proximus axi
circulus, austrinas qui stringit et obsidet Arctos.

The Celestial Circles described by Manilius as part of his serious Aratean cartography are in Ovid the arena for an erotic tale. Note the paradox in *Metamorphoses* 2.515–16, where the *nuper honoratas stellas* are described by Juno as *mea volnera*.[73] The crunch comes at 521: *esse hominem vetui: facta est dea*!

Ovid's inversion of the principles of catasterism is clearest at *Metamorphoses* 2.527–30, Juno's *peroratio*:

'at vos si laesae tangit contemptus alumnae,
gurgite caeruleo Septem prohibete triones,
sideraque in caelo, stupri mercede, recepta
pellite, ne puro tingatur in aequore paelex'.

In these lines of the *Metamorphoses* the idea of catasterism is ironically reversed. It is *stupri mercede* that carries the weight

[73] *Volnera* in the elegiac sense: for the usage, compare *Fasti* 4.5–6, *'num vetus in molli pectore volnus habes?' | 'scis, dea,' respondi, 'de volnere'.*

of the irony. Rather than being catasterised for some *virtus* or *officium*, Callisto, in Juno's eyes, is unjustly rewarded for her *stuprum*.

Catasterism is also eroticised. Bömer's parallels for the erotic motifs in the Callisto episode of the *Metamorphoses* reveal the extent to which the *sermo amatorius* permeates this passage.[74] Callisto gives us an identification of erotic subject matter and diction with the stars.

The theme of power is particularly highly developed in *Metamorphoses* 2. The passage begins *at pater omnipotens* (401), picked up by *arcuit omnipotens* in 505; note also *potentia* (416, 520) and *potestas* (522). This tale in the *Metamorphoses* is about characters vying for erotic power. The panegyrical formula of *maius* with the ablative of comparison is incorporated in the erotic context. In *Metamorphoses* 2.429, Callisto tells the false Diana (really Jupiter in disguise) that, in her opinion, she is 'greater than Jupiter, even if he himself were to hear': *audiat ipse licet, maius Iove*.[75] At *Metamorphoses* 2.430, Jupiter-in-disguise rejoices to hear himself preferred to himself, *sibi praeferri se gaudet*. The reader of *Metamorphoses* 15.850–1 (of Julius Caesar compared to Augustus), *natique videns bene facta fatetur | esse suis maiora et vinci gaudet ab illo*, might possibly recall Jupiter's reaction. The fact that Caesar's reaction to Augustus' greater deeds (*maiora*) is like Jupiter's on deceiving Callisto might seem worrying in the later panegyrical context. *Maius* with the ablative of comparison can, if pushed, show us the negative side of power.

It is ironic that, in *Metamorphoses* 2.436–8, the strength of Jupiter will indeed prove greater (*maior*) than that of Callisto, and this is what results in her fall from virtue, and rise to the stars:

> illa quidem pugnat; sed quem superare puella,
> quisve Iovem poterat? superum petit aethera victor
> Iuppiter . . .

[74] Bömer (1969–86) *ad loc*. On erotic contrasts between the *Fasti* and the *Metamorphoses* versions of Callisto, see Newlands (1995) 157.

[75] Compare Horace, *Odes* 1.12.19–20, *proximos illi (Iovi) tamen occupavit | Pallas honores*.

Victor Iuppiter here is the god victorious in his scurrilous enterprise. But *Victor Iuppiter* is also an official by-name of the Roman state god, as at *Fasti* 4.621–2:

> occupat Apriles Idus cognomine Victor
> Iuppiter: hac illi sunt data templa die.

We may recall the *Iuppiter invictus* of *Fasti* 5.126, a figure for Augustus victorious at Actium.

In the Callisto episode of the *Metamorphoses,* we have the ironic treatment of Jupiter as *pater omnipotens*; at *Fasti* 2.119–44 the panegyrical treatment of Augustus as *pater patriae*, followed by Ganymede and Callisto. Should Ovid's treatment of the power motif in the *Metamorphoses*, and to a lesser extent in the Callisto episode of the *Fasti*, affect our reading of the panegyric? If Augustus is Jupiter, the god who is responsible for the catasterism of Capella,[76] Jupiter is also responsible for the rape and catasterism of Callisto. Augustus was also, we remember, responsible for Caesar's catasterism.

Most importantly, should the negative catasterism of Callisto affect the way we approach imperial catasterism, especially given the geographical proximity of the *Sidus Iulium* and Callisto? Was there for the Roman reader a possibility of confusion between astral myth and astral encomium? Especially when new stars are now a result of arbitrary *vis*, perpetrated by the Father of Gods and Men.

How much should we allow Ovid's fuller treatment of the myth of Callisto in *Metamorphoses* 2, with its greater development of the theme of arbitrary power, to colour our reading of the story in *Fasti* 2? We know that the two works were written together. They are both in some sense aetiological works, and are mentioned by their author in the same context at *Tristia* 2.549–56. In addition, the similarities between the two works are most apparent in star myths. We have noted how Callisto in the *Fasti* is presented as a myth of metamorphosis; Ariadne in the *Fasti* is also described as *mutata* (*Fasti* 3.512). It is possible to argue that all star myths in the *Fasti*

[76] And the deification of Romulus, *Fasti* 2.475–512.

are myths of metamorphosis, even when the verb *mutare* is not explicitly present. To my mind a case can be made for reading the story of Callisto across Ovid's two works. Following Newlands, one might find support for a reading of Callisto as subverting comparisons of Augustus with Jupiter earlier in the poem. Equally, Callisto may influence our reading of Caesar's catasterism. By implication, imperial catasterism is connected with metamorphosis.

The connection between imperial apotheosis and metamorphosis might also be expressed by a couplet which stands as the first two lines of '*Fasti* 7' in some of the manuscripts:[77]

> tu quoque mutati causas et nomina mensis
> a te qui canitur, maxime Caesar, habes.

Servius Auctus says (*ad Georgics* 1.43): *Quintilis et Sextilis mutati sunt postea in honorem Iulii Caesaris et Augusti, unde sunt Iulius et Augustus. sic Ovidius in Fastis.* July and August are metamorphosed months (hence *mutati ... mensis*); the Caesars are the key to their aetiology and etymology (*causas et nomina*). Julius Caesar, to whom July now belongs, has become the agent of metamorphosis through the politics of calendrical reform. Caesar is metamorphosed himself, into a star, by his son Augustus. The Julians are both the agents and the beneficiaries of metamorphosis, and there are certain dangers inherent in this. These dangers can come out in Ovid's text by the closeness of myths of catasterism to imperial apotheosis.

[77] See Alton, Wormell and Courtney (1988) v.

EPILOGUE

Is the impulse which finds inspiration in both cosmography and myths of metamorphosis counter to the panegyrical spirit of the *Fasti*? Callimachus and Catullus showed, in the *Lock of Berenice*, that a gentle irony at least is not out of place in encomium.[1] It may be in that literary inheritance that the answer lies. Callimachus' praise of the Ptolemies in the *Coma Berenices*, which, as Philip Hardie says, 'reveals a deliberately oblique, even tongue-in-cheek, approach to another area where cosmology was at the time being re-integrated into more narrowly human concerns, namely astral apotheosis, particularly as claimed for the dead ruler',[2] underlies Ovid's references to the catasterism of Caesar, as we have seen in the preceding discussion. Following Callimachus, it was right for Roman poets like Ovid to treat imperial catasterism with a light touch. The conclusion of the *Metamorphoses* functions as part of a network of allusion, as well as being panegyric.

Lucan picks up the literary motif of imperial catasterism in his address to Nero at the beginning of the *Pharsalia*, changing Virgil's map at the beginning of *Georgics* I in a way that can exemplify the potential slide of catasterism towards the ridiculous:

te, cum statione peracta
astra petes serus, praelati regia caeli
excipiet gaudente polo: seu sceptra tenere,
seu te flammigeros Phoebi conscendere currus,
telluremque nihil mutato sole timentem
igne vago lustrare iuvet, tibi numine ab omni

[1] Barchiesi (1997) 82 points out that we are not bound to think that political *laudes* and playfulness are incompatible.

[2] Hardie (1986) 9.

cedetur, iurisque tui natura relinquet,
quis deus esse velis, ubi regnum ponere mundi.
sed neque in arctoo sedem tibi legeris orbe,
nec polus aversi calidus qua vergitur austri,
unde tuam videas obliquo sidere Romam.
aetheris inmensi partem si presseris unam,
sentiet axis onus. librati pondera caeli
orbe tene medio; pars aetheris illa sereni
tota vacet, nullaeque obstent a Caesare nubes. (*Pharsalia* 1.45–59)

When your watch on earth is over and you seek the stars at last, the celestial palace you prefer will welcome you, and the sky will be glad. Whether you choose to wield Jove's sceptre, or to mount the fiery chariot of Phoebus and circle earth with your moving flame – earth unterrified by the transference of the sun; every god will give place to you, and Nature will leave it to you to determine what deity you wish to be, and where to establish your universal throne. But choose not your seat either in the Northern region or where the sultry sky of the opposing South sinks down: from these quarters your light would look aslant at your city of Rome. If you lean on any one part of boundless space, the axle of the sphere will be weighed down; maintain therefore the equipoise of heaven by remaining at the centre of the system. May that region of the sky be bright and clear, and may no clouds obstruct our view of Caesar![3]

Lucan responds to Virgil's invocation of Octavian at the beginning of the *Georgics* and Ovid's concluding prayer in the *Metamorphoses* by taking the language of cosmography and pushing it over the edge. The balance of the Eudoxan centripetal universe as we saw it at *Fasti* 6.269–76 may not stand the weight.

For Domenicucci, this is merely *literary* polemic: a remapping of the sky in response to Virgil's invocation of Octavian. He reads Lucan's proem as praise: 'Lucan's praise of Nero is probably devoid of ironic intent.'[4] Hinds in his recent book gives a more subtle reading, taking Lucan's invocation of Nero as 'a patent parody of encomiastic rhetoric, and hence fully consistent with Lucan's attitude to Caesarism late in the poem'.[5] Hinds points out that the best commentary on Lucan's attitude may be the denunciation of apotheosis later in the poem (*Pharsalia* 7.454–9):

[3] Trans. Duff (1977). [4] Domenicucci (1996) 154. [5] Hinds (1998) 87–8.

mortalia nulli
sunt curata deo. cladis tamen huius habemus
vindictam, quantam terris dare numina fas est:
bella pares superis facient civilia divos;
fulminibus manes radiisque ornabit et astris
inque deum templis iurabit Romanus per umbras.

Man's destiny has never been watched over by any god. Yet for this disaster we have revenge, so far as gods may give satisfaction to mortals: civil war shall make dead Caesars the peers of gods above; and Rome shall deck out dead men with thunderbolts and haloes and constellations, and in the temples of the gods shall swear by ghosts.

For Hinds, a disillusioned Lucan denies Stoic providence: *mortalia nulli sunt curata deo*. It is civil war that will create gods equal to the ones above. Romans will deck their civil-war dead with stars and thunderbolts. Military achievements are the way to catasterism; but catasterism is an illusion. Hinds comments, 'This is a tale of debasement in the divine order': a black picture.

Yet the scholia appear to take the *laudes Neronis* as both praise, and a joke. On 1.52, a scholiast says *quis deus esse velis: adulatur Lucanus Neroni divinos ei promittens honores sicut et Virgilius Augusto 'an deus inmensi venias maris'*. Lucan praises Nero by promising him the same honours as Virgil had Augustus. At the same time, the scholiast registers a series of jokes:

1.57, sentiet axis onus – 'iocatus est. dicitur enim Nero obeso fuisse corpore.'
1.58, orbe tene medio – 'adlusit ad herniam eius.'
1.59, nullaeque obstent a Caesare nubes – 'ut placidus sis. sed adlusit ad calvitiem.'

Ridiculous as these explanations may be, it is still possible to get something out of them by noting the term the scholiast chooses. *Ad-ludo* is how the scholiast describes what Lucan is doing: he 'alludes to' Nero's physical defects (however implausible the explanations may seem). At the same time, the verb is apposite, since Lucan 'alludes to' Virgil, and 'plays on' the tradition. It seems out of place to discuss Lucan's sincerity: he plays with the *topoi* of catasterism. The game gives us pleasure.

Literary allusion can be loaded with political meaning. The value of imperial catasterism under Augustus may have given Ovid a reason which was more than purely poetic to read the *Phaenomena* of Aratus. By including the stars in a calendrical format which did not necessarily provide a place for them, Ovid orientates himself in the sphere of astral monarchy; appropriation of Aratus, a model at once poetic and (implicitly) monarchical, gave him a convenient form in which to do this.

Yet the further nexus we have seen between the *Fasti* and *Metamorphoses* plunges Ovid's Augustan *Phaenomena* into a universe of flux incompatible with the unified and teleological universe, both of Aratus' *Phaenomena*, when read as a Stoic poem, and of the Principate. The poet may equally well have chosen to read the *Phaenomena* as a source for myths of astral metamorphosis, which might form a way of linking his astronomy in the *Fasti* with the universe of his other long poem. Whatever the case, the consideration of the *Phaenomena*, the *Fasti* and the *Metamorphoses* together, against the frame of the Augustan régime, has shown us that the relationship between power and astronomy carries both positive and negative potential.

A reading of the *Fasti* through its stars has placed it in the intellectual and political setting of the late Augustan Principate, and has shown how the poem may both subscribe to, and pull against, world empire on the Alexander model. Aratus was a key text in the articulation of the celestial aspect of world rule, both in the Hellenistic age, and, to a limited extent, in the Roman republic. Ovid, therefore, cannot use the stars to disengage one register of his work from its political setting, but on the contrary exploits their twofold potential against the Augustan political background.[6]

Ovid's *Fasti* is a double metamorphosis: of Aratus, and of the Roman appropriation of the Aratean stars in the service of astral monarchy. The fragmentation of material from Aratus' text across the *Fasti*, and therefore the Roman year,

[6] *Pace* Martin (1985).

changes Aratus, in that his poem is now located on the margins of the Augustan régime, articulated through the festivals of the Julian calendar; at the same time, this is not entirely in harmony with the Augustan appropriation of the stars as part of the paraphernalia of Hellenistic rulership, since Aratean material is selected and organised to emphasise the closeness of imperial catasterism to astral myth of other kinds, and is fragmented by the Julian calendrical system which purported to *unify* time.

APPENDIX I: ARATEAN ECHOES IN THE *FASTI*

This Appendix provides a list of Ovid's constellations, in order of their first appearance in the *Fasti* (with the exception of Capella and the Bears, studied in detail elsewhere[1]), noting any similarities with Aratus. The list is comprehensive in that it collects all of the constellations in the *Fasti* and all of the Aratean references to these constellations; it is not comprehensive in the sense of isolating sources for the non-Aratean elements in Ovid's astronomical entries. Nor is it intended to 'correct' references in a technical sense, as Ideler (1825) did, but to assist in making a detailed comparison between Ovid and Aratus, a comparison designed to shed light on the relationship which scholars have postulated between the two poets.

The results of detailed study of Ovid's constellations in the light of Aratean influence are somewhat mixed. On the one hand, where influence may be discerned it is often very clear, as in the case of the Bears, Capella, Orion and the Pleiades (Capella and the Bears have been discussed in chapters 5 and 6, the Pleiades and Orion are numbers 8 and 19 below). In addition, Ovid may follow the earlier poet in choosing constellations about which to tell extended myths, even when drawing on contrasting mythographical material, as, again, in the instance of the Bears, whose tale we have studied in chapter 6. Constellations spatially or temporally juxtaposed in Aratus may be used as 'props' in a single myth in the *Fasti*, often without specifying the status of some of the elements in such a myth as independent constellations (possible examples of this are Orion, and the Centaur, number 22 below). Thus the learned reader gains pleasure from the *minutiae* of Ovid's games with his Aratean model.

On the other hand, the number of Ovidian constellations which display definite Aratean influence is smaller than one might expect: nine or ten out of twenty-five. It is obvious that Ovid intends the reader to recall the *Phaenomena* at certain points in the *Fasti*, and perhaps to bear Aratus' work in mind, in some wider sense, throughout the poem. To enumerate Ovid's repetition of Aratean motifs in the *Fasti* is only partially to explain the relationship between the two poets. Such a relationship is not directly quantifiable. My list of constellations has therefore been appended to the main discussion, which takes as its premise the interplay between Aratus' *Phaenomena* and Ovid's *Fasti* on a broader level.

[1] Above, pp. 127–53, 174–87.

1. Cancer: *Fasti* 1.311–14, 6.725–8 / *Ph.* 147, 446, 491–500, 539, 545, 569–91, 893, 996. In both poets the references are brief, Ovid's temporal, Aratus' spatial. Both mention the Crab as an indicator of the summer solstice, Ovid allusively, Aratus overtly. At *Fasti* 6.727, *Cancri signa rubescunt*; at *Phaenomena* 499–500, speaking of the Tropic of Cancer, Aratus says, 'The summer solstices are on it. This circle is fixed in the north in the latitude of the Crab.' This is the only similarity between the two. Ovid's adjective at *Fasti* 1.313, *octipes,* is designed to recall Roman aetiology, since it is found elsewhere only at Propertius 4.1.150.[2]

2. Lyre: *Fasti* 1.315–16, 653–4, 2.73–8, 5.415–16 / *Ph.* 268–74, 597, 615, 674.[3] In Ovid all references are brief, with a descriptive epithet attached to *Lyra* only once (*curva, Fasti* 5.415). In Aratus the Lyre is the constellation of Hermes: Λύρη ... Κυλληναίη (597), Ἑρμαίη ... Λύρη (674). There is no direct similarity between the two.

3. Dolphin: *Fasti* 1.457–8, 2.79–118, 6.469–72, 720 / *Ph.* 316–18, 597–8. At *Phaenomena* 597–8, Aratus notes the synchronic setting of the Lyre, the Dolphin and the Arrow. Ovid refers to two of these constellations one after the other (*Fasti* 2.73–8, the Lyre, *Fasti* 2.79–118, the Dolphin). As well as this, the motif of the Lyre carries over into the story of the Dolphin, where it is no longer a constellation but a prop in the story:

> illa nocte aliquis, tollens ad sidera voltum,
> dicet 'ubi est hodie quae **Lyra** fulsit heri?' (*Fasti* 2.75–6)
>
> quem modo caelatum stellis Delphina videbas,
> is fugiet visus nocte sequente tuos,
> seu fuit occultis felix in amoribus index,[4]
> Lesbida cum domino seu tulit ille **lyram**. (*Fasti* 2.79–82)

The answer to the question in 75–6 – 'Where is the lyre?' – is that, although the constellation has set, the lyre is now embedded in the story of Arion. Ovid tells the myth of Arion; Aratus does not tell a myth of catasterism but provides a longer than usual description of the Dolphin's configuration at *Phaenomena* 316–18. Ovid may be following Aratus in awarding some prominence to this bright constellation, while diverging from him in choosing to recount the myth.

[2] See above, pp. 30–4. The astronomical date is incorrect: Ovid has given rising for setting (Ideler (1825) 155–6).

[3] The date Ovid gives for the rising of the Lyre in *Fasti* 1 is perhaps an Alexandrian calculation which found its way into Caesar's calendar and thence to Ovid (Ideler (1825) 144–6).

[4] The alternative version of the myth, alluded to here by Ovid, is that the Dolphin was accessory to the love affair of Poseidon and Amphitrite (see Frazer (1929) *ad loc.*).

4. Capricorn appears only once in the *Fasti*, at 1.651. Ovid's reference, of the passing of the sun from one zodiacal sign into another, is too brief to detect any similarity with Aratus' numerous mentions of the constellation Aegoceros (*Ph.* 284–99, 316, 386, 501, 538, 547, 683–92, 702). Capricorn is the sign of the winter solstice; it was also Augustus' conception-sign.[5]

5. Aquarius (Hydrochoüs): *Fasti* 1.651–2, 2.145–6, 453–8 / *Ph.* 283–99, 389–401, 502, 548, 693. The end of the sailing season on 15 February is marked by Ovid as follows:

> orta dies fuerit, tu desine credere ventis;
> perdidit illius temporis aura fidem.
> flamina non constant, et sex reserata diebus
> carceris Aeolii ianua lata patet.
> iam levis obliqua subsedit Aquarius urna:
> proximus aetherios excipe, Piscis, equos. (*Fasti* 2.453–8)

If *tu* in line 453 is a sailor, Ovid can be seen as maintaining here the Aratean fiction, deriving ultimately from Hesiod, of presenting poetic stars as a useful navigational tool. Aratus also addresses his sailor in the second person singular:

> οὔτε κεν ἠοῖ
> πολλὴν πειρήνειας, ἐπεὶ ταχινώταταί εἰσιν,
> οὔτ᾽ ἂν τοι νυκτὸς πεφοβημένῳ ἐγγύθεν ἠὼς
> ἔλθοι καὶ μάλα πολλὰ βοωμένῳ. (*Phaenomena* 288–91)

Neither by day can you make much headway, for the days pass most swiftly then, nor in your terror by night will the dawn come soon, however much you cry out.

Phaenomena 283–99 is something of a purple passage, in which Aratus notes the spatial proximity of Pisces, Hydrochoüs and Aegoceros (Capricorn), before describing in detail the perils of navigation when the sun enters Capricorn. Capricorn is spatially conjunct with Aquarius, their movements therefore temporally proximate, as Ovid also tells us in the earlier passage of the *Fasti* in which he deals with Capricorn:

> haec ubi transierint, Capricorno, Phoebe, relicto,
> per iuvenis curres signa regentis aquam. (*Fasti* 1.651–2)

Ovid appears in *Fasti* 2.453–8 to have attached Aratus' navigational perils to Aquarius rather than to Capricorn. This is appropriate in a thematic sense, since Aquarius is Ganymede, the *iuvenis regentis aquam* (1.652). This alludes both to the identity of Aquarius as Ganymede, the cup-bearer of Jupiter, and the rainy nature of the constellation because of its proximity to Capricorn. This is typical of the mythical/technical interface in Ovid's astronomical references.

[5] On Capricorn and Augustus, see above, pp. 138–43.

6. Leo: *Fasti* 1.655–6, 2.77–8 / *Ph.* 148–55, 446, 491, 545, 590–5. Recourse to Aratus does not elucidate Ovid's two brief references to Leo.

7. The Hyades: *Fasti* 3.105, 4.677–80, 5.159–82, 6.197–8, 711–12 / *Ph.* 172–8. The Hyades are a leitmotif of the *Fasti*; Ovid purports to record their morning rising on no less than five separate occasions.[6] In contrast, they appear only once in Aratus, in association with Taurus, from which they are disjunct in Ovid. The closest they come to their host constellation in the *Fasti* is at 4.677, where they are separated from the Bull in line 717 by the intervening festival of the Cerealia. Ovid's myth of Hyas (*Fasti* 5.159–82) is not Aratean, but appears in Roman prose sources: Hyginus, Servius, and the scholia to Germanicus.[7]

8. The Pleiades: *Fasti* 3.105, 4.165–78, 5.81–110, 447, 599–602, 664 / *Ph.* 253–67, 1066, 1085. Aratus' Pleiades, a star group already identified by Homer and Hesiod,[8] appear both in the 'Phainomena' proper and in the 'Diosemeiai'. Ovid's Pleiades retain their twofold function, as star sign and as weather sign, and acquire a third, that of Maia the Pleiad, mother of Mercury.[9]

Aratus' description of the Pleiades at *Phaenomena* 257–67 sets up a contrast between tradition and perception:

ἑπτάποροι δὴ ταί γε μετ' ἀνθρώπους ὑδέονται,
ἓξ οἶαί περ ἐοῦσαι ἐπόψιαι ὀφθαλμοῖσιν.
οὐ μέν πως ἀπόλωλεν ἀπευθὴς ἐκ Διὸς ἀστήρ,
ἐξ οὗ καὶ γενεῆθεν ἀκούομεν, ἀλλὰ μάλ' αὔτως
εἴρεται. ἑπτὰ δὲ κεῖναι ἐπιρρήδην καλέονται
Ἀλκυόνη Μερόπη τε Κελαινώ τ' Ἠλέκτρη τε
καὶ Στερόπη καὶ Τηΰγέτη καὶ πότνια Μαῖα.
αἱ μὲν ὁμῶς ὀλίγαι καὶ ἀφεγγέες, ἀλλ' ὀνομασταὶ
ἦρι καὶ ἑσπέριαι, Ζεὺς δ' αἴτιος, εἱλίσσονται,
ὅ σφισι καὶ θέρεος καὶ χείματος ἀρχομένοιο
σημαίνειν ἐπένευσεν ἐπερχομένου τ' ἀρότοιο.

Seven in number they are in the lore of men, although there are only six apparent to the eye. No star at all had been lost from our ken in Zeus since our oral tradition began, but this is just what is said. Those seven are called by name Alcyone, Merope, Celaeno and Electra, Sterope, Taygete and honoured Maia. All alike they are small and faint, but they are famous in their movements at morning and evening, and Zeus is the cause, in that he authorised them to mark the beginnings of summer and winter and the onset of ploughing-time.

6 See Ideler (1825) 153–5.
7 See Frazer (1929) and Bömer (1957–8) *ad loc.*
8 *Iliad* 18.486 (the Shield of Achilles), *WD* 615. Compare *WD* 383 (Ἀτλαγενέων), and Virgil, *Geo.* 1.221 (*Atlantides*) with the patronymic *Atlanteas* (*Fasti* 3.105).
9 Mercury is addressed as *Pliade nate* at *Fasti* 5.447 (see also 5.663–4).

Ovid's note of the morning setting of the Pleiades, at *Fasti* 4.165–78, bears a strong resemblance to this passage, especially in its imitation of the six/seven motif, found only from Aratus onwards:[10]

> Nox ubi transierit, caelumque rubescere primo
> coeperit, et tactae rore querentur aves,
> semustamque facem vigilata nocte viator
> ponet, et ad solitum rusticus ibit opus,
> Pliades incipient umeros relevare paternos,
> quae septem dici, sex tamen esse solent:
> seu quod in amplexum sex hinc venere deorum
> (nam Steropen Marti concubuisse ferunt,
> Neptuno Alcyonen et te, formosa Celaeno,
> Maian et Electran Taygetenque Iovi),
> septima mortali Merope tibi, Sisyphe, nupsit;
> paenitet, et facti sola pudore latet:
> sive quod Electra Troiae spectare ruinas
> non tulit, ante oculos opposuitque manum.

Ovid's translation of this motif in his *Phaenomena* survives, quoted by Probus *ad* Virgil, *Georgics* 1.138. Perhaps, therefore, Ovid is recalling his own translation of Aratus at this point in the *Fasti,* as well as the Greek original. Ovid has varied the order in the catalogue of names, and interspersed the Pleiades with their mythical lovers as befits a poet of erotic elegy, especially in a book presided over by the goddess Venus, as is Book 4 of the *Fasti.*

At *Fasti* 5.601–2 the Pleiades are a weather sign:

> tum mihi non dubiis auctoribus incipit aestas,
> et tepidi finem tempora veris habent.

The primary meaning of *non dubiis auctoribus* is of course that the rising of the Pleiades is the clearest possible indication of the beginning of summer, as their setting is a sure premonition of winter in Aratus, *Phaenomena* 1066 and 1085. But Ovid's *non dubiis auctoribus* could also be interpreted as referring, with some levity, to the opposition between literary and pragmatic tradition.

Cicero, in his translation of *Phaenomena* 259–61, develops Aratus' distinction between tradition and perception into what seems like a comment on the role of the literary tradition in shaping how the *vulgus* perceives the stars, following Homer and Hesiod rather than their own observation:

> sed frustra, temere a vulgo, ratione sine ulla,
> septem dicier, ut veteres statuere poetae ... (*Aratea* 32–3)

Read with the help of Cicero, Ovid's *non dubiis auctoribus* might be interpreted as follows: for reliance on the Pleiades as a meteorological sign, there is no need of reference to the *dubii auctores* belonging to a poetic tra-

[10] Le Boeuffle (1977) 199.

dition, but the mythology of the stars (as it has been told at *Fasti* 4.165–78) is subject to multiple interpretations.[11]

9. Arctophylax: *Fasti* 2.153–92, 3.403–6, 5.733, 6.235–6 / *Ph.* 91–5, 579–85, 721–3. Ovid may allude, with *piger* at *Fasti* 3.405, to Bootes' 'late' or slow setting (ὀψὲ δύοντι, *Ph.* 585), which is due to his proximity to the never-setting Bears (*Ph.* 721–3).[12]

Ovid's treatment of Arctophylax shows a general debt here to Aratean astronomical style, although direct echo of the model is not apparent. Appeals to the reader's powers of perception, such as Ovid's *aspicies*, *Fasti* 2.154, are characteristic of astronomical didactic poetry: note (one among innumerable examples) Aratus' ἑσπερόθεν κεν ἴδοιο Θυτήριον, *Phaenomena* 710. *Geminos pedes* (*Fasti* 2.154) is also characteristic, the segregation of anthropomorphic constellations into body parts adding a pleasingly grotesque touch to the Alexandrian model, as at *Phaenomena* 96–7, Ἀμφοτέροισι δὲ ποσσὶν ὕπο σκέπτοιο Βοώτεω | Παρθένον ... The most bizarre example of this phenomenon in Aratus is his description of the setting of Cassiepeia at *Phaenomena* 654–7:

τὰ δ' οὐκέτι οἱ κατὰ κόσμον
φαίνεται ἐκ δίφροιο, πόδες καὶ γούναθ' ὕπερθεν,
ἀλλ' ἥ γ' ἐς κεφαλὴν ἴση δύετ' ἀρνευτῆρι
μειρομένη καμάτων ...

... but the part of her seen in the chair, feet and knees uppermost, is no longer comely: she goes down headfirst like a tumbler, having her own share of trouble ...

Note in *Phaenomena* 656 the simile 'like a tumbler, like someone diving', figurative language typical of Aratean astronomical style. A similar expression is used of Bootes himself at *Phaenomena* 91, ἐλάοντι ἐοικώς, 'as though he were driving', referring to the position of Bootes/Arctophylax behind the Bears, which are also called the Wagons.[13] Ovid keeps the idea of likeness at *Fasti* 2.189–90, where Bootes is not just following the Bear, but 'has the form of somebody following along behind':

signa propinqua micant: prior est, quam dicimus Arcton,
Arctophylax formam terga sequentis habet.

[11] Compare *non dubiis auctoribus* with Virgil's passage on the role of the moon, *Geo.* 1.432–5:

sin ortu quarto (namque is certissimus auctor)
pura neque obtunsis per caelum cornibus ibit,
totus et ille dies et qui nascentur ab illo
exactum ad mensem pluvia ventisque carebunt.

[12] Ideler (1825) 140–3. For the myth of the Bear, Callisto, at *Fasti* 2.153ff., see above, pp. 175–80.

[13] *Ph.* 26–7: δύω δέ μιν ἀμφὶς ἔχουσαι | Ἄρκτοι ἅμα τροχόωσι, τὸ δὴ καλέονται Ἅμαξαι. For an extended discussion of the Bear, see above, chapter 6.

10. The Raven, Snake and Bowl: *Fasti* 2.243–66 / *Ph.* 443–9. Ovid may have in mind the passage of Aratus, but he appears to equate spatial juxtaposition with temporal proximity. This misunderstanding results in the following astronomical errors:

(i) Ovid has the three constellations rising on the same day, whereas the Hydra, because of its size, rises over a very long period.
(ii) The Crater rises for the last, not the first, time on 14 February.
(iii) Ovid says it rises at night, whereas its rising closest to this date is in the morning.[14]

However, false conjunction of the three constellations allows Ovid to tell the associated myth, found in Eratosthenes, *Catasterismoi* 41 and Hyginus, *De Astronomia* 2.40, rather than in Aratus, who concentrates on spatial mapping.[15]

11. Pisces: *Fasti* 2.457–74, 3.399–402 / *Ph.* 239–47, 282, 357, 362, 548, 700–2. At *Fasti* 3.399–402, Ovid is like Aratus in mentioning the north and south winds:

> nam duo sunt: Austris hic est, Aquilonibus ille
> proximus; a vento nomen uterque tenet. (*Fasti* 3.401–2)

> οἱ δ᾽ ἄρ᾽ ἔτι προτέρω, ἔτι δ᾽ ἐν προμολῇσι νότοιο
> Ἰχθύες. ἀλλ᾽ αἰεὶ ἕτερος προφερέστερος ἄλλου
> καὶ μᾶλλον βορέαο νέον κατιόντος ἀκούει. (*Phaenomena* 239–41)

Still further ahead and more in the approaches to the south are the Fishes; but one is always more prominent than the other and hears more the fresh onset of the north wind.

In *Fasti* 2.457–74, however, noting the sun's passage from Aquarius to Pisces, Ovid chooses to tell a non-Aratean myth.[16]

12. Vindemitor (Protrygeter): *Fasti* 3.407–14 / *Ph.* 137–40. Aratus' reference is very brief, and bears no relation to Ovid's aetiology.

13. Pegasus: *Fasti* 3.449–58 / *Ph.* 205–24. Both poets give an aetiology for the constellation of the Horse. Both emphasise the number of stars in Pegasus; Ovid's appeal to perception (*suspice*, 450) can be compared to Aratus' verbs of seeing at *Phaenomena* 223–4 (ὄψεαι | θηήσασθαι). The neck of the horse (*colla*, *Fasti* 3.450) is also mentioned in Aratus (αὐχήν, *Ph.* 211). Both authors refer to the *aition* of Hippocrene: τὸ δ᾽ ἀθρόον αὐτόθεν ὕδωρ | ἐξέχυτο πληγῇ προτέρου ποδός ... (*Ph.* 219–20); *cum levis Aonias ungula*

[14] See Ideler (1825) 165.
[15] For a critical interpretation of Ovid's juxtaposition of these three constellations in terms of poetic programme, see Newlands (1991).
[16] Which is found in Hyginus, *Astr.* 2.30 (Viré (1992) 76–7).

fodit aquas (*Fasti* 3.456). Ovid differs from Aratus, however, in technique and style. While Aratus' passage is primarily descriptive of the glory and size of the constellation (paralleled in *Fasti* 3.458), Ovid presents the reader with a complex piece of mythography. He has conflated two events of the Pegasus myth, the foundation of the fountain of the Muses on Mount Helicon, and the capture of Pegasus by Bellerophon at the fountain of Pirene near Corinth. The second does not appear in the Aratean version.[17]

14. The Knossian Crown: *Fasti* 3.459–516 / *Ph.* 71–3, 572–4, 625–6, 660. All of Aratus' references are brief. Even the longest (*Ph.* 71–3) tells the myth of Dionysus' love for Ariadne in shorthand form, with a glance at the relative position of the constellation:

αὐτοῦ κἀκεῖνος Στέφανος, τὸν ἀγαυὸν ἔθηκε
σῆμ' ἔμεναι Διόνυσος ἀποιχομένης Ἀριάδνης,
νώτῳ ὕπο στρέφεται κεκμηότος εἰδώλοιο.

There too the famous Crown, which Dionysus established to be an illustrious memorial to the departed Ariadne, circles close to the back of the labouring figure.

Ovid, in contrast to Aratus, turns the episode into a quasi-epyllion in answer to Catullus 64.[18] In Aratus, the Crown is a memorial of Ariadne's death; in Ovid, it is a memorial of her reconciliation with Dionysus after a lovers' tiff. Ovid changes the timing of the catasterism in order that he can precede it by a *Heroides*-like lament.[19] In the *Fasti*, the Crown of Ariadne is a location where the stars and erotic elegy coincide.[20]

15. Scorpio: *Fasti* 3.711–12, 4.163–4, 5.417, 5.493–544 / *Ph.* 85–6, 304–7, 402–3, 437–8, 505–6, 546, 634–46, 667. Ovid's references to the constellation Scorpio are succinct, as are Aratus'. A general similarity (not necessarily a sign of direct debt, needless to say) is that both poets refer more than once to the 'sting' of Scorpio (*Ph.* 305 ἐγγύθι κέντρου, 505–6 κέντρον | Σκορπίου, *Fasti* 4.163 *elatae metuendus acumine caudae* | *Scorpios,* 5.542, *curva . . . spicula*). More significant perhaps is Ovid's allusion, in an *aition* explaining the relative positions of Scorpio and Orion, to *Phaenomena* 634–46, at the end of his version of the Orion myth (*Fasti* 5.493–544). This will be treated in detail when we come to Orion.

[17] For programmatic readings of Ovid's Pegasus, see Hinds (1987a) 4–24 and Newlands (1995) 48.

[18] Compare *Fasti* 3.473 with Catullus 64.133, *Fasti* 3.475 with Catullus 64.143, and so on.

[19] Compare line 470 to *Heroides* 10.16 and 47; line 472 to *Her.* 10.150; 473 to *Her.* 10.76, 477 to *Her.* 10.77.

[20] Newlands (1995) 48 mentions the story of Ariadne in the context of 'generic play', but does not develop a detailed reading.

16. Milvus (The Kite): *Fasti* 3.794. A constellation which appears nowhere else except in Pliny the Elder.[21] My suspicion that Ovid may have confused a weather sign with a star sign has been confirmed by correspondence with John Ramsey, who speculates that some almanac maker must have given this date for the return of the bird, not the constellation, to Italy, a sign of spring. Ovid then copied this, converting the bird into a constellation.

17. Aries: *Fasti* 3.851–76, 4.715–16, 903 / *Ph.* 225–32, 238, 357, 515–17, 549, 709, 713. In Ovid the Ram is never named, and always incorporated in the myth of Helle and Phrixus, which is not Aratean.[22] The Aratean references describe only his spatial position and his marking of the Equator.

18. Libra (Chelae): *Fasti* 4.385–6 / *Ph.* 89–90, 231–2, 438, 520–1, 546, 607–26. Ovid's single reference bears no similarity to Aratus. Ovid's reference to Rome's sacred sign is comic (*plura locuturi subito seducimur imbre*, *Fasti* 4.385): Ovid and his interlocutor run for shelter as Libra tips its scales.[23]

19. Orion: *Fasti* 4.387–8, 5.493–544, 6.719, 785–90 / *Ph.* 232, 310, 322–5, 361, 518, 586–9, 634–46, 677, 730, 754–5.[24] Ovid's version of the catasterism of Orion (*Fasti* 5.493–544) can be seen as a response to Aratus, *Phaenomena* 634–46. Ovid follows Aratus in choosing to expound the myth of the constellation Orion, alluding to the earlier poet but differing from him in certain ways. Here is the Aratean version:

καμπαὶ δ' ἂν Ποταμοῖο καὶ αὐτίκ' ἐπερχομένοιο
Σκορπίου ἐμπίπτοιεν ἐϋρρόου ὠκεανοῖο,
ὅς καὶ ἐπερχόμενος φοβέει μέγαν Ὠρίωνα.
Ἄρτεμις ἱλήκοι· προτέρων λόγος, οἵ μιν ἔφαντο
ἑλκῆσαι πέπλοιο, Χίῳ ὅτε θηρία πάντα
καρτερὸς Ὠρίων στιβαρῇ ἐπέκοπτε κορύνῃ,
θήρης ἀρνύμενος κείνῳ χάριν Οἰνοπίωνι.
ἡ δέ οἱ ἐξ αὐτῆς ἐπετείλατο θηρίον ἄλλο,
νήσου ἀναρρήξασα μέσας ἑκάτερθε κολώνας,
σκορπίον, ὅς ῥά μιν οὖτα καὶ ἔκτανε πολλὸν ἐόντα
πλειότερος προφανείς, ἐπεὶ Ἄρτεμιν ἤκαχεν αὐτήν.
τοὔνεκα δὴ καί φασι περαιόθεν ἐρχομένοιο
Σκορπίου Ὠρίωνα περὶ χθονὸς ἔσχατα φεύγειν. (*Phaenomena* 634–46)

[21] *NH* 18.237: *Caesar Cancri exortu id fieri observavit, maior pars auctorum vindemitoris inmersu – VIII idus aquilonii piscis exortu et postero die Orionis; in Attica milvum apparere servatur. Caesar et idus Mart. ferales sibi notavit scorpionis occasu, XV kal. vero April. Italiae milvum ostendi, XII kal. equum occidere matutino.* For a programmatic reading of the Kite see Newlands (1995) 48.

[22] But is found in Apollodorus, *Bibl.* 1.9.1, Eratosthenes, *Catast.* 19, Hyginus, *Astr.* 2.20, *Fabulae* 3 (see Frazer (1929) *ad Fasti* 3.851, Bömer (1957–8) *ad Fasti* 3.852).

[23] For Libra as Rome's foundation sign, see Manilius, *Ast.* 4.769–77, Abry (1988). Again it is surprising that Ovid does not make more of Libra, since it is the location for Virgil's catasterised Augustus at *Geo.* 1.33, who will be 'between Virgo and the Claws' (another name for Libra).

[24] Ideler (1825) 161–3: Ovid may have used two different parapegmata for his dates.

> The windings of the River will plunge into the fair stream of Ocean as soon as the Scorpion arrives, which also puts great Orion to flight at its coming. May Artemis be gracious! It is a tale of the ancients, who said that stalwart Orion seized her by her robe, when in Chios he was smiting all the wild creatures with his stout club, striving to secure a hunting gift for Oenopion there. But she immediately summoned up against him another creature, breaking open the centre of the island's hills to left and to right, a scorpion that stung and killed him for all his size, emerging even more massive, because he had outraged Artemis herself. That is why they say that when the Scorpion comes over the horizon, Orion flees round the earth's boundary.

Both poets announce their intention to give Orion's *aition*: Aratus, characteristically, relies on tradition, with his προτέρων λόγος; Ovid is more of an individualist, with *signi causa canenda mihi* (*Fasti* 5.494).

In Aratus, the reason for expounding the myth is immediately apparent: he is purporting to explain the synchronicity of the settings of the constellations Orion and Scorpio, in answer to the putative question, 'Why does Scorpio set just after Orion?' Knowledge of the prior version sheds light on Ovid's seemingly inexplicable intention to tell the myth of an absent constellation ('If you look for Boeotian Orion in the midst of these, you'll be wrong', *Fasti* 5.493). In Aratus, a reference to Scorpio precedes Orion, and Aratus gives the myth as an explanation for this; in Ovid, Scorpio appears inside the myth of Orion, which begins abruptly, since Ovid has possibly lifted the tale from Aratus without its proper context. The Aratean passage may help to explain the fact that Ovid's introductory couplet appears to contain a *non sequitur*, in that his proposal is to give the *aition* of a constellation which is not there.

Aratus' Orion is a hunter who dies for his *hubris* towards Diana. Ovid, in contrast, heroicises Orion: in the *Fasti*, the giant interposes himself between Latona, whose bodyguard he is, and a scorpion sent by Tellus to attack her.

The tale of the hero's birth (left untreated by Aratus) is presented by Ovid as a less-than-reverent version of the *topos* of mortal hospitality towards the gods in which an old man, Hyrieus, is rewarded for his piety to Jupiter and Mercury by the gift of a strangely conceived son, Orion. This story is introduced from other sources.[25] It is only with the giant's death (*Fasti* 5.539–44) that we recognise the Aratean material which has been lurking all along behind Ovid's decision to recount the *aition* of the constellation, despite the fact that Ovid himself does not attempt to identify the scorpion which attacked Orion specifically as the constellation Scorpio, which in Aratus chases Orion to the Western horizon, but leaves the reader to make the connection through knowledge of the earlier version.[26]

20. Taurus: *Fasti* 4.717–20, 5.603–20 / *Ph.* 167–78, 322, 515–17, 549, 712–20. In both passages of the *Fasti* Ovid tells the myth of the constellation,

[25] See Frazer (1929) *ad Fasti* 5.494 and Bömer (1957–8) *ad Fasti* 5.493.

[26] For another interpretation of the Orion episode, see Newlands (1995) 110–15.

allusively in the first, explicitly in the second (the story of Europa).[27] Aratus' references are spatial and temporal.

21. Canis/Sirius: *Fasti* 4.901–42, 5.723–4 / *Ph.* 326–37, 340. In *Fasti* 4, Ovid has transformed a reference by Aratus to the agricultural effect of Sirius, the brightest star in the Dog,[28] into the aetiology of an agricultural festival. Ovid gives a different version of the Dog's identity from that of Aratus, alluding in *Fasti* 4.939 and 5.723 to the myth of the faithful dog of Icarus and Erigone, rather than that of Orion which appears in Aratus' version (*Ph.* 326). In addition, Ovid transfers Sirius' rôle as destroyer of crops (*Ph.* 332–5, Cicero, *Aratea* 113–19) to Robigo, the goddess of Blight, on whose festival the star is said to rise (nearly four months early[29]). One can only assume that the erroneousness of Ovid's date for Sirius' rising is due to his desire to connect the Dog Star with a festival in which a dog is sacrificed to Blight.

22. Chiron (Centaurus): *Fasti* 5.379–414 / *Ph.* 431, 436–42, 447, 505, 625–6, 661–4, 695, 700. Ovid's initial description of the constellation in *Fasti* 5.380, *semivir et flavi corpore mixtus equi,* may be compared with Aratus, *Phaenomena* 437–8:

τοῦ γάρ τοι τὰ μὲν ἀνδρὶ ἐοικότα νειόθι κεῖται
Σκορπίου, ἱππούραια δ' ὑπὸ σφίσι χηλαὶ ἔχουσιν.

You will find this constellation lying below two others: part of it, resembling a man, lies beneath the Scorpion, and the Claws have the horse's hind-part under them.

Two levels of seeming and reality are involved: on the one hand the Centaur itself is both *like* a man and *like* a horse, and on the other, the form of the constellation is *like* this creature. It seems that both poets strive to reflect this contortion, Aratus in his coining of the compound adjective ἱππούραια (a *hapax legomenon*), and Ovid in the somewhat tautological syntax of line 380.

Aratus' description at *Phaenomena* 436–42 is of the spatial position of the Centaur only; Ovid tells the myth of Chiron, Achilles and Hercules. In this myth Hercules comes to visit Chiron and the young Achilles, and the centaur is accidentally killed by one of Hercules' poisoned arrows.[30]

Is it possible that there is some play between Aratus' later note of the synchronic rising of the Bow with, among other constellations, the Centaur and Lyre (*Ph.* 663–78)? Compare *Fasti* 5.398, *laevo fixa sagitta pede est,* with *Phaenomena* 663–4:

[27] Found also in *Metamorphoses* 2.833–75. For sources, see Frazer (1929) *ad Fasti* 5.604 and Bömer (1957–8) *ad Fasti* 5.605.

[28] A Hesiodic star (*WD* 417–22, 587). See Fantham (1998) *ad loc.*

[29] Ideler (1825) 163–4, Fantham (1998) *ad loc.*

[30] See Eratosthenes, *Catast.* 40, scholiast on Germanicus, Robert (1878) 184–7; Hyginus, *Astr.* 2.38. For modern interpretations of Ovid's Chiron episode, see Brookes (1994), Newlands (1995) 115–22.

τοὶ δ' αὖθι μένουσι
τόξον ἐπερχόμενον πρότεροι πόδες ἱπποτάφηρος.

The forefeet of the rider-beast wait where they are for the rising of the Bow.

In Aratus the constellation of the Bow is spatially conjunct with Chiron's front feet – in one of which (in Ovid's version) Hercules' arrow becomes embedded.[31] The lyre, played by Achilles, is also present in *Phaenomena* 674 and *Fasti* 5.386. Although in Ovid the lyre and the arrow from Hercules' bow are not constellations but props in his myth of catasterism, whereas both are constellations in Aratus, it would not be without precedent in the *Fasti* for allusion to Aratus to be made in this fashion: creatures which are constellations in their own right in Aratus are several times made ancillary to one particular star myth in Ovid. As in the case of the Raven, Snake and Bowl, and of Orion and the Scorpion, the spatial juxtaposition of constellations in the Aratean heaven may induce Ovid to link them in an aetiological tale.

23. Gemini: *Fasti* 5.693–720, 6.727 / *Ph.* 147, 450, 481, 549, 717, 725. Overlap between Ovid and Aratus occurs only in reference to the proximity in the Zodiac of Cancer and Gemini (*Fasti* 6.727, *Ph.* 147).

24. Aquila: *Fasti* 5.731–2, 6.195–6 / *Ph.* 313–15, 522–3, 591, 691. Ovid's *grata Iovi . . . avis* (*Fasti* 5.732) is parallel in the broadest sense to Aratus' Ζηνὸς . . . μέγας ἄγγελος (*Ph.* 523).

25. Anguitenens (Ophiuchus): *Fasti* 6.733–62 / *Ph.* 74–87, 488, 521, 577–8, 665–8, 724–6. Ovid chooses to tell a myth, identifying Anguitenens with Hippolytus/Aesculapius, while Aratus merely gives the spatial co-ordinates of the constellation. Again similarities are more general than specific: compare for instance *et gemino nexas porrigit angue manus* (*Fasti* 6.736), with ἀμφότεραι (χέρες) δ' Ὄφιος πεπονήαται (*Ph.* 82).[32]

[31] Brookes (1994) 446–9 emphasises the role of Chiron's arrow-struck foot in conveying his human, rather than hybrid, nature, in order to gain the reader's sympathy: 'The word *pes* is a general term, applicable to all species. Its use here, in preference to the word *ungula*, which applies specifically to a horse's hoof, plays down the centaur's hybrid nature. Moreover, the phrase *laevo pede* cannot usefully designate which hoof it was that the arrow struck, for, as a centaur, Chiron has four legs, and two left feet!' (446).

[32] For a programmatic reading of the Aesculapius episode in the *Fasti*, see Newlands (1995) 192–7.

APPENDIX 2: TECHNICAL PROBLEMS OF OVID'S ASTRONOMY

One may attempt to explain Ovid's astronomical errors, following the method of Ideler, by the various factors I shall go on to list in this appendix.[1] Many of these errors may be a result of Ovid's promiscuous use of calculations taken by different observers at different latitudes. Others may be a product of confusion between rising and setting, and between true and apparent movements of stars, which I shall explain below. Still others are inexplicable.

With the aid of computer programmes, one might calculate the exact dates of rising and setting of a given star at a given latitude in any particular year. It would then be possible to take each of Ovid's astronomical entries and tabulate them on the basis of whether they represent rising or setting, whether they represent true or apparent movement of a star, and whether the observation they appear to be based on was taken at Rome, Alexandria, or somewhere else in the Mediterranean. A pattern might emerge which might show us the provenance of some of the sources Ovid followed: Alexandrian calculations might, for example, point towards Sosigenes and hence to Caesar's calendar. Results from the use of computer software cannot be presented here, since my research in this area is not yet far enough advanced; it may be of some interest, however, to outline the parameters of the problems in Ovid's astronomy.

It should be stated that, while technical inquiry can provide vital information on the accuracy of astronomical calendars in Greece and Rome, and especially on the provenance of the data in Caesar's calendar, it cannot be an end in itself with regard to the *Fasti*. Astronomical 'errors' should perhaps be understood as part of the poet's thematic and allusive repertoire, since in certain cases (such as that of the Robigalia, *Fasti* 4.901–42) the use of a particular star at a particular juncture enables Ovid to play with a theme or *topos*. In addition, it was more important for Ovid (as, arguably for Caesar himself) to maintain the fiction of astronomical knowledge, since that knowledge carried, and bestowed, privileged status. Seen in this light, accuracy is less important than symbolic value.

Bearing all this in mind, we can look at some of the factors which may have caused Ovid to err:

[1] See Ideler (1825) 139–40.

(i) Ovid does not distinguish between the true and apparent risings and settings of constellations.[2] These are a result of the fact that, in geocentric terms, the starry sphere moves slightly faster around the earth than does the sun; so, for example, the morning setting of a given star (i.e. when it passes below the western horizon) will be about four minutes earlier every day in relation to sunrise. In the simplest terms of modern astronomy this is a result of the two different movements of the earth, its rotation on its axis and its orbit round the sun, which mean that an observer on the earth sees the sun against a slightly different background of stars every day. The stars rise and set, visibly or invisibly, throughout the twenty-four hours of the day, because the earth's movement is continuous, but their significant positions are calculated by the course of the sun. Confusion arises from the fact of trying to reconcile two essentially different sorts of time and motion: the sidereal day, which is 23h 56m 4.091s, and the solar day of an average of 24h.

There are eight possible combinations of risings and settings in ancient astronomy by which the poet and his sources may become confused:[3]

REFERRING TO THE MORNING RISING OF A STAR:

1. True cosmical rising – a star and the sun rise together, hence the star is invisible, since there is too much sunlight for it to be seen.
2. Heliacal rising – first visible appearance of a star on the eastern horizon before sunrise, when it has preceded the rising sun by long enough to be seen.

EVENING RISING:

3. True acronychal rising – the star rises as the sun sets and hence is invisible.
4. Apparent acronychal rising, or the last visible rising of a star in the evening before it rises early enough for the sun's light to obscure it as it appears

[2] According to Ideler (1825), Ovid refers to all his risings and settings as if apparent (i.e. visible). Of the Greek parapegmatists, Meton, Eudoxus and Euctemon (see Soubiran (1969) 208–10) give apparent motions; Geminus, following Callippus (Soubiran (1969) 209), gives true risings and settings. On the parapegmatists as technical astronomers, see Dicks (1970) 84–6, 107, 188–9, 210.

[3] See Dicks (1970) 13–14, Mair and Mair (1921) 203–4. Various ancient sources explain the disctinction; Pliny, *NH* 18.218 is the clearest: *exortus occasusque binis modis intelleguntur, aut enim adventu solis occultantur stellae et conspici desinunt, aut eiusdem abscessu proferunt se (ut emersum hoc melius quam exortum consuetudo dixisset et illud occultationem potius quam occasum)*. Servius, commenting on Virgil, *Geo.* 1.218, *averso cedens Canis occidit astro*, seems to be aware of the different star motions: *nam ortus et occasus duo sunt: unus* ἡλιακός, *id est solaris, et alter* κοσμικός, *id est mundanus: unde fit, ut ea signa, quae cum sole oriuntur, a nobis non possint videri, et ea, quae videmus, quantum ad solis rationem pertinet, videantur occidere. secundum quod nunc ait 'occidit canis'; nam canis paratellon est cancri, id est cum eo oritur.* Arnulf of Orleans, a twelfth-century commentator on the *Fasti*, quotes this passage of Servius in his introductory preamble (the manuscript I have seen is thirteenth-century, *Reginensis Latinus* 1548). On this commentary see Buonocore (1994) 140, and Alton (1930).

above the eastern horizon before sunset. Having risen, it will be visible during the night.

MORNING SETTING:

5. True cosmical setting – a star sets as the sun rises, and hence cannot be seen, because there is too much light by the time it reaches the western horizon.

6. Apparent cosmical setting – first visible setting of a star in the morning, when its disappearance takes place long enough before sunrise to be seen.

EVENING SETTING:

7. True acronychal setting – star and sun set together, so the star is invisible.

8. Heliacal setting – the final setting of a star in the evening before it begins to set while there is still too much light before sunset for it to be seen.

(ii) Ovid's own references to the passing of time are sometimes oblique. The marks of date which have appeared since the mid nineteenth century in Ovid's text (see, for example, Courtney's 1988 Teubner edition) were not fixed by the poet himself, and may in fact add unwanted clarity to his astronomical references.[4] Likewise, it is not always clear whether he is referring to the rising or setting of a star, or whether the movement he refers to is in the morning or evening, as in the following reference to Delphinus:

> interea Delphin clarum super aequora sidus
> tollitur et patriis exserit ora vadis.

At *Fasti* 1.457–8 we are in the dark as to whether Ovid means the morning or evening rising of the constellation.

(iii) Points of calculation: a star rises or sets at different times according to the point on the globe from which one observes it (the angle of observation). Because of this, the various calendars used by Ovid as sources may have different dates, which the poet may conflate.

(iv) The particular star the poet (or his sources) used to calculate risings and settings of constellations affects the rising and setting dates of any given constellation. Different parts of constellations, especially large ones like Pegasus or the Hydra, rise or set on different dates.

(v) There are several potential problems with Ovid's sources. A problem with Ovid's use of much earlier sources like the fifth and fourth-century

[4] The date-markings, which appear in Alton, Wormell and Courtney (1988) in bold type, surrounded by interstices, are of a kind which seems to have originated in Merkel's importation of the date-markings of epigraphical convention into the *Fasti* in his second edition of the text, of 1851. Admittedly there is a precedent for the appearance of such date-markings in some of the later manuscripts (e.g. Vat. Lat. 3263). However, it is likely that they would have been absent from Ovid's own text, and they do not appear in the earliest manuscripts such as the Ursinianus (Vat. Lat. 3262).

parapegmatists (or his encountering of such sources through the agricultural calendars of his Roman predecessors) is precession of the equinoxes, the fact that the earth's axis of rotation does not in fact maintain a constant orientation, because of inequalities of motion due to the earth not being a perfect sphere. This means, for example, that in the Greek astronomer Meton's time (fifth century BC) in the latitude of Athens the Pleiades set on 16 May, but in Ovid's time in the latitude of Rome on 28 May.

Again, one is very rarely presented with a complete set of risings and settings for every star in the ancient agricultural calendars we have looked at in chapter 1. Take Capella as an example: I have tried to collect a set of dates from Varro, Pliny and Columella; Varro does not appear to give any dates for this star, and the dates in the other two are as follows:

Columella, *De Re Rustica* 11
Morning rising 29 April (and, inexplicably, 25, 26, 27 May) – *DRR* 11.2.37 and 11.2.43
Morning setting 23 December – *DRR* 11.2.94
Evening rising not given
Evening setting not given

Pliny, *Naturalis Historia* 18
Morning rising 8 May – *NH* 18.248
Morning setting not given
Evening rising 9 September – *NH* 18.310
Evening setting 21 May – *NH* 18.255

Ideler's opinion is that Ovid and Columella both followed Greek parapegmata, either Meton's or Eudoxus'.[5] Pliny follows Caesar and Sosigenes, since the date given at *NH* 18.248 may be appropriate for the latitude of Alexandria. But because of the incomplete dates in the sources, it is hard to get a full picture of where, for instance, Ovid and Pliny followed a common source, such as Caesar's calendar, and where they diverge.

Finally, it seems that a sort of game of Chinese whispers is going on among Ovid and his sources and their sources: the information is slightly altered, perhaps through misunderstanding,[6] each time it passes from one to another. Ideler in his article of 1825 tried to fit Ovid's recorded risings and settings to the closest significant date for any given star calculated from the latitude of Rome, a methodology whose conclusions seem unavoidably tentative, and which fails to explain the presence and function of astronomy in the *Fasti*. Thus my primary purpose has been to deal with Ovid's astronomy not on the level of technical error or exactitude, but on that of literary history and poetic structure.

[5] Ideler (1825) 143–4. See Columella, *DRR* 9.14.12 (quoted in chapter 1, p. 13).
[6] As in the case of the Kite: see above, p. 201.

BIBLIOGRAPHY

Ancient texts

Anthologia Graeca: Paton, W. R. (1925), *The Greek anthology*, 5 volumes, London and Cambridge, MA

Anthologia Latina: Riese, A., ed. (1906), *Anthologia Latina*, vol. 1.2, second edn, Leipzig

Aratus: Kidd, D. A. (1997), *Aratus: Phaenomena*, Cambridge

Maass, E., ed. (1893), *Arati Phaenomena*, Berlin

Mair, A. W. and Mair, G. R., eds. (1921), *Callimachus: Hymns and Epigrams; Lycophron, Aratus*, London and Cambridge, MA

Martin, J., ed. (1956a), *Arati Phaenomena*, Florence

Scholia on Aratus: Maass, E., ed. (1898), *Commentariorum in Aratum reliquiae*, Berlin

Archimedes: Mugler, C., ed. (1970–2), *Archimède*, 4 volumes, Paris

Augustus: Malcovati, H., ed. (1928), *Caesaris Augusti Imperatoris operum fragmenta*, Turin

Callimachus: McLennan, G. R., ed. (1977), *Callimachus: Hymn to Zeus*, Rome

Mair, A. W. and Mair, G. R., eds. (1921), *Callimachus: Hymns and Epigrams; Lycophron, Aratus*, London and Cambridge, MA

Pfeiffer, R. (1949–53), *Callimachus*, 2 volumes, Oxford

Cato: Goujard, R., ed. (1975), *Caton: de l'agriculture*, Paris

Hooper, W. D., ed. (1934), *Marcus Porcius Cato: On agriculture, Marcus Terentius Varro: On agriculture*, London and Cambridge, MA

Catullus: Godwin, J., ed. (1995), *Catullus: Poems 61–68*, Warminster

Mynors, R. A. B., ed. (1958), *C. Valerii Catulli Carmina*, Oxford

Cicero, *Aratea*: Soubiran, J., ed. (1972), *Cicéron: Aratea, fragments poétiques*, Paris

De Natura Deorum: Pease, A. Stanley, ed. (1955–8), *M. Tulli Ciceronis De Natura Deorum Libri*, 2 volumes, Cambridge, MA

Walsh, P. G. (1997), *Cicero: the nature of the gods*, Oxford

De Re Publica: Keyes, C. W., ed. (1928), *Cicero: De Re Publica, De Legibus*, London and Cambridge, MA

Powell, J. G. F., ed (1990), *Cicero: Laelius on friendship, and the dream of Scipio*, Warminster

Cleanthes: Long, A. A. and Sedley, D. N. (1987), *The Hellenistic philosophers*, 2 volumes, Cambridge

Powell, J. U. (1925), *Collectanea Alexandrina*, Oxford

Columella, *De Re Rustica*: Forster, E. S. and Heffner, E. H., eds. (1941–55), *Columella, De Re Rustica: On agriculture*, 3 volumes, London and Cambridge, MA

Cornutus, *Theologiae Graecae Compendium*: Lang, C., ed. (1881), *Cornutus: Theologiae Graecae Compendium*, Leipzig

Ennius, *Annales*: Skutsch, O., ed. (1985), *The Annales of Q. Ennius*, Oxford

Vahlen, J., ed. (1928), *Ennianae poesis reliquiae*, Leipzig

Scaenica: Ribbeck, O., ed. (1897), *Scaenicae Romanorum poesis fragmenta*, 2 volumes, Leipzig

Festus: Lindsay, W. M., ed. (1913), *Sexti Pompei Festi De Verborum Significatu*, Leipzig

Firmicus Maternus: Monat, P., ed. (1992–7), *Firmici Materni Mathesis*, 3 volumes, Paris

Germanicus: Gain, D. B., ed. (1976), *The Aratus ascribed to Germanicus Caesar*, London

Scholia on Germanicus: Eyssenhardt, F., ed. (1866), *Martianus Capella, accedunt scholia in Germanici Aratea*, Leipzig

Hesiod, *Fragments*: Merkelbach, R. and West, M. L., eds. (1967), *Fragmenta Hesiodea*, Oxford

Theogony: West, M. L., ed. (1966), *Hesiod: Theogony*, Oxford

West, M. L., ed. (1988), *Hesiod: Theogony and Works and Days*, Oxford (World's Classics)

Works and Days: West, M. L. (1978), *Hesiod: Works and Days*, Oxford

Homer, *Iliad*: Hammond, M., trans. (1987), *Homer, the Iliad*, London (Penguin)

Edwards, M. W. (1991), *The Iliad: a commentary*, vol. v, Cambridge

Odyssey: Rieu, E. V., trans. (1946), *Homer, the Odyssey*, London (Penguin)

Horace: Nisbet, R. and Hubbard, M., eds. (1970–8), *A commentary on Horace Odes*, 2 volumes, Oxford

West, D., ed. (1995), *Horace Odes I: carpe diem*, Oxford

Hyginus, *De Astronomia*: Viré, G., ed. (1992), *Hygini De Astronomia*, Leipzig

Fabulae: Marshall, P. K., ed. (1993), *Hygini Fabulae*, Leipzig

Lucan: Duff, J. D., ed. (1977), *Lucan: the Civil War*, London and Cambridge, MA

Scholia on Lucan: Usener, H., ed. (1869), *M. Annaei Lucani commenta Bernensia*, Leipzig

Lucretius: Bailey, C., ed. (1947), *Titi Lucreti Cari De Rerum Natura Libri Sex*, 3 volumes, Oxford

Costa, C. D. N., ed. (1984), *Lucretius, De Rerum Natura 5*, Oxford

Lydus: Wachsmuth, C., ed. (1863), *Ioannis Laurentii Lydi liber de ostentis*, Leipzig

Macrobius, *Saturnalia*: Davies, P. V. (1969), *Macrobius, the Saturnalia*, New York and London

Manilius: Goold, G. P., ed. (1977), *Manilius, Astronomica*, London and Cambridge, MA

Goold, G. P., ed. (1985), *Manilius: Astronomica*, Leipzig

Housman, A. E., ed. (1903–30), *M. Manilii Astronomica*, 5 volumes, London

Ovid, *Amores*: McKeown, J. C., ed. (1987–9), *Ovid: Amores*, 2 volumes, Leeds

Fasti: Alton, E. H., Wormell, D. E. W. and Courtney, E., eds. (1988), *Ovidius: Fasti*, Leipzig

Bömer, F., ed. (1957–8), *P. Ovidius Naso: Die Fasten*, 2 volumes, Heidelberg

Frazer, J. G., ed. (1929), *The Fasti of Ovid*, 5 volumes, London

Merkel, R., ed. (1841), *P. Ovidi Nasonis Fastorum Libri Sex*, Berlin

Merkel, R. (1851), *P. Ovidius Naso Tom. III: Tristia, Ibis, Ex Ponto Libri, Fasti, Halieutica*, Leipzig

Schilling, R. (1992–3), *Ovide, les Fastes*, 2 volumes, Paris

Metamorphoses: Bömer, F., ed. (1969–86), *P. Ovidius Naso: Metamorphosen*, 7 volumes, Heidelberg

Pliny: Rackham, H., ed. (1950), *Pliny, Natural History*, London and Cambridge, MA

Plutarch: Perrin, B. (1917), *Plutarch's Lives*, vol. v, London and Cambridge, MA

Propertius: Barber, E. A., ed. (1953), *Sexti Properti Carmina*, Oxford

Butler, H. E. and Barber, E. A., eds. (1933), *The Elegies of Propertius*, Oxford

Goold, G. P., ed. (1990), *Propertius: Elegies*, London and Cambridge, MA

Theocritus: Gow, A. S. F., ed. (1950–2), *Theocritus*, 2 volumes, Cambridge

Varro, *Antiquitates*: Agahd, R., ed. (1898), *M. Terenti Varronis Antiquitatum Rerum Divinarum Libri 1, 14, 15, 16*, Leipzig

De Re Rustica: Hooper, W. D., ed. (1934), *Marcus Porcius Cato: On agriculture, Marcus Terentius Varro: On agriculture*, London and Cambridge, MA

Virgil, *Aeneid*: Gransden, K. W., ed. (1976), *Virgil, Aeneid Book 8*, Cambridge

Georgics: Thomas, R. F. (1988), *Virgil, Georgics Books 1–2*, Cambridge

Eclogues: Coleman, R., ed. (1977), *Virgil, Eclogues*, Cambridge

Vitruvius: Granger, F., ed. (1934), *Vitruvius, On architecture*, London and Cambridge, MA

Soubiran, J., ed. (1969), *Vitruve, de l' architecture livre 9*, Paris

Modern works

Abry, J.-H. (1988), 'Auguste: la Balance et le Capricorne', *REL* 66: 103–21

Alton, E. H. (1930), 'The medieval commentators on Ovid's *Fasti*', *Hermathena* 20: 119–51

Alton, E. H., Wormell, D. E. W. and Courtney, E. (1977), 'A catalogue of the manuscripts of Ovid's *Fasti*', *BICS* 24: 37–61
Arnaud, P. (1984), 'L' Image du globe dans le monde romain', *MEFRA* 96.1: 53–116
Arnold, E. (1911), *Roman Stoicism*, Cambridge
Aujac, G. (1979), 'Regards sur l'astronomie grecque', in G. Aujac and J. Soubiran, eds., *L' astronomie dans l'antiquité classique*, Paris, 35–54
Barchiesi, A. (1991), 'Discordant muses', *PCPS* 37: 1–21
(1997), *The poet and the prince*, Berkeley and Los Angeles
Barton, T. (1994a), *Ancient astrology*, London
(1994b), *Power and knowledge: astrology, physiognomics and medicine under the Roman empire*, Ann Arbor
(1995), 'Augustus and Capricorn: astrological polyvalency and imperial rhetoric', *JRS* 85: 33–51
Bayet, J. (1939), 'L'immortalité astrale d'Auguste, ou Manilius commentateur de Virgile', *REL* 17: 141–71
Beard, M. (1980), 'The sexual status of the Vestal Virgins', *JRS* 70: 12–27
(1987), 'A complex of times: no more sheep on Romulus' birthday', *PCPS* 213: 1–15
Bing, P. (1988), *The well-read muse: present and past in the Hellenistic poets*, Göttingen
(1990), 'A pun on Aratus' name in verse 2 of the *Phainomena*?', *HSCP* 93: 281–85
(1993), 'Aratus and his audiences', *MD* 31: 99–110
Boardman, J. (1981–) *et al.*, eds., *Lexicon iconographicum mythologiae classicae*, Zürich/Munich
Boisacq, E. (1950), *Dictionnaire étymologique de la langue greque*, fourth edn, Heidelberg
Boyle, A. J. (1997), 'Postscripts from the edge: Exilic *Fasti* and Imperialised Rome', *Ramus* 26: 7–28
Bowersock, G. (1990), 'The pontificate of Augustus', in K. A. Raaflaub and M. Toher, eds., *Between Republic and Empire*, Berkeley, 380–94
Bram, J. R. (1975), *Ancient astrology, theory and practice: Matheseos Libri VIII by Firmicus Maternus*, New Jersey
Brendel, O. (1977), *Symbolism of the sphere*, Leiden
Brind 'amour, P. (1983), *Le calendrier romain*, Ottawa
Brookes, I. (1994), 'The death of Chiron: *Fasti* 5.379–414', *CQ* 44: 444–50
Brown, R. D. (1987), 'The palace of the sun in Ovid's *Metamorphoses*', in M. Whitby, P. R. Hardie and M. Whitby, eds., *Homo Viator*: classical essays for John Bramble, Bristol, 211–20
(1990), 'The structural function of the song of Iopas', *HSCP* 93: 315–34
Brugnoli, G. (1989), 'Augusto e il Capricorno', in Cervellera and Liuzzi (1989): 17–32

Buchheit, V. (1966), 'Mythos und Geschichte in Ovids *Metamorphosen*', *Hermes* 94: 80–108

Buchner, E. (1982), *Die Sonnenuhr des Augustus*, Mainz

(1988), 'Horologium Solarium Augusti', in W.-D. Heilmeyer *et al.*, eds., *Kaiser Augustus und die verlorene Republik*, Berlin, 240–5

Bulloch, A. W. (1985), 'Hellenistic Poetry', in P. Easterling and B. Knox, eds., *Cambridge history of classical literature*, vol. I, Cambridge, 541–621

Buonocore, M. (1994), *Aetas Ovidiana*, Sulmona

Cairns, F. (1972), *Generic composition in Greek and Roman Poetry*, Edinburgh

Cameron, A. (1995), *Callimachus and his critics*, Princeton, NJ

Cervellera, M. A. and Liuzzi, D., eds. (1989), *L'astronomia a Roma nell' età augustea* (Università degli studi di Lecce, Dipartimento di filologia classica e medioevale, Testi e studi 2), Lecce

Clavel, V. (1868), *De M. T. Cicerone Graecorum Interprete*, Paris

Courtney, E. (1990), 'Greek and Latin acrostichs', *Philologus* 134: 3–13

(1993), *The fragmentary Latin poets*, Oxford

Degrassi, A. (1963), *Inscriptiones Italiae*, vol. XIII.2, Rome (Istituto poligrafico dello stato)

Devallet, G. (1989), 'Apothéoses romaines: Romulus à corps perdu', in A.-F. Laurens, ed., *Entre hommes et dieux*, Paris, 107–26

Dicks, D. R. (1970), *Early Greek astronomy to Aristotle*, London

Diels, H., ed. (1929), *Doxographi Graeci*, Leipzig

Diels, H. and Kranz, W., eds. (1951–2), *Die Fragmente der Vorsokratiker*, 2 volumes, Berlin

Dijksterhuis, E. J. (1987), *Archimedes*, trans. C. Dikshoorn, Princeton, NJ

Domenicucci, P. (1989), 'I "Capretti" di Virgilio. Note sul catasterismo di Giulio Cesare', in Cervellera and Liuzzi (1989): 93–106

(1996), *Astra Caesarum: Astronomia, astrologia e catasterismo da Cesare a Domiziano*, Pisa

Dumézil, G. (1966), *La religion romaine archaïque*, Paris

Dunbar, H. (1971), *A complete concordance to the Odyssey of Homer*, revised by B. Marzullo, New York

Dwyer, E. (1973), 'Augustus and the Capricorn', *Mitteilungen des deutschen archäologischen Instituts, Römische Abteilung* 80: 59–67

Effe, B. (1977), *Dichtung und Lehre: Untersuchungen zur Typologie des antiken Lehrgedichts* (Zetemata: Monographien zur klassischen Altertumswissenschaft 69), Munich

Fantham, R. E. (1983), 'Sexual comedy in Ovid's *Fasti*', *HSCP* 87: 195–216

(1985), 'Ovid, Germanicus and the composition of the *Fasti*', *Papers of the Liverpool Latin Seminar* 5: 243–81

(1995), 'Rewriting and rereading the *Fasti*: Augustus, Ovid and recent classical scholarship', *Antichthon* 29: 42–59

(1997), 'Images of the City: Propertius' new-old Rome', in Habinek and Schiesaro (1997): 122–35
(1998), *Ovid: Fasti 4*, Cambridge
Farrell, J. (1991), *Vergil's Georgics and the traditions of ancient epic*, Oxford
Feeney, D. C. (1991), *The gods in epic: poets and critics of the classical tradition*, Oxford
(1992), '*Si licet et fas est*: Ovid's *Fasti* and the problem of free speech under the principate', in Powell (1992): 1–25
(1998), *Literature and religion at Rome*, Cambridge
Fowler, D. P. (1995), 'Horace and the aesthetics of politics', in S. J. Harrison, ed., *Homage to Horace*, Oxford, 248–66
Fränkel, H. (1969), *Ovid, a poet between two worlds*, Berkeley and Los Angeles
Fraser, P. M. (1972), *Ptolemaic Alexandria*, 2 volumes, Oxford
Frede, M. (1978), 'Principles of Stoic grammar', in J. M. Rist, ed., *The Stoics*, Berkeley and Los Angeles, 27–76
Friedländer, P. (1941), 'Pattern of sound and atomistic theory in Lucretius', *AJP* 62: 16–34
Gale, M. (1994a), *Myth and poetry in Lucretius*, Cambridge
(1994b), 'Lucretius 4.1–25 and the proem to the *De Rerum Natura*', *PCPS* 40: 1–17
Galinsky, K. (1996), *Augustan culture: an interpretative introduction*, Princeton, NJ
Green, P. (1990), *Alexander to Actium*, London
Griffiths, F. T. (1979), *Theocritus at court*, Leiden
Habinek, T. (1989), 'Science and tradition in *Aeneid* 6', *HSCP* 92 (1989): 223–55
(1998), *The politics of Latin literature: writing, identity and empire in ancient Rome*, Princeton, NJ
Habinek, T. and Schiesaro, A., eds. (1997), *The Roman cultural revolution*, Cambridge
Hardie, P. R. (1985a), '*Imago Mundi*: cosmological and ideological aspects of the shield of Achilles', *JHS* 105: 11–31
(1985b), 'Cosmological patterns in the *Aeneid*', *PLLS* 5: 85–98
(1986), *Virgil's Aeneid: cosmos and imperium*, Oxford
(1991), 'The Janus episode in Ovid's *Fasti*', *MD* 26: 47–64
(1992), 'Augustan poets and the mutability of Rome', in Powell (1992): 59–82
(1995), 'The speech of Pythagoras in Ovid *Metamorphoses* 15: Empedoclean *epos*', *CQ* 45: 204–14
(1997), 'Questions of authority: the invention of tradition in Ovid *Metamorphoses* 15', in Habinek and Schiesaro (1997): 182–98
Harries, B. (1989), 'Causation and the authority of the poet in Ovid's *Fasti*', *CQ* 38: 164–85

Harrison, J. E. (1912), *Themis: a study in the social origins of Greek religion*, Cambridge

Haury, A., (1964), 'Cicéron et l'astronomie: à propos de *Rep.* 1.22', *RÉL* 42: 198–212

Heinze, R. (1919), *Ovids elegische Erzählung* (Berichte über die Verhandlungen der Sächsischen Akademie der Wissenschaften zu Leipzig, Philologisch-historische Klasse 71.7), Leipzig

(1993), *Virgil's epic technique*, trans. D. & H. Harvey, Bristol

Herbert-Brown, G. (1994), *Ovid and the Fasti: an historical study*, Oxford

Hill, P. (1989), *The monuments of ancient Rome as coin types*, London

Hinds, S. (1987a), *The metamorphosis of Persephone*, Cambridge

(1987b), 'Generalizing about Ovid', *Ramus* 16: 4–31

(1992), '*Arma* in Ovid's *Fasti*', *Arethusa* 25: 81–153

(1998), *Allusion and intertext: dynamics of appropriation in Roman poetry*, Cambridge

Hölscher, T. (1965), 'Ein römischer Sternziegel mit Victoria und Capricorni', *Jahrbuch des Zentralmuseums Mainz* 12: 59–73

Holzberg, N. (1997), *Ovid: Dichter und Werk*, Munich

Hopkinson, N. (1984), 'Callimachus' *Hymn to Zeus*', *CQ* 34: 139–48

(1988), *A Hellenistic anthology*, Cambridge

Horsfall, N. (1985), 'Augustus' sundial: architecture, astronomy and propaganda', *Omnibus* 11: 5–7

Housman, A. E. (1913), 'Manilius, Augustus, Capricornus and Libra', *CQ* 7: 109–14

Hunter, R. L. (1995), 'Written in the stars: poetry and philosophy in the *Phaenomena* of Aratus', *Arachnion: a journal of ancient literature and history on the web* 2: 1–34

(1996), *Theocritus and the archaeology of Greek poetry*, Cambridge

Hutchinson, G. O. (1988), *Hellenistic poetry*, Oxford

Ideler, J. (1825), 'Über den astronomischen Theil der *Fasti* des Ovid', *Abhandlungen der königlichen Akademie der Wissenschaften zu Berlin aus den Jahren 1822–3*, Berlin, 137–69

Innes, D. C. (1979), 'Gigantomachy and natural philosophy', *CQ* 29: 165–71

Jacoby, F., ed. (1923–58), *Die Fragmente der griechischen Historiker*, Berlin

James, A. W. (1972), 'The Zeus hymns of Aratus and Cleanthes', *Antichthon* 6: 28–38

Johnson, W. R. (1978), 'The desolation of the *Fasti*', *CJ* 74: 7–18

Kennedy, D. F. (1992), '"Augustan" and "Anti-Augustan": reflections on terms of reference', in Powell (1992): 26–58

Kenney, E. J. (1979), 'The typology of didactic', *CR* 29: 71–3

Kidd, D. A. (1981), 'Notes on Aratus' *Phaenomena*', *CQ* 31: 355–62

Knox, P. E. (1986), *Ovid's Metamorphoses and the traditions of Augustan poetry* (Cambridge Philological Society supplementary volume no. XI), Cambridge

Kraft, K. (1967), 'Zum Capricorn auf den Münzen des Augustus', *Jahrbuch für Numismatik und Geldgeschichte* 17: 17–27
Lafaye, G. (1904), *Les Métamorphoses d'Ovide et leurs modèles grecs*, Paris
Lapidge, M. (1978), 'Stoic Cosmology', in J. M. Rist, ed., *The Stoics*, Berkeley and Los Angeles 161–86
Le Boeuffle, A. (1964), 'Quelques erreurs ou difficultés astronomiques chez Columelle', *RÉL* 42: 324–33
(1977), *Les noms latins d'astres et de constellations*, Paris
Levitan, W. (1979), 'Plexed artistry: three Aratean acrostics', *Glyph* 5: 55–68
Lieberg, G. (1982), *Poeta creator: Studien zu einer Figur der antiken Dichtung*, Amsterdam
Little, D. (1970), 'Richard Heinze: Ovids elegische Erzählung', in E. Zinn, ed., *Ovids Ars Amatoria und Remedia Amoris: Untersuchungen zum Aufbau*, Stuttgart, 64–105
Little, D. (1982), 'Politics in Augustan poetry', *ANRW* 2.30.1: 254–370
Long, A. A. (1975–6), 'Heraclitus and Stoicism', *Philosophia* 5–6: 133–53
(1992), 'Stoic readings of Homer', in R. Lamberton and J. Keaney, eds., *Homer's ancient readers*, Princeton, NJ, 41–66
L'Orange, H. P. (1953), *Studies in the iconography of cosmic kingship*, Oslo
Maass, E. (1892), *Aratea*, Berlin
Macdonald, W. L. (1976), *The Pantheon*, London
McKeown, J. C. (1984), '*Fabula proposito nulla tegenda meo*: Ovid's *Fasti* and Augustan politics', in D. West and A. Woodman, eds., *Poetry and politics in the age of Augustus*, Cambridge, 169–87
Mackie, N. (1992), 'Ovid and the birth of *Maiestas*', in Powell (1992): 83–97
Macurdy, G. H. (1932), *Hellenistic queens: a study of woman-power in Macedonia, Seleucid Syria, and Ptolemaic Egypt*, Baltimore, MD
Maltby, R. (1991), *A lexicon of ancient Latin etymologies*, Leeds
Manitius, C., ed. (1894), *Hipparchi in Arati et Eudoxi Phaenomena commentariorum libri tres*, Leipzig
Martin, C. (1985), 'A reconsideration of Ovid's *Fasti*', *ICS* 10: 261–74
Martin, J. (1956b), *Histoire du texte des Phénomènes d'Aratos*, Paris
(1979), 'Les *Phénomènes* d'Aratos: étude sur la composition du poème', in Aujac and Soubiran (1979): 91–104
Mattingly, H. (1923), *Coins of the Roman Empire in the British Museum*, vol. 1, Augustus to Vitellius, London
Meincke, W. (1965), *Untersuchungen zu den enkomiastischen Gedichten Theokrits*, Diss., Kiel
Miller, J. F. (1991), *Ovid's elegiac festivals: studies in the Fasti*, Frankfurt
(1992), 'The *Fasti* and Hellenistic didactic', *Arethusa* 25: 11–31
Mommsen, T., ed. (1863), *Corpus inscriptionum latinarum* 1.1 (second edition), Berlin

Myers, K. S. (1994), *Ovid's causes: cosmogony and aetiology in the Metamorphoses*, Ann Arbor

Neugebauer, O. (1975), *A history of ancient mathematical astronomy*, 3 volumes, Berlin

Newlands, C. E. (1991), 'Ovid's ravenous raven', *CJ* 86: 244–55

(1992), 'Ovid's narrator in the *Fasti*', *Arethusa* 25: 33–54

(1995), *Playing with time: Ovid and the Fasti*, Cornell

Nicolet, C. (1991), *Space, geography and politics in the early Roman empire*, Ann Arbor

O' Hara, J. (1992), 'Naming the stars at *Georgics* 1.137–8 and *Fasti* 5.163–82', *AJP* 113: 47–61

Otis, B. (1970), *Ovid as an epic poet*, Cambridge (second edition)

Pendergast, G. L. (1971), *A complete concordance to the Iliad of Homer*, revised by B. Marzullo, New York

Pfeiffer, R. (1968), *A history of Classical scholarship from the beginnings to the end of the Hellenistic age*, Oxford

Platner, S. and Ashby, T. (1929), *A topographical dictionary of ancient Rome*, Oxford

Pollini, J. (1990), 'Man or god: divine assimilation and imitation in the late republic and early principate', in K. A. Raaflaub and M. Toher eds., *Between republic and empire*, Berkeley and Los Angeles, 334–63

Porte, D. (1985), *L' Étiologie religieuse dans les Fastes d'Ovide*, Paris

Postgate, J. P. (1910), 'On Ovid *Fasti* 6.263 sqq.', *CQ* 4: 196–200

(1914), 'On the text of the *Stromateis*', *CQ* 8: 237–46

(1918), 'A note on Ovid *Fasti* 6.271f', *CQ* 12: 139

Powell, A., ed. (1992), *Roman poetry and propaganda in the age of Augustus*, Bristol

Ramsey, J. T. and Licht, A. L. (1997), *The comet of 44 BC and Caesar's funeral games*, (American Philological Association American classical studies 39), Atlanta, GA

Reeve, M. D. (1983), 'Aratea', in L. D. Reynolds, ed., *Texts and transmission*, Oxford, 18–24

Repellini, F. R. (1993), 'Matematica, astronomia e meccanica', in G. Cambiano, L. Canfora and D. Lanza, eds., *Lo spazio letterario della Grecia antica*, vol. 1, tom. 2, Rome, 305–68

Rist, J. M. (1969), *Stoic Philosophy*, Cambridge

Robbins, F. (1913), 'The Creation Story in Ovid, *Met.* 1', *CP* 8: 401–35

Robert, C., ed. (1878), *Eratosthenis Catasterismorum reliquiae*, Berlin

Rzach, A., ed. (1913), *Hesiodus: Carmina*, Leipzig

Santini, C. (1975), 'Motivi astronomici e moduli didattici nei *Fasti* di Ovidio', *GIF* n.s. 6: 1–26

Scheid, J. (1992), 'Myth, cult and reality in Ovid's *Fasti*', *PCPS* 38: 118–31

Schiesaro, A. (1994), 'The Palingenesis of the *De Rerum Natura*', *PCPS* 40: 81–107

Schütz, M. (1990), 'Die Sonnenuhr des Augustus auf dem Marsfeld', *Gymnasium* 97: 432–57
Scott, A. (1991), *Origen and the life of the stars*, Oxford
Simon, E. (1986), *Augustus*, Munich
Snodgrass, A. (1987), *An archaeology of Greece: the present state and future scope of the discipline*, Berkeley and Los Angeles
Stahl, H.-P. (1985), *Propertius: 'love' and 'war': individual and state under Augustus*, Berkeley and Los Angeles
Syme, R. (1978), *History in Ovid*, Oxford
Taylor, L. R. (1931), *The divinity of the Roman Emperor*, Middletown, CT
Thibault, J. C. (1964), *The mystery of Ovid's exile*, Berkeley and Los Angeles
Traina, A. (1956), 'Variazioni omeriche in Arato', *Maia* 8: 39–48
Turcan, R. (1989), *Les cultes orientaux dans le monde romain*, Paris
Van Keuren, F. (1986), 'Cosmic symbolism of the Pantheon on the cuirass of the Prima Porta Augustus', in R. Winkes, ed., *The age of Augustus*, Providence, RI, 177–87
Von Arnim, H., ed. (1903–1924), *Stoicorum veterum fragmenta*, 4 volumes, Leipzig
Wallace-Hadrill, A. (1985), Review of E. Buchner, *Die Sonnenuhr des Augustus*, Mainz 1982, *JRS* 75: 246f.
(1987), 'Time for Augustus: Ovid, Augustus and the *Fasti*', in M. Whitby, P. Hardie and M. Whitby eds., *Homo viator: classical essays for John Bramble*, Bristol, 221–30
(1997), '*Mutatio morum*: the idea of a cultural revolution', in Habinek and Schiesaro (1997): 3–22
Weinstock, S. (1971), *Divus Julius*, Oxford
West, D. (1993), 'On serial narration and the Julian star', *Proceedings of the Virgil Society* 21: 1–16
Wheeler, S. M. (1995), '*Imago Mundi*: another view of the creation in Ovid's *Metamorphoses*', *AJP* 116: 95–121
White, P. (1988), 'Julius Caesar in Augustan Rome', *Phoenix* 42: 334–56
Wilkinson, L. P. (1955), *Ovid recalled*, Cambridge
Williams, Gareth (1991), 'Vocal variations and narrative complexity in Ovid's Vestalia: *Fasti* 6.249–468', *Ramus* 20: 183–204
Williams, Gordon (1978), *Change and decline: Roman literature in the early empire*, Berkeley and Los Angeles
Winkes, R., ed. (1986), *The age of Augustus*, Providence, RI
Wiseman, T. P. (1995), *Remus: a Roman myth*, Cambridge
Witt, R. E. (1971), *Isis in the Graeco-Roman world*, London
Wright, M. R. (1995), *Cosmology in antiquity*, London
Zanker, P. (1988), *The power of images in the age of Augustus*, trans. A. Shapiro, Ann Arbor

INDEX OF PASSAGES DISCUSSED

Major discussions are indicated in **bold** type

GENERAL INDEX

Lightning Source UK Ltd.
Milton Keynes UK
UKOW01f1347020916

282056UK00001B/29/P

9 780521 101776